FLORIDA STATE
UNIVERSITY LIBRARIES

MAY 1 0 2001

TALLAHASSEE, FLORIDA

Deviant Street Networks

Deviant Street Networks

Prostitution in New York City

Bernard Cohen
Queens College,
City University of New York

Lexington Books
D.C. Heath and Company
Lexington, Massachusetts
Toronto

HQ
146
.N7
C63

Robert Manning Strozier Library

JUN 25 1981

Tallahassee, Florida

Library of Congress Cataloging in Publication Data

Cohen, Bernard, 1937-
 Deviant street networks.

 Bibliography: p.
 Includes index.
 1. Prostitution—New York (City) 2. Social sciences—Field work. I. Title.
HQ146.N7C63   306.7'4'097471   80-8039
ISBN 0-669-03949-7

Copyright © 1980 by D.C. Heath and Company

All rights reserved. No part of this publication may be reproduced or transmitted in any form or by any means, electronic or mechanical, including photocopy, recording, or any information storage or retrieval system, without permission in writing from the publisher.

Published simultaneously in Canada

Printed in the United States of America

International Standard Book Number: 0-669-03949-7

Library of Congress Catalog Card Number: 80-8039

To my parents

Contents

	List of Figures and Tables	xi
	Foreword	xiii
	Preface	xv
	Acknowledgments	xvii
Chapter 1	**Introduction**	1
	Background	2
	Rationale	3
	Specific Aims	5
	Issues	5
Chapter 2	**Research Strategy**	9
	Visible Deviant Street Condition	9
	Street Survey	10
	Deviant Street Networks	10
	Deviant Street Circuits	14
	Stability of Location	14
	Research Techniques	16
	Ethical Issues	23
	Safety	25
Chapter 3	**Deviant Street Network Profiles**	29
	The Lower East Side	29
	Park and Fifth Avenues	31
	Ninth Avenue	32
	Eighth Avenue	34
Chapter 4	**Characteristics and Patterns of Visible Street Deviance**	37
	Prostitutes	37
	Transvestite Prostitutes	52
	Deviant Managers	55
	The Patron	60
	Hangers-on	66

Chapter 5	**The Police**	71
	Police Presence	74
	Arrests by Race	76
Chapter 6	**The Division of Deviance**	83
	Spatial Distribution of Street Deviance	83
	Deviance Segregation	85
	The Typicality of Deviance	86
	Deviant Sorting	87
	Stratified Street Order	90
Chapter 7	**Deviant Street Network Stratification**	95
	Female Prostitutes	95
	Male Transvestite Prostitution	100
	Deviant Management	101
	Johns	102
	Hangers-on	102
	Deviant Spacing	103
	Order within Deviant Street Networks	104
	Order within Deviant Street Location	105
	Deviant Distancing	108
Chapter 8	**Determinants of Deviant Street Locations**	111
	Ecological Factors	112
	Economic Base	115
	Sociodemographic Factors	115
	Community Tolerance	117
	The Bowery and Delancey Street	121
	10th to 14th Streets	123
	32nd Street and Madison Avenue	126
Chapter 9	**The Deviant Street Location Cycle**	131
	Emergence	131
	Expansion	133
	Equilibrium	135
	Dissolution	136
Chapter 10	**Maintaining Deviance**	139
	Economic-Social Model	139
	Normative Succession Theory	143

Contents

	Territorial Exclusivity of Street Deviance	146
	Deviance Stratification	148
	One-Sex Peer Group	151
Chapter 11	**Recommendations**	155
Appendix A	**Prostitution: A Complex Phenomenon**	159
Appendix B	**Letter of Identification**	181
	Bibliography	183
	Index	189
	About the Author	201

List of Figures and Tables

Figures

2-1	Thirteen Deviant Street Locations	11
2-2	Deviant Street Networks	13
2-3	Deviant Street Circuits	15
6-1	Deviant Street Clusters	84
8-1	The Bowery and Delancey Street	122

Tables

4-1	Number, Percent, and Average per Hour of Prostitutes at Four Deviant Street Networks	38
4-2	Number, Percent, and Average per Hour of Prostitutes at Thirteen Deviant Street Locations	40
4-3	Estimated Number of Prostitutes during Nighttime at Thirteen Deviant Street Locations	41
4-4	Number and Percent of Prostitutes by Race and Deviant Street Networks	43
4-5	Number and Percent of Prostitutes by Race and Thirteen Deviant Street Locations Ordered According to Ethnic Majority	45
4-6	Average Number of Prostitutes per Hour by Race at Deviant Street Networks	46
4-7	Average Number of Prostitutes per Hour by Race and Time Period	47
4-8	Average Number of Prostitutes per Hour at Different Times of Day and Night for Deviant Street Networks	49
4-9	Age of Prostitutes by Race and Deviant Street Networks	52
4-10	Number and Percent of Transvestite Prostitutes by Race and Deviant Street Networks	54
4-11	Number and Percent of Deviant Managers by Race and Deviant Street Networks	58

4-12	Average Age of Deviant Managers by Race		59
4-13	Estimated Age Differential between Prostitutes and Managers		60
4-14	Relationship of Manager and Prostitute by Race		60
4-15	Relationship of Prostitute and Patron by Race and Deviant Street Networks		62
4-16	Number and Percent of Hangers-on by Race and Deviant Street Networks		67
4-17	Number and Average Size of Groups of Hangers-on by Race		68
5-1	Percent of Police on Beat and in Cars by Deviant Street Networks		74
5-2	Average Number per Hour of Prostitutes and Police by Time of Day and Night		75
5-3	Number and Percent of Prostitutes Arrested by the Police and Identified through Field Counts		76
5-4	Police on Beat and in Cars for Black, White, and Mixed Deviant Street Locations		78
5-5	Average Number per Hour of Prostitutes and Police by Ethnic Areas and Time of Day and Night		79
7-1	Approximate Order of Locations from High to Low Socioeconomic Status within Deviant Street Networks		104
7-2	Approximate Area Covered by Each Deviant Street Location		105
8-1	Comparison of Structures on 32nd Street and 33rd to 35th Streets		127
10-1	Patterns of Human Behavior		145

Foreword

This is a fascinating study for several reasons. To many students of society, the subject matter is intrinsically interesting. But this is not merely a study of heterosexual prostitution; it is a work clearly blessed with craftsmanship and enlightened by that kind of sociological imagination that makes for skillful analysis. Journalism and investigative reporting are honorable forms of describing phenomena, but they are not usually sociology because they lack the conceptualization of, and the ideational association with, the units of analysis traditionally found in social science. *Deviant Street Networks* is quality sociology. There are theoretical propositions, there are precise descriptions, there is full disclosure of limitations, and there are conclusions that have transferability to other places, other times.

Another important aspect of this work is the felicitous combination of qualitative and quantitative data. Micro-ethnographic and macro-quantitative research are rarely wedded as they are in this study. The author refers to this union as *ethnometrics*, and he deserves our praise for making the marriage so effective in providing through both methods a chiaroscuro that a singular approach sometimes fails to yield.

The norm violator and the norm violation dichotomy, with the binary yes-no cell distribution clearly reminiscent of Merton, is a contribution that I suspect will be cited and used constructively by scholars in future studies.

This important book includes an economic-social model, an analysis of ethnic distributions, and very practical recommendations both for the police and for prostitutes.

Street observations are neither easy to make nor simple to describe. The author of this book is right in being surprised that more street sociology has not been done and in suggesting that many other kinds of social deviance, as well as conforming human behavior, can well be studied this way.

Bernard Cohen is a fully seasoned scholar whose background gives him that classic Talmudic precision of analysis and whose sociological insights render these street observations with a selective participation that is uncommon in its scope. William Whyte, Erving Goffman, and Elliot Liebow should be pleased at the emulation that this study represents. They should also be satisfied by the extension of their approach that Bernard Cohen has done so well.

It is especially gratifying to me who first knew this gentle and careful scholar when he was a student. My respect for his mind has grown with his continued production, of which this study represents a significant contribution.

Marvin E. Wolfgang
University of Pennsylvania

Preface

The idea for this book on deviant street networks in New York City emerged during one of the many hours over several years that I accompanied New York City police on patrol as part of a series of research projects on job performance. I noticed, in full public view, substantial ongoing street deviance, including gambling, drug abuse, homosexual prostitution, heterosexual prostitution, transvestite prostitution, and alcoholism. I observed dozens of illegal acts occurring without the intervention of passersby, neighborhood residents, or the police.

I wondered why more researchers had not taken advantage of numerous opportunities to conduct field research on street deviance and, for that matter, ordinary street behavior. Street scenes are packed with subject matter and data for sociologists, including human interaction and status hierarchies. Moreover, no special permission is required to observe these phenomena. Yet a paucity of sociological description exists on deviance in its natural settings. Sociological research is rich in descriptive materials and summaries from interviews, questionnaires, and official records, but little attention is devoted to activities that unfold before the researcher. Moreover, most previous studies that gathered data visible to the naked eye never fully utilized or applied this method because of reliance on other sources of information. As useful as this other information may be, it cannot replace data obtained through direct observation. It is my opinion that many previous field studies could have derived additional insights from direct observation. This book presents informal interviews that were held only after all avenues of direct field observation were thoroughly exhausted. It has been asserted that more may be learned about street deviance from police officers than from street observation. This position only serves to underscore the present viewpoint, and my study is especially instructive for proponents of this argument.

I was also puzzled that, in this age of technology, despite the high cost of gasoline, an automobile was not used more often as an instrument of social research. An observer in a car can traverse large areas or distances in a short time and capture integrated ongoing social structures or patterns that would appear unrelated and fragmented to an observer on foot. The routes followed by cruising johns illustrate this point quite well. It would have been virtually impossible to identify these special street circuits without the aid of an automobile.

I also thought that more than qualitative impressions ought to be obtained from field observation. I could never understand why most field research concentrated only on qualitative information, nearly always at the expense of quantitative data. I decided that quantitative information on street deviance would also be an integral part of my data-collection strategy. I entered my car, left the safety and confines of home and university, and drove around city streets at all hours of day and night. I quickly discovered that a car and field observation go hand in hand. In the study of heterosexual street prostitution, a car is especially useful as a research tool for gathering quantitative as well as qualitative field data. Street prostitution is a highly visible activity spread over a large area and is sufficiently stable for accurate counts of people and acts. I urge other researchers to conduct field studies on street life, which after all is one of the natural spheres of the social scientist.

Acknowledgments

I wish to pay tribute to my friend and colleague, Dean Savage, who reviewed and revised my final manuscript with care, patience, and expertise. Many of his excellent suggestions found their way into this book.

I would like to take this opportunity to acknowledge Lauren H. Seiler and Robert E. Kapsis for numerous, insightful comments and suggestions on early drafts of this book. Also, I am grateful to Stephen H. Leinen, a long-time friend and colleague, who provided substantial inputs on techniques for street observation and on police tactics for controlling visible deviance. His combined training in sociology and police work was particularly suited for this purpose.

Several individuals provided valuable assistance. These include Swapna Bhattacharya, Betsy Goldberg, Norma Gayne, Vlachos Athanassios, Jean Martin, Eileen Piervencenti, Robert Rediger, Elizabeth Beazley, Teresa Martin, and Florence Levitt.

**Deviant Street
Networks**

1 Introduction

Control over street deviance is a perennial problem for urban communities and police. Deviant street behavior has always fascinated the public, and the mass media have not been too shy to exploit this keen interest. Although the media constantly feed the public's fantasies on forms of deviance visible in the street, such as prostitution, gambling, alcoholism, and drug abuse, and a vast literature exists on these types of deviance, they have not been studied in a systematic and scientific manner as examples of street deviance. The public's perception and perhaps even that of specialists (for example, the police and scholars) is that street deviance is a random, disorganized, and unordered phenomena concentrated in a city's deteriorated and slum neighborhoods. As I will demonstrate, this is very far from the truth; visible street deviance is highly ordered and distributed socially and ecologically. Therefore, the overall objective of the research for this book is to determine the incidence, genesis, and persistence of visible street deviance. As part of this task the focus is on the spatial, temporal, and ecological distribution of thirteen locations of visible street deviance in New York City and the characteristic conditions and interaction patterns associated with them.

Deviance in this book is conceived as law-violating behavior scorned or disavowed but not considered beyond the limits of tolerance by a substantial proportion of the population. These violations of legal norms often consist of a voluntary exchange of strongly desired though illegal goods or services.[1] They have been termed victimless or marginal crimes and include prostitution, gambling, drug abuse, and alcoholism. In the street these forms of deviance occur in full public view. This definition of street deviance excludes predatory street crimes where real or potential violence or property loss may ensue (for example, homicide, rape, robbery, burglary, larceny, auto theft, and weapons violations). These acts are not tolerated by the public and tend to be hidden from public view.

It is important to study street deviance for several reasons. First, a substantial proportion of crime handled by the police involves visible street deviance or results directly from it. According to the President's Commission on Law Enforcement and Administration of Justice, drunkenness and disorderly conduct, both law-violating behaviors likely to be visible in the street, are the two most frequent offenses accounting for 41.5 percent of all offenses.[2] Also, current crime statistics show that nearly a third of all arrests are for offenses likely to result from street deviance, such as prostitution, gambling, drunkenness, vagrancy, disorderly conduct, loitering, suspicion, and narcotic-related offenses.[3] Moreover, predatory street crime including homicide, rape, robbery, and aggravated assault may in some ways be related to visible street deviance. Although the extent of serious crime that results from visible street deviance is not known, the President's Crime Commission found that about 64 percent of all robberies occurred outside or on the streets, while 46.8 percent of major crimes against males and 30.7 percent of crimes against females occurred in the street.[4] A significant proportion of police work involves visible street deviance. Research leading to innovative approaches for its control might free the police for attention to more serious crime.

Second, regardless of the level of crime, little tends to undermine the fabric of a city more than visible street deviance. Street deviance is highly visible and it creates an offensive atmosphere, especially for children. It is not unusual for a man, sometimes even when accompanied by his family, to be solicited by prostitutes or accosted by derelicts or drug peddlers, and upon refusal to be harassed. The negative ambiance emanating from visible street deviance may be one significant determinant for why families flee cities for the suburbs. A study of visible street deviance allows us to learn about the interaction among crime, criminals, the police, passersby, and storekeepers in their natural habitat. Of particular interest is the extent to which so-called ordinary citizens encourage or even become involved in street deviance.

Finally, the community's attitude toward police is shaped by the action of individual officers in the field. Visible street deviance provides an ideal setting for learning about police discretion and enforcement of laws against victimless crimes.

Background

Several previous studies have undertaken observations of streets and street corners,[5] but these works have been limited either to an analysis of a single street-corner group or the personal social-psychological interaction among persons who frequent one particular street corner or neighborhood.[6] Moreover, the primary focus of these studies was neither on law-violating behavior, on the conditions leading to crime, nor on the way in which agencies of social control interact with law violators. An urban study still in progress dealing with street deviance on West 42nd Street has uncovered many interesting findings, including perceptions New Yorkers have of street deviance in the 42nd Street area; however, it also focuses primarily on a single location comprising two city blocks.[7]

Introduction

This book is not concerned as much with the personal social-psychological interaction among participants of a particular street condition as it is with the relationships between patterns of visible street deviance, the police, and the wider ecological and social environment. The personal interaction between individuals or members of groups who make up these conditions, although a part of this book, are treated only to the extent that it influences or is influenced by the structure, patterns, and social control of visible street deviance. This approach draws on the ecological works of the early and later Chicago School, including Park, Burgess, Shaw, McKay, Wirth, Suttles, and Kapsis.[8] These studies examine deviance and crime in relationship to a neighborhood's social, demographic, and physical characteristics. This book also attempts to integrate the insights of recent research dealing with environmental design,[9] the police, behavior in public places, and prostitution.[10]

Rationale

In an attempt to find practical solutions to law-violating behavior, academicians, scholars, and practitioners have conducted thousands of studies covering nearly every conceivable aspect of crime and the criminal-justice system including homicide, domestic disputes, forcible rape, organized crime, gang delinquency, crimes without victims, drug abuse, the police, the prosecutorial system, courts, and corrections. Most of these studies identify a particular crime or agency of social control and focus on selective dimensions for closer analysis. For example, in research on drug abuse, basic information may consist only of those aspects officially recorded by the police.

Some studies have gone beyond official-agency data, having utilized interviews, questionnaires, or even field observations. Most of these have chosen a select group of law violators or a special agency of social control where interaction was examined from the point of view of either the alleged criminal or the agency of social control. These studies, though useful, are limited by the perceptions, habits, and styles of the subjects chosen for analysis.

A less frequenlty used approach for learning about law-violating behavior is direct observation of crime and its participants within natural surroundings. It is a difficult method but one that promises to provide needed information for understanding the dynamics and control of deviance. Accordingly, in this book we attempt to learn about law violation and law violators by direct observation of social interaction in its actual setting. Visible street deviance in New York City is studied, utilizing female heterosexual prostitution as the primary illustrative example. The prostitute who works in full public view in the street, known as the *streetwalker*, is the focus of this book, not call girls, bar girls, or other prostitutes who work inside locations. A thorough literature review revealed that prostitution is rarely viewed as a street deviation (see appendix A).

Female heterosexual street prostitution was selected for analysis because it is one of the most visible forms of deviant behavior. Certainly it is easier to observe than other forms of street deviance such as drug abuse, an activity more surreptitious and covert because of greater law enforcement and harsher penalties. Moreover, noncommercial homosexual encounters in the street often are mistaken for transactions involving male homosexual prostitutes. Signals utilized by male prostitutes compared to female prostitutes are more subtle and discreet. Therefore they are harder to detect. Also, it is relatively difficult to distinguish the prostitute from the patron in a homosexual encounter. Female heterosexual street prostitution in New York City is an open affair in which prostitutes and clients initiate contact in full public view. These activities may be observed at numerous locations in different parts of the city.

Although female heterosexual prostitution in full public view is one of the most convenient examples for the study of street deviance, visible male homosexual prostitution, male transvestite prostitution, alcoholism, or drug abuse might have been highlighted as well. Thus these forms of deviance are introduced whenever they shed additional light on patterns of visible female street prostitution.

A unique aspect of this book is that we examine ethnologically an extensive area containing numerous separate pockets of deviance at several different locations. Most previous studies of street deviance in actual settings have focused on one or even several neighborhoods, but few if any have attempted to explore the variability among numerous locations spread over a substantial area.[11] This procedure allows for identification of certain uniformities and patterns that characterize visible deviant locations that otherwise would go undetected with only one or even several deviant locations. Moreover, generalizations based on this approach are more reliable than inferences drawn from a single location. Certain significant issues also can be explored when a substantial number of units are available for analysis. These issues include: determination of common sets of social, demographic, and ecological elements that characterize deviant street locations; determination of the effects of neighborhood's socioeconomic status on street deviance; whether or not a visible deviant location once suppressed reemerges somewhere close by; whether police patterns of enforcement differ by neighborhoods; and whether locations of visible deviance are near precinct boundaries so that participants may simply cross the street to avoid arrest.

Introduction

Specific Aims

A significant proportion of individuals are attracted to street deviance because of its high visibility and easy access. Therefore a reduction in visibility and other opportunities leading to street deviance may well result in an overall decrease in deviant conditions without requiring increased law enforcement. If this is so, it is extremely important to learn about the dynamics underlying the genesis and persistence of visible street deviance. At the same time the effects of current means to control street deviance must be determined. Utilizing female street prostitution as the primary illustration, specific foci for this book include: the spatial and temporal distributions of visible street deviance, including why and when it surfaces in certain neighborhoods on certain sides of the street; the relationships between ecological and physical structures and opportunities for street deviance; the relationships between sociodemographic characteristics of neighborhood "users" (for example, residents, shoppers, workers, passersby) and opportunities for street deviance; the sociodemographic characteristics of participants drawn by opportunities for street deviance; whether street deviance at different times of day and night result from the same group of persons; the types of crime related or unrelated to street deviance; methods utilized by the police and the community to control or eliminate street deviance; a better theoretical understanding of street deviance.

Issues

Several interesting and useful issues on visible street deviance uncovered during the initial research were explored. The field observations were conducted for approximately two years. This provided a sufficient period to assess certain issues related to the stability and change in patterns of street deviance. These issues include:

1. Increased police enforcement (for example, harassment, street stops, searches, arrest and detention) may actually increase the incidence of street deviance because street actors are forced to disperse and occupy new nearby locations. This increases the overall number of deviant street locations and opportunities.

2. Visible deviant street conditions may not be eliminated as a result of community action but instead may be displaced to other neighborhoods.

3. Police enforcement of visible street deviance varies according to a neighborhood's socioeconomic status. It tends to be more repressive in lower socioeconomic areas than in prime areas. (Repression, however, is not necessarily absent from well-to-do locations.)

4. The presence of certain forms of deviance in a specific neighborhood (for example, prostitution and drug abuse) represses certain other forms of deviance and crime (for example, gang delinquency, muggings, and homicides).

5. Visible street deviance is likely to emerge in areas where it does not clash with competing legitimate or illegitimate interests. The emergence process may be facilitated by local interests that benefit from street deviance.

6. Visible street deviance is likely to emerge in neighborhoods exhibiting an absence of community opposition to these activities. These neighborhoods are characterized by an overrepresentation of single adult males and an underrepresentation of families, young children, elderly persons, shoppers, and business people.

7. Visible street deviance is likely to emerge at facilitative locations that provide convenient places for business and escape. These locations are characterized by the presence of parks, alleys, seedy hotels, cheap roominghouses, empty lots, abandoned buildings, late-hour coffee shops, and bars.

8. Different forms of visible street deviance are territorially segregated and ordered hierarchically by the socioeconomic status of neighborhood. The groups with most power, prestige, and wealth occupy higher socioeconomic areas while the least powerful groups occupy lower socioeconomic areas. For example, we would expect gamblers to occupy areas of higher socioeconomic status than derelicts because they have more money, power, and prestige.

9. Similar forms of visible street deviance at different locations are hierarchically ordered according to socioeconomic status. For example, more desirable and higher priced male prostitutes (that is, they possess greater power and prestige) occupy higher socioeconomic status areas than their less desirable and lower priced counterparts.

Notes

1. See Edwin M. Schur, *Interpreting Deviance* (New York: Harper & Row, 1979), p. 451.

2. *Task Force Report: Crime and Its Impact—An Assessment*, The President's Commission on Law Enforcement and Administration of Justice (Washington, D.C.: U.S. Government Printing Office, 1967), p. 17.

3. *Crime in the United States. Uniform Crime Reports 1978*, United States Department of Justice (Washington, D.C.: U.S. Government Printing Office, 1979), p. 186.

4. *Task Force Report*, pp. 63 and 82.

5. For example: William F. Whyte, *Street Corner Society* (Chicago: University of Chicago Press, 1943).

6. For example: Elliot Liebow, *Tally's Corner* (Boston: Little, Brown & Co., 1967).

7. William Kornblum et al., *West 42nd Street: The Bright Light Zone*, 1978 (Unpublished Monograph).

8. See Robert E. Park, Ernest W. Burgess, and Roderick D. McKenzie, *The City* (Chicago: University of Chicago Press, 1925); Louis H. Wirth, "Urbanism as a Way of Life," *American Journal of Sociology* 44, no. 1 (July 1938):1-24; Clifford R. Shaw and Henry D. McKay, *Juvenile Delinquency and Urban Areas* (Chicago: University of Chicago Press, 1967); Gerald D. Suttles, *The Social Order of the Slum* (Chicago: University of Chicago Press, 1968); Gerald D. Suttles, *The Social Construction of Communities* (Chicago: University of Chicago Press, 1972); Robert E. Kapsis, "Residential Succession and Delinquency," *Criminology* 15, no. 4 (February 1978):459-486; Robert E. Kapsis, "Black Street Corner Districts," *Social Forces* 57, no. 4 (June 1979):1212-1228.

9. Thomas A. Reppetto, "Crime Prevention through Environmental Policy," *American Behavioral Scientist* 20 (November/December 1976):275-288; Oscar Newman, *Defensible Space* (New York: Macmillan, 1972); C. Ray Jeffery, *Crime Prevention through Environmental Design* (Beverly Hills, Calif.: Sage Publications, 1971); and Jane Jacobs, *The Death and Life of Great American Cities* (New York: Vintage Books, 1961).

10. See Charles Winick and Paul M. Kinsie, *The Lively Commerce* (Chicago: Quadrangle Books, 1971). See also appendix A of this book for a review of the literature on prostitution focusing on the streetwalker; James Q. Wilson, *Varieties of Police Behavior* (Cambridge, Mass.: Harvard University Press, 1968); Erving Goffman, *Behavior in Public Places* (New York: The Free Press, 1963); and Erving Goffman, *Relations in Public* (New York: Basic Books, 1971).

11. Studies by Paul G. Cressey, *The Taxi-Dance Hall* (Chicago: University of Chicago Press, 1932) and Frederic M. Thrasher, *The Gang* (Chicago: University of Chicago Press, 1927) have explored taxi-dance halls and gangs spread over an extensive area. However, Cressey and Thrasher only briefly discuss the activities of taxi-dance halls and gangs within the context of specific deviant locations.

2 Research Strategy

New York City, like other large cities, has endemic patterns of visible street deviance which concern the community and occupy substantial police time and resources. This study was limited to the area from 59th Street to the southern tip of Manhattan because of its manageable size; it is a compact natural area bounded by water on three sides and Central Park on a portion of the northern boundary. In addition, this area includes nearly every type of social class and residential neighborhood. Moreover, it is the center of New York and draws on the outlying population to sustain a large number of deviant street locations.

Visible Deviant Street Condition

A *visible deviant street condition* consists of several persons who gather together in the same public street location at predictable moments, over a substantial period of time and overtly and repeatedly engage in behavior that is in violation of law. A *deviant street condition* is characterized by the visible presence of deviants openly transacting illegal business on the street, such as prostitutes soliciting customers, derelicts accosting passersby, and drug pushers selling drugs. Visible deviant street conditions may persist for periods of only a few months, but most endure for several years. The relative stability of street deviance in one sense may make it easier to control than more fleeting forms of crime.

This definition of visible street deviance excludes norm-violating behavior in nonstreet locations including bars, after-hours clubs, and parks. Acts of deviance engaged in solely by individuals are omitted from this definition. Therefore, a location used by a single prostitute, homosexual, transvestite, derelict, or drug addict does not fall within the scope of this book. Also, visible deviant street conditions exclude groups that gather spontaneously or coalesce for short periods such as a few hours, days, or even several weeks. Likewise, it excludes roving gangs or groups who do not consistently use the same particular location for delinquent activity. Mobile aggregates are more fluid and less constant than the forms of street deviance studied, and they must be considered in a different framework. Robbery, mugging, assault, rape, homicide, and other street crimes also are excluded from this definition because these events usually do not involve several persons gathering in the same public locations at predictable times over a substantial period who repeatedly engage in law-violating behavior in full public view.

Street Survey

Most field work for this book was conducted during 1977 and 1978. An extensive and systematic survey of streets was undertaken at different times of day and night from 59th Street to the southern tip of Manhattan to determine locations of visible female street prostitution. Every avenue and street was visited several times during the morning, afternoon, and evening to determine the location and persistence of visible street conditions.

Efforts to identify visible street deviance resulted in the following thirteen key locations: (1) the Bowery and Delancey Street; (2) Forsythe Street, between Delancey and Grand Streets; (3) Third Avenue and East 6th Street; (4) Third Avenue between East 10th and East 14th Streets; (5) Lexington Avenue and East 25th Street; (6) Park Avenue and East 26th Street; (7) Fifth Avenue and East 32nd Street; (8) Lexington Avenue between East 44th and East 50th Streets; (9) Eighth Avenue between West 42nd and West 49th Streets; (10) Eighth Avenue between West 38th and West 42nd Streets; (11) Ninth Avenue and West 42nd Street; (12) Ninth Avenue and West 46th Street; and (13) Tenth Avenue and West 42nd Street, (figure 2-1).

Deviant Street Networks

The thirteen separate locations of visible street deviance formed four major *deviant street networks*. These included Park and Fifth Avenues, Eighth Avenue, Ninth Avenue, and the Lower East Side. Each street network included two to four separate locations that were sociologically related, contiguous, and strikingly alike in sociodemographic and neighborhood characteristics. The present concept of network is similar to the description offered by J.A. Barnes and refined by Frank Ianni in *Black Mafia*. Both applied *network* to a social field when people are directly and indirectly in touch with one another. Barnes explained, "Each person is, as it were, in touch with a number of other people, some of whom are directly in touch with each other and some of whom are not . . . I find it convenient to talk of a social field of this kind as a network."[1] A deviant street network is based on certain social relationships and patterns; it is not determined primarily by distance. Therefore it did not matter that several deviant street locations in the same network were a further distance from each other than certain networks.

Research Strategy

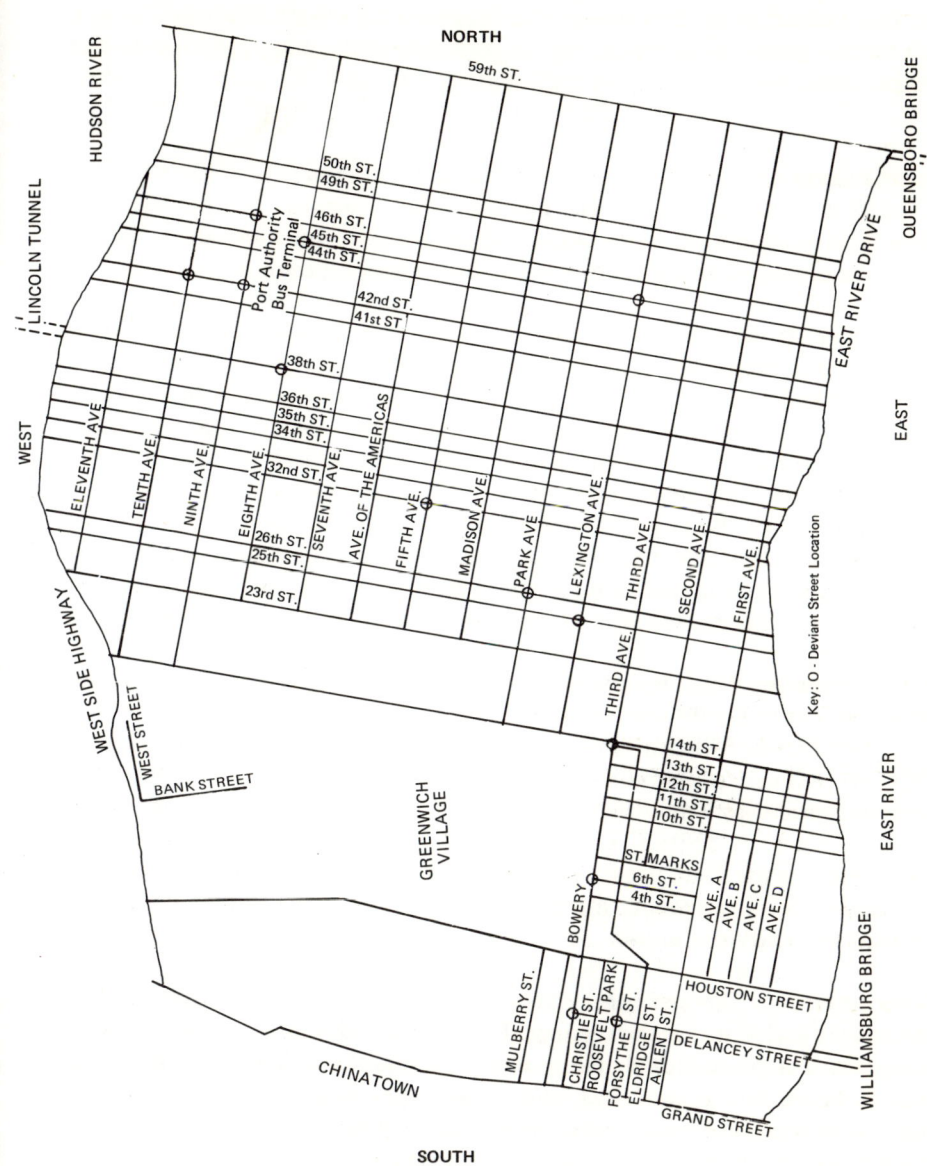

Figure 2-1. Thirteen Deviant Street Locations

In this book many prostitutes in a single network were likely to know or at least recognize one another, were in many instances managed by the same pimps, competed for the same pool of johns, and on occasion worked several different locations within the network. Also the price, method of operation, and overall temporal patterns were similar for locations comprising the same network. On the other hand, substantial differences existed between deviant street networks on these same factors. The networks of varying socioeconomic status were utilized as a key independent variable. They are arranged below from high to low socioeconomic status.

Park and Fifth Avenues. This area extends primarily from East 23rd Street to East 53rd Street between Fifth and Lexington Avenues. This deviant street network includes the following four street locations of visible female prostitution: 25th Street and Lexington Avenue; 26th Street and Park Avenue; 32nd Street and Fifth Avenue; and 44th to 50th Streets and Lexington Avenue. This network is situated in New York City's East Side and it includes some of the city's most desirable neighborhoods. It is the highest ranking socioeconomic area studied in this book.[2] Visible street deviance in this configuration, in addition to female heterosexual prostitution, consists mainly of male homosexual prostitution (see figure 2-2).

Eighth Avenue. This area extends from Eighth Avenue and 38th Street to Eighth Avenue and 49th Street. It includes two contiguous but separate conditions of female prostitution: 38th Street to 42nd Street and 42nd Street to 49th Street. These streets comprise the Eighth Avenue Red Light Zone. This area is adjacent to Times Square and 42nd Street and includes part of the Broadway theatre district. Eighth Avenue ranks second in socioeconomic status among the four networks. Many forms of street deviance occur in this area including female, male, and transvestite prostitution, gambling, alcoholism, and drug abuse.

Ninth Avenue. This network extends primarily from 42nd Street to 46th Street on Ninth and Tenth Avenues. It is in a mixed residential and business area comprising individuals from many racial and ethnic groups, including blacks, Hispanics, Irish, Poles, and Greeks. This configuration ranks third highest in socioeconomic status. Female and transvestite prostitution and gambling are the main forms of street deviance in the Ninth Avenue network.

The Lower East Side. This area mainly includes the territory from Delancey Street, Forsythe Street and the Bowery, north to 14th Street on Third Avenue. The four separate deviant conditions at the Bowery and Delancey Street, Forsythe Street, 6th Street, and 10th to 14th Streets are

Research Strategy

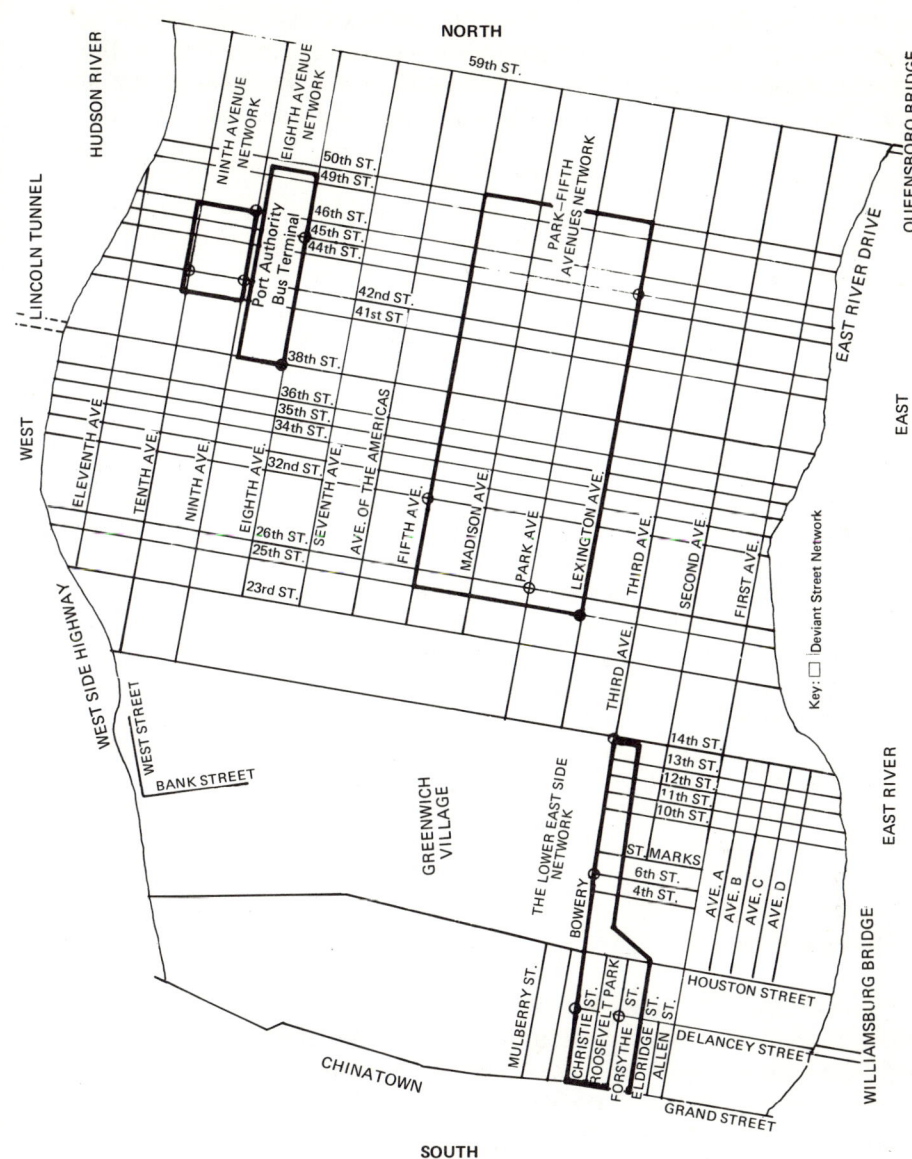

Figure 2-2. Deviant Street Networks

part of this street network. This deviant complex consists of several different types of deviant street conditions including female prostitution, transvestite prostitution, and alcohol abuse. Relatively few male prostitutes work this area. This configuration is less desirable and of lower socioeconomic status than the other three networks of female street prostitution.

Deviant Street Circuits

A *deviant street circuit* consists of several deviant street networks easily accessible by car. Virtually no link exists between separate deviant street networks comprising a single circuit other than convenient access. A deviant street circuit's shape is determined primarily by cruising johns who frequently drive up and down the circuits searching for prostitutes. In one sense these cruising patterns establish an open-air market for shopping by johns in cars. Cruising johns have greater mobility than prostitutes and even the police who are confined to precinct boundaries. This mobility provides a certain measure of protection from dangerous and threatening street encounters because johns need not remain for long periods at any one location or network. The two street circuits in this book included Eighth to Ninth Avenues (West Side circuit) and Park and Fifth Avenues—the Lower East Side (East Side circuit). The East Side circuit covers eight deviant street locations and takes approximately ten to fifteen minutes to traverse in light traffic. The West Side circuit covers five deviant street locations and traveling time is about five to ten minutes depending on traffic conditions (figure 2-3).

Stability of Location

Each visible deviant street location was visited at least once a week for several months to determine its permanence. It has since been determined that most deviant locations have persisted for many years. These thirteen locations do not exhaust all visible deviant street locations involving female prostitution in New York City or even for the area covering 59th Street to the southern tip of Manhattan. Groups of female prostitutes worked at several other locations, but at least during 1977 and 1978 these conditions were either not permanent or arose after the field work was undertaken. Therefore they were excluded from the present analysis. For decades, prostitutes "worked" on Sixth and Seventh Avenues, between 42nd and 59th Streets, but during this research they constantly were on the move and did not concentrate at any one street location. Female prostitution also surfaced on 37th Street and Ninth Avenue subsequent to the outset of the present research, consisting of several black prostitutes who frequented this loca-

Research Strategy

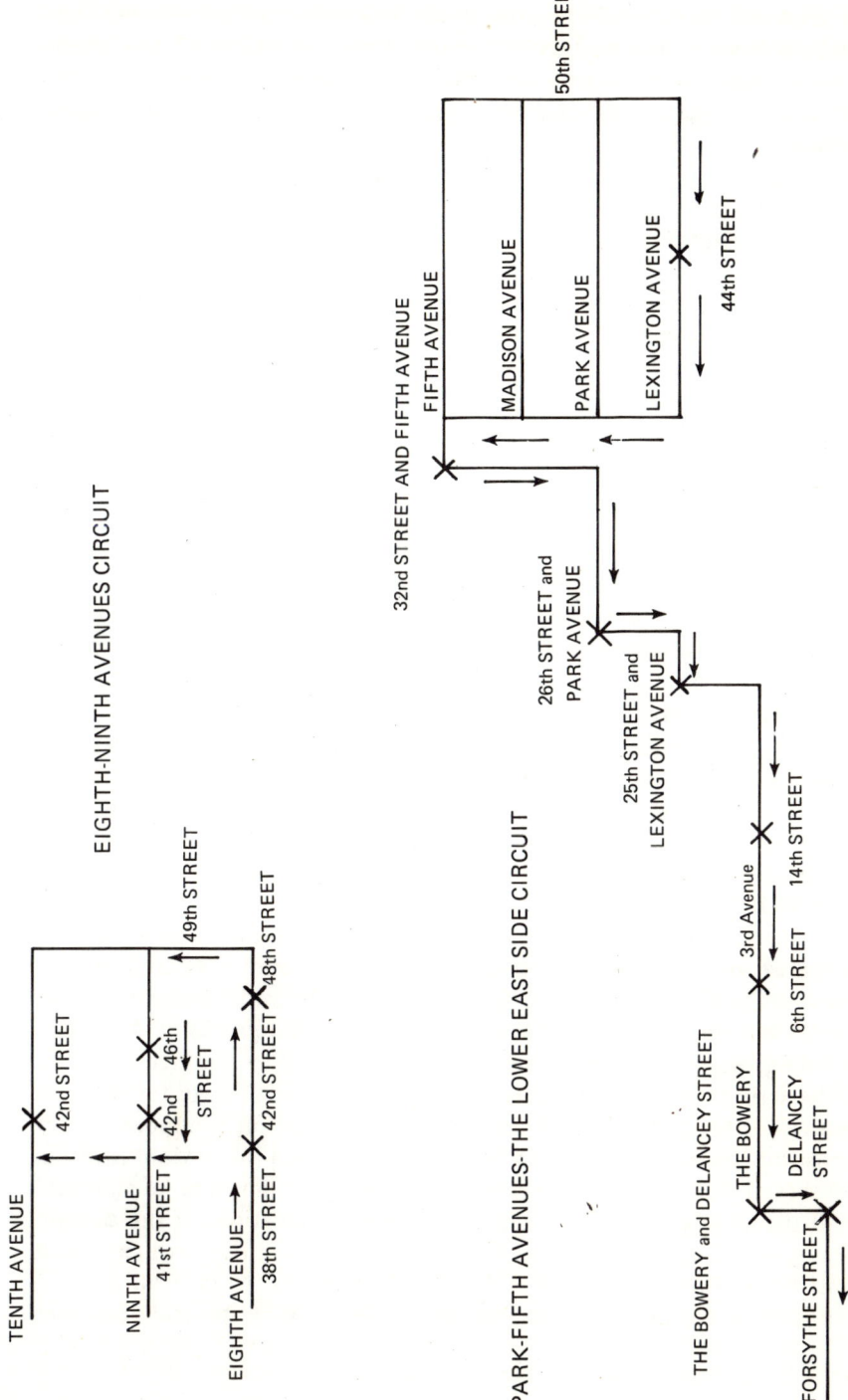

Figure 2-3. Deviant Street Circuits

tion during evening hours. Later, several additional conditions of female prostitution developed, including one in the 30's between Tenth Avenue and the Hudson River in the vicinity of the old West Side Highway and one in Greenwich Village at Bank and West Streets. Chapter 9 provides a description of the life cycle of deviant street locations including the process of emergence.

Research Techniques

The primary methodological techniques employed were field observation and selective participant observation.

Field Observation

Numerous visits were made to each area of visible street deviance to become familiar with the neighborhood. Each street location was then placed under systematic observation. Usually I would approach a location in a car, park in an unobtrusive spot, and observe the ongoing visible street deviance. At other times I left the car and either stood or walked in the area for hours. Nearly all field observations were entered into a tape recorder from the car. In this way various counts were made of police, places, patrons, prostitutes, pimps, and passersby.

Deviant street conditions are relatively constant especially over a short period of time. Moreover, networks are arranged in such a way that a driver can pass all thirteen street locations in less than an hour. During late evening hours when traffic diminished, this time is reduced to thirty minutes. Therefore several visits at key hours of morning, afternoon, evening, and night were sufficient for gathering most appropriate data. A rigid touring schedule was avoided because this would lessen the flexibility desired.

A typical observation tour took three to four hours beginning with a visit to a deviant street location. Upon finding substantial activity, a half hour or so was spent taking field notes of the street interaction and events. After a deviant condition became stable, I proceeded to another location.

If the activity at a location was dormant for the first five or ten minutes the researcher proceeded to yet another deviant location. Suppose one or two prostitutes were present and a few passersby. Then the deviant location was observed for about twenty minutes and after nothing meaningful changed the observer traveled to the next deviant location. If the deviant location was active, the researcher then would remain in this area for about one-half hour. In this way it was feasible in one tour to visit all thirteen locations of street deviance several times. By visiting several locations numerous times in one field-observation tour, the researcher could determine whether or not the same street actors were present at the same or different locations over time. In addition to the hundreds of hours of intensive field observations, a distinct set of fifty-six hours of observation of approximately equal duration was undertaken where standardized field counts were made at the thirteen deviant street locations. The results of these specific field counts are presented in chapters 4 and 5.

Not only were locations of deviant street conditions observed, but adjacent streets and neighborhoods where deviant conditions did not persist also were monitored in order to determine the elements that might account for the observed differences. An automobile was an important instrument because its speed and mobility facilitated the study of social activities spread over a substantial geographical area. Also, *mobile ethnography* provides a certain measure of safety, convenience, and concealment not available to researchers on foot. This tactic is particularly appropriate for studying deviant circuits and networks whose shape is partially determined by johns in cars.

Selective Participant Observation

Selective participant observation occurs when the researcher enters a milieu and attempts to gather information through observation, conversation, and unstructured interviews. Selective participant observation differs from ordinary participant observation in that the researcher does not enter the milieu completely nor does he attempt to become part of the social system. This method is useful where there is concern that total participation over time might disturb the milieu and influence the behavior of the subjects.[3]

I conducted observations unobtrusively either from a distance (for example, scouting the general neighborhood) or close by as part of the social milieu (for example, walking near but past street actors; standing among other bystanders in heavy pedestrian traffic; "hanging out"). Then I approached a street or corner, usually when several prostitutes were present, and I waited for them to initiate conversation. Prostitutes frequently attempted to solicit my business. They spelled out numerous details including price, place, and amount of time for services. After a few minutes I tried to direct the conversation to the research. It was not difficult to extend the conversation, probe, and ask various kinds of questions dealing with deviant locations, street positions, and police activity. Sample questions included: Why do you work in one area (neighborhood, block, side of street) rather than another? Why do you work on the street where arrest is likely? Why do the police often ignore your behavior even when it is obvious that you are violating the law? Why does street deviance exist on this block and not the next one?

Although I did not participate fully in the social milieu, I spent many hours at each location attempting to fit into the street scene through hanging out and conversation. Eventually I established rapport with several prostitutes who volunteered information. Some finally offered to provide detailed accounts, self-descriptions, and life histories. However, this went beyond the limited aims of this study. Informal interviews were held primarily with prostitutes because they were willing at the outset to converse with ordinary citizens.

A combination of field observation and selective participant observation is useful where entrance and total immersion in a particular milieu is difficult, as with a group of drug addicts, street gamblers, or street prostitutes. It is also useful for initial preservation of the natural environment. Only after the street interaction is observed without penetrating the milieu is it breached more fully.

Techniques of field observation and selective participant observation need not automatically vitiate quantitative data or the precision of replication studies testing for reliability, validity, and range of applicability. In addition to qualitative data, careful counts and other numerical information can be gathered from field observation. These *hard data* were gathered in the present study and they represent actual counts of deviance location users (for example, police, patrons, prostitutes, pimps). In one sense these data are more precise and accurate than census information which is mainly derived from responses to questionnaires by area residents, many of whom reside in nondeviance areas surrounding deviant locations. (Wherever feasible these data were compared to census information and police arrest data.) This approach is called *ethnometrics* or gathering hard, quantitative data through field observation. Other researchers have utlized observation techniques, including William Whyte, Erving Goffman, and Elliot Liebow, but they relied exclusively or heavily on qualitative descriptions, only rarely attempting to quantify observations. One early attempt at ethnometrics was Thrasher's classic study of 1313 Chicago gangs; a well-known, more recent effort is Gerald Suttles' research on the slums.[4] Both utilized information based upon counts obtained through observation, and the present research is an attempt to apply, expand, and refine these methods.

Although the unit of analysis was the deviant street location, observation also focused on neighborhood characteristics, groups and individuals. Interest was in observable, personal and sociodemographic characteristics, acts, actions, and behavior rather than in thoughts or attitudes. I was searching for uniformities and patterns associated with certain locations, neighborhoods, and deviant conditions rather than personal motivation. Accordingly the number and position of persons in the street, whether and by whom they were managed, their race, approximate age (child, youth, adult, elderly), sex, dress, and method of operation were important.

Research Strategy

Neighborhood and ecological characteristics including the design of buildings, streets, and parks also were significant, especially if they provided or encouraged escape routes, routine nondangerous contacts with passersby, or a special means of concealing deviant acts. For example, the location and orientation of a building with regard to the corner of a block, an alleyway, or passing traffic might be important. Most of these particulars could fairly well be determined or estimated by field observation. Selective participant observation provided more detailed information on these items.

This study is exploratory and designed to shed light on the structural patterns of visible deviant street conditions. The task at hand was to develop basic knowledge and data about visible street prostitution. At the outset of this research the thirteen locations of female street prostitution in midtown and lower Manhattan representing all known "permanent" conditions for this type of deviance were deemed adequate for this task. The restriction of locations to thirteen visible deviant street conditions in Manhattan South made their selection more attractive. The same number of street locations scattered over a larger area would have obscured important patterns governing interactions between adjacent deviant street conditions. Moreover, the logistics for observing locations over a more extensive area go beyond the resources available for this study.

The thirteen deviant street locations selected do not possess idiosyncratic characteristics. These locations represent a wide variety of neighborhoods and are not atypical of street conditions. A comparison of these thirteen locations with two other street conditions of female street prostitution on the city's upper West and East sides failed to show any meaningful differences, however, like those studied, they are in mixed business, residential, and ethnic areas that are not part of the city's ghettos. Perhaps visible street prostitution or any other form of deviance might differ in deteriorated slum areas. Although the range of applicability of findings in the present study must be tested by future research, there is no indication whatsoever that the patterns, regularities, and uniformities characterizing the thirteen street locations are unique and not also descriptive of other deviant areas in similar neighborhoods of New York City or other large cities.

Prostitute Indicators

One crucial problem was to distinguish female prostitutes from other women. It is quite common to find women not engaged in prostitution standing alone or in groups of two or three on many streets in New York City. Various indicators were utlized to identify prostitutes including location, time, gesture, walk, clothing, and reaction to police. Given these and other similarly visible indicators, it was not difficult to identify prostitutes.

Streets, blocks, corners, and doorways were places prostitutes expropriated for illicit activities. Ordinary women rarely used these same locations for leisure and recreation. The same prostitutes usually stood or walked together in groups day after day at typical locations of active visible street deviance. Ordinary women were reluctant to mix with prostitutes or even be seen at these known locations either because of threat of bodily harm, loss of reputation, harassment by johns, or fear of arrest. Consequently most women who spent time in the area were probably prostitutes. The location at the Bowery and Delancey Street illustrated these patterns. A string of about five to thirty prostitutes lined the block or walked along the streets at different set times of day and night. Ordinary women almost never used these same streets.

It was rare for ordinary women to remain at any of the thirteen street locations when visible street deviance was active. This was even more so during evening hours when pedestrian and vehicular traffic usually diminished. The location of street deviance at 32nd Street and Madison Avenue illustrated these patterns. During daylight hours the condition was dormant and the streets empty of prostitutes. Instead the streets were filled with middle-class persons who worked and shopped in the areas' businesses and stores. After the stores and office buildings closed for the night, the area was deserted. The first wave of prostitutes appeared at approximately 8:30 p.m. Beyond this hour until early each morning ordinary women did not appear except to pass hastily through the area. As evening wore on, prostitutes and patrons were observed discussing transactions and on occasion entering hotels or cars together.

At most locations of visible street deviance, prostitutes openly solicited male passersby on foot and in cars. They approached and engaged males by overt hand signals (waving, gesturing with their index finger signifying "come to me" or "come here," and so forth) and verbal gestures. Typical verbal gestures included "Honey, do you want a date?," "Do you want some sport?," "Would you like some fun?" There was a willingness to initiate conversation with almost any male. New York City, despite its epithet "Fun City," is not a town where ordinary women routinely stand in the street to chat with strangers. At times the prostitutes were extremely persistent. They followed male passersby, grabbed their arms or jackets, and held the door of a waiting car standing so close that often the driver was hesitant to accelerate because of fear of injuring the prostitute. Prostitutes continuously searched and waited for a connecting eye. Some girls made a head movement to attract males; others simply stared. Most legitimate women waiting for someone or for transportation tended to look downward and they ignored approaches by male strangers. When they did throw a glance they turned away immediately. When the police were thought to be in an area the prostitutes simply stood and waited for a male to approach them. When this happened a cautious conversation ensued.

Prostitutes frequently stood together in one spot for substantial periods of time (fifteen to thirty minutes) or they constantly walked back and forth on the same block, often talking to each other. Most prostitutes assumed a sexually inviting posture designed to attract potential customers. Ordinary women were never observed in known locations of street deviance continuously walking up and down peering in every direction.

A prostitute's clothing often provided clues about the profession. Traditional prostitute garments included weather coats, high boots, miniskirts, hot pants, pantyhose, tight pants and open halters. When these garments were in style, prostitutes had a tendency to wear their clothes more prominently and conspicuously than others. For example, oftentimes they wore their skirts shorter, and dungarees tighter than nonstreet women. Many prostitutes also wore showy and prominent wigs, had on excess makeup, and frequently carried umbrellas and handbags with long shoulder straps ostensibly for protection.

When police passed the area, prostitutes usually darted from their *spots* and entered coffee shops, bars, and hotels or they attempted to hide behind cars, in doorways, alleys, or other places of concealment. Ordinary women simply stood their ground. On numerous occasions prostitutes attempted to mislead the police. Some prostitutes have become sidewalk artists. They have developed skills for blending into the local scene. They wear unobtrusive clothing, walk in a relaxed manner, exude a nonchalant air, and perform numerous tricks with doorways, phone booths, cars, bus queues, shopping bags, packages, and taxis. In most cases these tactics do not succeed. The prostitutes are recognized and either threatened with arrest or forced momentarily to leave the area.

On a few occasions the police arrested ordinary women who were mistaken for prostitutes. In one instance late in the evening, women dressed in attractive clothing were standing in the vicinity of Lexington Avenue and 25th Street. They were arrested despite vehement protestations that they were waiting for friends. Most lawsuits arising from this type of error, so long as there is probable cause and proper police behavior, result in relatively small settlements of $10,000 or less.[5]

None of these factors alone were used to identify the vast majority of prostitutes. However, when taken together they served as reliable indicators of street prostitutes. Two cases from the field notes illustrate how distinctions were made between ordinary women and street prostitutes.

> On August 2, 1977 at 10:30 p.m. I observed two women on 32nd Street and Fifth Avenue. Although at this time several prostitutes were present at this

location I concluded that these women were not part of the permanent street scene. Unlike prostitutes, these women scurried through the block in a direction away from the visible deviant street location. They held packages which appeared to be record discs and they were talking to each other but not to anyone else. Both were dressed in what appeared to be conservative and expensive clothes. They were not dressed in a promiscuous manner nor did they have on excess makeup. They did not pay attention to the constant flow of traffic circling the block or to a police radio car. In fact they kept very much to themselves staring downward toward the sidewalk or looking at each other but avoiding eye contact with other street actors. After a few minutes they disappeared from view and were never seen again by this researcher.

Although in an active location of visible street deviance, it was decided that these two women were not prostitutes because of significant differences in their behavior compared to deviant street participants.

On May 30, 1978 at 4:55 a.m. a white woman about thirty-six years of age was walking on 59th Street and Eighth Avenue. She was dressed in a white blouse and a black skirt a little bit above the knees. I was in my car waiting for a traffic light to change. This woman passed my car and didn't look toward me. All of a sudden she threw a sudden furtive glance at me and then turned quickly away. She seemed to be afraid as she walked the streets. She darted into a luncheonette. I remained out of sight at this location for at least ten minutes to determine whether or not this woman might leave the luncheonette and position herself on the street.

I decided this woman was not a street prostitute working this location because she did not return to the street, walk back and forth, gesture to passersby, or talk to anyone. She removed herself entirely from the street scene. It was also significant that 59th Street and Eighth Avenue was not a known location for visible street deviance.

Obtrusiveness

The presence of the researcher almost never appeared to interfere with the usual conduct of business. In most instances while the researcher was in the car, he was totally unnoticed or, if noticed, wholly ignored. Prostitutes conducted business in open view of passersby whether the observer was parked and stationed in his car, in heavy steady traffic, or completely hidden from view. Once while conducting observations from the car, a prostitute followed a male in a business suit across the street directly in front of the "research" car. She obviously was not successful in convincing him to come with her, so she turned back past the car, glanced in, and returned right back to her former spot. The presence of the researcher seemingly had no effect in terms of disturbing the natural setting. It was business as usual and the naturalness of the setting was preserved.

On only a few occasions, especially when I left my car to conduct observations from the street, was I suspected of being a police officer. Prostitutes either desisted from routine deviant activities or left the area until somehow they allayed their suspicions or summoned enough courage to covertly carry on. Several prostitutes asked me whether I was a cop. I answered "no" and afterward most prostitutes returned to business as usual. Most often, however, when I left the car I was perceived as a potential client, bystander, or passerby. Prostitutes frequently approached me on the street and treated me like any other adult male.

Nonobtrusiveness by the researcher and the preservation of the natural setting probably varied with time and place. For example, during daylight hours at 44th Street and Lexington Avenue observations were made from across the street. I stood near the building with a newspaper or briefcase in hand and pretended to be waiting for someone. Between the hours of 5 p.m. and 9 p.m. there was fairly heavy pedestrian traffic; people stood about waiting for taxis, friends, and associates. Here it was feasible to blend in with the natural setting simply by dressing appropriately.

After 9 p.m. when most of the area's businesses were closed, observation became more difficult. Pedestrian traffic diminished significantly and occupied cars, parked near the street setting, were noticed more easily. The problem became more acute as evening continued because pedestrian and vehicular traffic diminished further.

Since it might seem strange if an observer were to stand directly across the street or on the same block as the prostitutes during hours of light pedestrian movement, I usually observed them from about a block away in my automobile.

The fact that I was a middle-class, white, male adult was useful because many bystanders and johns fit this general description. My presence was probably a good deal less obtrusive than researchers in many other well-known field studies. Elliot Liebow, for example, observed unemployed, uneducated, unmarried blacks who hung around street corners despite the fact that he was white, married, educated, employed, resided elsewhere, and spoke in a manner markedly different from street people.[6] Despite these differences his presence did not interfere with routine activities or influence them in any meaningful way.

Ethical Issues

Key ethical issues in the present research are whether physical, psychological, social, or any other form of harm may have existed for the human subjects; whether the researcher's identity should have been revealed; and whether the human subjects should have been informed about the nature of this research.

In the present study no reasonable chance existed that bodily, psychological, social, or any other form of harm would be inflicted on the subjects. The anonymity of each subject was assured and information that might identify subjects was not revealed. All information was organized so that it could not be associated with individuals. Quantitative counts, for example, were presented in statistical or aggregate form. The conversations with subjects ought not to have harmed anyone because these take place in the street all the time.

Whether or not to reveal the researcher's identity has been debated by several scholars with ambiguous and conflicting opinions (for example, Kai T. Erikson, Julius Roth, Raymond L. Gold).[7] In the present study the researcher's identity was not routinely revealed because there was no reasonable likelihood of injury. Also, routine disclosure definitely would have disturbed the natural environment.

Most information was gathered by observation in public locations without disturbing or distracting the subjects who voluntarily entered into certain agreements. Nearly all the data were collected in the streets of New York City where prostitutes and johns routinely made contact and members of the New York City Police Department carried out their patrol functions. At times the researcher stood in the street and peered into coffee shops or other commercial establishments that serve the public. The researcher did not require special permission from anyone at any time to stand, walk, or work in any place. The focus of the research was not on a single individual; there was no requirement that any subject had to be known personally. Therefore, I did not routinely inform the subjects that they were part of a study. Nor did I regularly identify myself as a researcher or announce my research intentions.

On certain occasions when a conversation was held and it moved beyond a routine exchange where it lasted for more than a few minutes or where several conversations were held with the same subject, I explained the research objectives. However, written consent was not feasible because the subjects were reluctant to provide a record of their identity. At the same time I assured them that responses under no circumstances would be associated with individuals. The conversations were conducted by the principal investigator, and they were terminated as soon as the subjects showed reluctance to continue.

During the course of this research I observed illegal behavior, but not more, in a qualitative sense, than encountered by ordinary citizens in New York City. On the few occasions I observed assaults or robberies I acted the way I would have under ordinary conditions (for example, I phoned for the police). Because I was not a participant observer I could easily switch roles from researcher to ordinary citizen.[8]

Research Strategy

Safety

An important issue in this type of field research is the safety and security of those who conduct the study. During two years or so in the field several potentially dangerous and threatening incidents occurred involving prostitutes and police.

About 4 a.m. in the vicinity of the Bowery and Delancey Street a prostitute approached my car and attempted to solicit my business while I was waiting for a traffic light. When I declined she suddenly pulled an object from her handbag and sprayed me with mace. Only a small quantity penetrated because simultaneously I made an evading movement and closed my window. The burning and choking sensation in my throat lasted about one and one-half hours even after several glasses of water, obtained in a nearby restaurant.

I had parked in the Park and Fifth Avenues network at approximately 1 a.m. and several prostitutes approached my car. Two "men" were lurking in the background. I explained to the prostitutes that I was conducting social research. One prostitute remarked that I was a police officer and then leaned through the car's front window to frisk me for a gun. Close contact of this nature can result in physical harm.

In the vicinity of Eighth Avenue and 49th Street about 3 a.m., two males approached me on the street and asked for a light. Simultaneously they began speaking in an aggressive tone. I quickly crossed the street and left the area.

On numerous occasions prostitutes spilled coffee and banged my car presumably because I declined their solicitations.

On several occasions while parked in my car police officers approached and in a hostile tone asked what I was doing. I explained I had stopped momentarily to fix some papers and that I was ready to leave the area. Typical responses by the officers included "Get the hell out of here," or "If we catch you in this neighborhood again we will arrest you."

On several occasions while waiting for a traffic light or hanging out on the street, police officers with drawn revolvers pursued fleeing suspects. In two incidents shots were fired by the police.

Certain precautionary techniques may help avoid dangerous situations and increase safety. These include: remain alert at all times even while in a parked or waiting vehicle; constantly check rear and side view mirrors; do not remain in one parking position for more than fifteen minutes and if a suspicious looking person approaches depart immediately; always allow sufficient space to be able to leave a parking spot in a single forward motion; keep doors and windows secured at all times; gauge your speed when approaching a traffic light for a green signal so you need not stop. If you must stop, position your vehicle several feet behind the last car in the queue. In the event of an emergency this tactic will allow a few extra seconds by moving the car forward or by maneuvering to either side of the forward car. Position your car first in line at a traffic signal to avoid being blocked by another vehicle. This tactic is especially feasible on wide streets where there are several car lanes; be especially cautious approaching stops with a concentration of males; in general a man and woman team in a car is safer than either a single individual or two males because they are less obtrusive at deviant street locations; defensive driving is a must; and be certain to have in your possession a statement on an official letterhead from someone in authority (that is, department chairperson, dean, police commissioner) explaining your study and requesting cooperation (see appendix B), although I had no occasion to display my letter.

Notes

1. J.A. Barnes, "Class and Communities in a Norwegian Island Parish," *Human Relations* 7, no. 1 (1954):38-39, as cited in Francis A.J. Ianni, *Black Mafia* (New York: Simon and Schuster, 1974), p. 62.

2. A network's socioeconomic status was determined by income level, education, and a thorough on-site survey of buildings, streets, and street users.

3. Raymond L. Gold, "Sex Roles in Sociological Field Observations," *Social Forces* 36, no. 220 (March 1958):217-223. These methods differ from Gold's "Observer-as-Participant" where the researcher spends substantial time observing and only a brief period in the milieu. For this book, in addition to observations the researcher spent substantial time acquiring information from the subjects through conversations and unstructured interviews. Nevertheless, no attempt was made to participate fully in the street scene. Also see: George J. McCall and J.L. Simmons, eds., *Issues in Participant Observation* (Reading, Mass.: Addison-Wesley Publishing Co., 1969); William J. Filstead, ed., *Qualitative Methodology* (Chicago: Markham Publishing Co., 1970); Rosalie H. Wax, *Doing Fieldwork* (Chicago: University of Chicago Press, 1971); Alcira Kreiner, "Environmental Preferences: A Critical Analysis of Some Research Methodologies," *Journal of Leisure Research* 9, no. 2 (1977):88-97; Robert S. Weppner, ed., *Street Ethnography* (Beverly Hills, Calif.: Sage Publications, 1977); and Francis A.J. Ianni, *Black Mafia* (New York: Simon and Schuster, 1974).

4. Frederic M. Thrasher, *The Gang* (Chicago: University of Chicago Press, 1927); and Gerald D. Suttles, *The Social Order of the Slum* (Chicago: University of Chicago Press, 1962).

5. See *The New York Times*, 4 August 1978, p. 24; 10 November 1979, p. 27; 5 February 1978, p. 6; 10 March 1976, p. 23; 16 April 1976, p. 27; and 16 October 1976, p. 27.

6. Elliot Liebow, *Tally's Corner* (Boston: Little, Brown & Co., 1967).

7. Kai T. Erickson, "A Comment on Disguised Observation in Sociology," pp. 252-260 and Julius A. Roth, "Comments on Secret Observation," pp. 278-280, in *Qualitative Methodology*, edited by William J. Filstead (Chicago: Markham Publishing Co., 1970). Also see "Roles in Sociological Field Observations," in *Issues in Participant Observation*, edited by George J. McCall and J.L. Simmons (Reading, Mass.: Addison-Wesley Co., 1969), pp. 30-38.

8. See discussion on this subject in Jerome Skolnick, *Justice Without Trial: Law Enforcement in Democratic Society* (New York: John Wiley & Sons, 1966) and Bernard Cohen and Stephen H. Leinen, *Research on Criminal Justice Organizations: The Sentencing Process* (Santa Monica, Calif.: The Rand Corp., 1976), R-2018DOJ, pp. 8-10.

3 Deviant Street Network Profiles

In 1626 from the time Peter Minuit purchased Manhattan until 1874 when the West Bronx was annexed, New York City was confined to the island of Manhattan.[1] This borough is the busiest and most vibrant of the five (Manhattan, Bronx, Brooklyn, Queens, Richmond), although its area is only twenty-two square miles. North of 59th Street, Manhattan consists mainly of residential communities including the Upper East and West Sides, Harlem, Spanish Harlem, Morningside Heights, and Washington Heights. Central Park also is included in this area. Manhattan, south of 59th Street, the area covered by this research, has relatively few inhabitants although Chelsea, the Lower East Side, Greenwich Village and parts of East and West Midtown have substantial residential communities of nearly every race and nationality. Manhattan South consists of some of the world's largest and most famous office buildings, retail stores, museums, theaters, and concert halls (for example, the Empire State Building, Macy's Department Store, the Museum of Modern Art, Shubert Theater, Carnegie Hall). Overall, Manhattan South has a highly concentrated and transient population in dynamic and rapid movement. During a given work day more than a million people enter Manhattan South, partly from the metropolitan area including New Jersey, Connecticut, and Long Island, to work and shop in its thriving commercial districts or visit its many famous historical, cultural and theatrical institutions. Anonymity is easily achieved in this environment.

The Lower East Side

The Lower East Side was settled in 1651 when Peter Stuyvesant obtained a patent for a farm that included a substantial parcel of land in the Eastern section of Lower Manhattan between 4th and 17th Streets.[2] During the remaining half of the seventeenth century the Lower East Side was a summer vacation spot for the wealthy. The large immigrant influx began around 1710 and by the year 1800 the area was a mecca for immigrants. First came the Irish and Germans, soon followed by the Italians and the Jews. The immigrants experienced poverty, unemployment, and crowded living quarters. Parents worked long hours to support their families, and children often earned money as newsboys, beggars, and petty thieves. Nearly every Jewish male child attended Hebrew school at an early age. Orthodox Jewish women with kerchiefs and men with skullcaps (*yarmulkes*) mixed with the pushcarts that lined the crowded streets. Yiddish was the main language and store signs used Hebrew letters. Two of the area's main thoroughfares were Delancey Street and Grand Street. This was the center of the shopping district where one could purchase every conceivable type and variety of portable merchandise. Grand Street was noted for its shops specializing in dry goods and apparel.

The Lower East Side continued to attract Jewish immigrants from Eastern Europe through the 1930s. After World War II and into the fifties the area's ethnic makeup began to change. The traditional Jewish quarter, which was east of the Bowery, shrank and blacks and Hispanics moved into the area. Today the area is a bustling retail center, but the buildings and neighborhoods are run down and dilapidated. The area still retains a distinctly Jewish flavor. Most stores are closed for the Sabbath and the big shopping day is Sunday when thousands of shoppers arrive to search for bargains.

The most famous thoroughfare in the Lower East Side is the Bowery (the Dutch term for farm).[3] This neighborhood is the home for drunkards, derelicts and homeless men. The dormitory-style hotels, referred to as *flophouses* by neighborhood denizens, had nearly 3500 beds in 1957, but today this has diminished to about 800. This area now consists mainly of commercial establishments, but many declining buildings, flea-bag hotels, and cheap bars remain.

The northern end of Third Avenue around 14th Street was considered a Polish enclave comprised of Jewish and non-Jewish Poles. The streets were lined with tenements and stores.

At Third Avenue and 6th Street is Cooper Square, one of the area's most famous historical landmarks. It is named after the American engineer and philanthropist Peter Cooper who in 1859, founded the Cooper Union as a free, coeducational institute of science and art, without racial or religious restrictions.[4] About a block away is McSorley's Old Ale House, one of the oldest and most famous saloons in America. Established in 1854, it has resisted everything from riots to real-estate brokers.[5]

Today the vicinity immediately surrounding the Bowery and Delancey Street consists of dilapidated tenements and abandoned buildings. Most area stores sell lighting fixtures, electrical supplies, and restaurant equipment. Also, a run-down hotel, a sleazy pool hall, numerous vacant stores, and several small fast-food restaurants are interspersed among the area's commercial establishments. Not many persons reside in this neighborhood.

Forsythe Street between Delancey and Grand Streets is bounded on its west side by Roosevelt Park and on its east side by decaying tenements. The block is populated primarily by Puerto Ricans and a few Chinese. The handful of neighborhood establishments include a *bodega* (a Spanish-American grocery store catering mainly to Hispanics) and two Hispanic churches.

Sixth Street and Third Avenue, two blocks south of St. Mark's Place, the core of East Village, has become a haven for artists, bohemians, and persons who cannot afford the rising rents of Greenwich Village. The area is primarily occupied by Ukranians, Poles, and Jews, but there are also substantial numbers of Italians, blacks, and Hispanics. This mixed community has contributed to its exciting atmosphere for in the space of a few blocks there are a kosher delicatessen, a Spanish storefront church, a Ukranian bookstore, and an Italian restaurant.[6] The new bohemians are enjoying the European flavor and low rents, and the older residents appear to be energized by the youth and creativity. The corner of 6th Street and Third Avenue where Cooper Union stands forms the end of a block with an elementary school and several brownstones. Across the street is the Cooper Union library and a small safety island used by pedestrians to cross the unusually wide avenue.

Tenth to 14th Streets on Third Avenue is a mixed commercial and residential area. Although the side streets are lined with well-kept brownstones and small apartment houses, Third Avenue itself consists mainly of numerous retail and commercial establishments including bars, two run-down "welfare" hotels, coffee shops, a pawn shop, a cheap movie house showing old, grade B films, a pornographic bookstore, a drugstore, a cigar store that used to sell loose cigarettes for a nickel each, a school for barbers, a gypsy palm reader, and a store selling camping goods. Three large parking lots take up nearly the entire three-block area on the east side of Third Avenue between 9th and 12th Streets. Many area residents live in a large apartment house on Third Avenue between 13th and 14th Streets. Overall the four deviant street locations comprising the Lower East Side network are sparsely populated with lower-income individuals.

Park and Fifth Avenues

The Park and Fifth Avenues area includes the city's Murray Hill and Madison Square section.[7] The Murray Hill section was part of the Robert Murray estate. During the Revolution, Mrs. Mary Murray delayed the British troops pursuing Washington's army by inviting the redcoat officers for tea. Although this area has numerous undistinguished postwar buildings, enough of the old town houses remain to provide a distinctive nineteenth century flavor. In the nineteenth century the Murray estate was divided into several small plots of land. Eventually expensive town houses were built on these individual lots. In 1897 a law passed barring businesses from parts of the area. This law was overturned in 1960, but strict zoning laws remain.

The area around 25th to 26th Streets between Lexington and Madison Avenues is known as Madison Square. The site occupied by the New York Life Insurance Company's skyscraper since 1925 initially was the old Union Depot. The depot was converted to Barnum's Hippodrome in 1871 and later into the original Madison Square Garden.

Park and Fifth Avenues between 23rd Street to 34th Street is primarily a commercial district concentrating on textiles, furniture, and book publishing. The Metropolitan Life Insurance Company occupies a two-block stretch on the east side of Madison Square, and the New York Life Insurance Company nearby covers a block and a half.[8] The area's residential stock is over a hundred years old and many town houses and apartment buildings have been renovated. A deteriorated hotel and bar occupy the southeast corner of Lexington Avenue at 25th Street. Another small decaying hotel is situated on the northeast corner. Several large buildings dominate the area including a National Guard Armory, an industrial building, and a small middle-income apartment house. Several coffee shops and Indian restaurants are within a few blocks of this location.

Park Avenue at 26th Street is primarily a commercial area. Tall office buildings take up three corners of the intersection while the fourth northeast corner is occupied by a small, seedy, physically run-down hotel. Several expensive apartment houses and town houses are in the immediate vicinity.

Thirty-second Street and Madison Avenue is nearly all commercial. There are many tall office buildings, lofts, and fine retail shops. Stores display special lingerie, exotic perfume, and designer linens. There are several small declining welfare hotels and numerous coffee shops in this area, including one open twenty-four hours a day.

Lexington Avenue between 44th and 50th Streets is also primarily a commercial area. It contains several luxury hotels including the world famous Waldorf Astoria. Interspersed between these expensive buildings are several fast-food restaurants open twenty-four hours and a small deteriorated hotel situated over a pub. The Park and Fifth Avenues network is one of the most expensive and prime residential areas in New York City. It contains the heaviest concentration of office buildings in the city including the corporate headquarters for many of the nation's leading businesses and the United Nations. Also this network boasts the city's most expensive and fashionable hotels, restaurants, private clubs, art-movie theaters, nightclubs, and shops.[9]

Ninth Avenue

The deviant street network on Ninth Avenue lies in the infamous area that was known as "Hell's Kitchen."[10] There are several stories on how this area got its name. The most enduring legend is that the name emerged from a conversation between two police officers, one a veteran of the force, the other a rookie. These officers encountered a small riot on West 39th Street. "This place is hell itself," the rookie is said to have remarked.

"Hell's a mild climate," retorted the veteran officer. "This is hell's kitchen, no less."[11]

The opening of the Hudson River Railroad in 1851 brought a sudden influx of industry into the area. Wooden tenements were erected in the spaces between industrial buildings. Irish and German immigrants crowded into them and made up a pool of cheap labor. During the next fifty years this area was the foulest and most dangerous slum in New York City. Criminal gangs such as the Gophers and Dead Rabbits roamed and ruled the streets. Eventually the New York Central Railroad recruited a private army that crushed the mobs after several months of bloody warfare. The Lincoln Tunnel and the Port Authority Bus Terminal eliminated a large chunk of these overcrowded tenements. Also since the mid-fifties new construction occurred in the area including the building of a dozen motor lodges and several major commercial buildings. Today newspapers and city agencies refer to this area as "Clinton."[12]

The area survives as a residential and shopping thoroughfare with many food stores selling wholesale as well as retail. The merchandise reflects the current ethnic composition including Italians, Greeks, Puerto Ricans, Yugoslavs, and Irish. Upcoming young actors also reside in this neighborhood because the theater district is nearby and it is also cheap. By now, many tenements between Eighth and Ninth Avenues have been remodeled and several small new buildings have been built on side streets.[13]

Forty-sixth Street on Ninth Avenue is part of a mixed residential and commerical area. The avenue is lined with small retail shops catering to neighborhood residents who live in old dilapidated brownstones and tenements on side streets. Most of the tenants are poor. Several families belong to a Protestant church located in about the middle of 46th Street between Ninth and Tenth Avenues. On the southwest corner of 46th Street there is a bar and on the northeast corner a grocery store that is open twenty-four hours. A similar store is open all the time on Ninth Avenue and 45th Street.

Forty-second Street on Ninth Avenue is nearly opposite the Port Authority Bus Terminal, the city's busiest and largest bus station. Currently it is undergoing expansion and as a result there is much construction. Few residents live in the immediate vicinity although several stores sell produce, meat, fish, and spices. Most buildings are old and declining. Heavy vehicular traffic flows toward the Lincoln Tunnel, but few pedestrians use these streets especially at night.

Forty-second Street and Tenth Avenue was nearly all commercial until about 1978 when a huge middle- to high-income apartment complex, known as Manhattan Plaza, was built on the northeast side of the street. It takes up one square block. Most deviance observed for this location occurred before construction of this apartment complex when the area was nearly all commercial. Several public parking garages now dot the area. Also within a block radius of 42nd Street and Tenth Avenue is a large retail record shop, an elevator company, and a Travel Inn Motor Lodge. An old, decaying, coffee shop in a row of run-down tenements is situated on the southwest corner. Recently several small theaters opened for business.

Eighth Avenue

Eighth Avenue is the eastern boundary of Hell's Kitchen but also serves as the western boundary of the Times Square entertainment district.[14] Rapid transportation reached the Times Square area in 1904 with the opening of the first subway line and played a significant role in development of the district. Eventually the area became known for its theaters, theatrical restaurants, and hotels. In 1925 the second home for Madison Square Garden was constructed at 50th Street and Eighth Avenue. This revitalized the entire Eighth Avenue theater district. The center of this network is 42nd Street and Eighth Avenue. The blocks off Eighth Avenue are lined with hotels, shops, restaurants, movie houses, theaters, and nightclubs. The area is part of the 42nd Street "crossroads" because on an average day, about half of the persons in the vicinity are visitors. It is a highly transient area consisting of employees and shoppers but few residents. Recently newspaper accounts have referred to the stretch on Eighth Avenue from about 38th Street to 49th Street as the "Minnesota Strip." It is so named for the teenage prostitutes from the Midwest attracted or brought to the area by pimps because of the large amount of money to be earned from prostitution.

Part of the area extending from 38th to 42nd Streets on Eighth Avenue is situated across from the Port Authority Bus Terminal. Pedestrian traffic is heavy, and taxis form a continuous queue on the west side of the avenue waiting for travelers entering the city from the bus station. The four blocks are dotted with bars, sleazy hotels, shops selling cheap merchandise, discount stores, fast-food establishments, and pizza parlors. These commercial establishments are situated in old run-down buildings of four to seven stories. There are few places for permanent residence in the immediate vicinity of these four blocks. Most of the persons on these streets are black or Hispanic adult males.

Forty-second to 49th Street on Eighth Avenue is similar to its southern counterpart between 38th and 42nd Streets, except that it appears somewhat more stable and slightly more desirable. The area has several movie houses and higher priced restaurants and it is an offshoot of the Seventh Avenue-Broadway theater district. On the other hand it is heavily dotted with porno shops, adult sexual entertainment centers, live sex shows, movie houses that show X-rated films, twenty-five-cent peep shows, massage parlors,[15] rundown hotels, and fast-food-take-out places. Perhaps the brownstones and tenements that line the side streets and the area's expensive restaurants catering to the theater crowd have contributed to its modest stabilization.

Notes

1. Gilbert Tauber and Samuel Kaplan, *New York City Handbook* (New York: Doubleday and Company, 1968), pp. 456-458.
2. See Michael Karmmen, *Colonial New York* (New York: Charles Scribner & Sons, 1975); Maxwell F. Marcuse, *This Was New York* (New York: Carlton Press, 1965); Robert E. Humphrey, *Children of Fantasy* (New York: John Wiley & Sons, 1978); Fred W. McDarrah, *Greenwich Village* (New York: Cornith Books, 1963).
3. Tauber and Kaplan, *New York City Handbook*, p. 475.
4. McDarrah, *Greenwich Village*, p. 72.
5. Ibid.
6. Ibid., p. 80.
7. Tauber and Kaplan, *New York City Handbook*, pp. 462-464 and *The New York City Planning Commission, Plan for New York City*, Vol. 4 (Manhattan, 1969), pp. 76 and 82.
8. Tauber and Kaplan, *New York City Handbook*, pp. 485-488.
9. Ibid., pp. 462-463.
10. Ibid., pp. 498-503.
11. Richard O'Connor, *Hell's Kitchen* (Philadelphia: J.B. Lippincott Co., 1968), p. 12.
12. Tauber and Kaplan, *New York City Handbook*, p. 500.
13. Ibid., p. 503.
14. See Stanley Buder, "Forty-Second Street at the Crossroads: A History of Broadway to Eighth Avenue," in *West 42nd Street: The Bright Light Zone*, edited by William Kornblum et al. (New York: Graduate School and University Center, City University of New York, 1978), pp. 53-81.
15. Most massage parlors have been closed by the police and other city agencies after special ordinances were passed prohibiting these types of establishments.

4 Characteristics and Patterns of Visible Street Deviance

The quantitative data gathered at the thirteen locations of visible deviance during fifty-six hours of field observations is presented in this chapter. These fifty-six hours do not include hundreds of hours of intensive observation at these same street locations to familiarize myself with deviant conditions, examine in detail patterns and characteristics of street actors, and gather extensive information on routine activities. The data obtained from the fifty-six hours of standardized quantitative counts confirmed the information gathered during qualitative field observations in nearly every case. The few instances where differences arose are pointed out in the text.

Approximately the same amount of observation time was spent at each of the thirteen deviant street locations. However, more time was spent during those hours when conditions were active. In this way most observations were conducted when deviant street participants were present, interacting, and working, while less effort was expended at times when locations were virtually desolate. Accordingly, a total of approximately six hours was spent visiting locations during the morning from 7:00 a.m. to 1:00 p.m., twelve hours during the afternoon from 1:00 p.m. to 7:00 p.m., fourteen hours during the early evening from 7:00 p.m. to 1:00 a.m., and twenty-four hours during late evening from 1:00 a.m. to 7:00 a.m. These time intervals are an approximation, and they were not followed to the exact minute. Moreover, they represent a series of sets of observations over several months and not a standardized, steady, or consecutive flow of observations over a short period of time.

Prostitutes

Prostitutes were counted each time they were observed during different observation tours. A total of 1189 prostitutes were sighted at the thirteen deviant street locations during fifty-six hours of field counts, for an average of 21.3 prostitutes per hour (table 4-1). A decision was made to derive averages, dividing each quantity by the total number of hours of observation per time frame (that is, six hours from 7:00 a.m. to 1:00 p.m.; twelve hours from 1:00 p.m. to 7:00 p.m.; fourteen hours from 7:00 p.m. to 1:00 a.m.; twenty-four hours from 1:00 a.m. to 7:00 a.m.), or the total number

Table 4-1
Number, Percent, and Average per Hour of Prostitutes at Four Deviant Street Networks

Deviant Street Networks	Number	Percent	$\overline{X}$
Lower East Side	493	41.5	8.8
Ninth Avenue	96	8.1	1.7
Eighth Avenue	334	28.1	6.0
Park and Fifth Avenues	266	22.4	4.8
Total	1189	100.1	21.3

of hours for all time frames (fifty-six hours). Thus the

$$\frac{\text{number of prostitutes at a specific location}}{\text{total number of hours of observation per time frame, or total number of hours for all time frames}}$$

were used rather than dividing averages by the precise amount of time at a specific location,

$$\frac{\text{number of prostitutes at a specific location}}{\text{total number of hours at a specific location}}$$

The reason the total time spent during a tour was used as the denominator and not the fraction of time is that prostitutes observed at a deviant street location worked many hours and nearly always remained on the street beyond the completion of the tour. Also every location was observed each tour for about an equal amount of time. Although time spent at each site was physically interrupted by visits to other locations, I constantly revisited each site and found the scene much the same except for the appearance of additional prostitutes. Very little changed at these sites over a period of a few hours. Therefore, it was as if each site was under constant observation for the entire tour.

Suppose an observation tour began at 8:00 p.m. and took three hours. I arrived at one of the thirteen deviant street locations and counted five prostitutes. Then I traveled to each of the other locations and made counts. Many street locations are less than a minute from each other so that by driving around for a few minutes several locations could be observed numerous times. Also, all thirteen locations could usually be covered in about one hour. At 9:00 p.m. I returned to the original street location and once again made field counts. Suppose I counted the initial five and then ten additional prostitutes. Now a total of fifteen prostitutes were at this location. Once again I made field counts at the remaining twelve street locations. I returned to the initial street location at 10:00 p.m. for the third consecutive time. Suppose now five additional prostitutes were observed for a total of twenty.

I concluded that for a three-hour period a total of twenty prostitutes were observed because it was likely that all prostitutes initially spotted remained on the street for the entire observation tour. Whatever the advantages or limitations of utilizing this method of computation compared to a denominator with the precise amount of time at a particular location, the relative results between locations for both methods are the same.

Most prostitutes worked the Lower East Side (493 or 41.5 percent); next Eighth Avenue (334 or 28.1 percent); and then Park and Fifth Avenues (266 or 22.4 percent); Ninth Avenue had the fewest prostitutes (96 or 8.1 percent). The average number of prostitutes per hour for the Lower East Side was 8.8; Eighth Avenue, 6.0; Park and Fifth Avenues, 4.8; and Ninth Avenue, 1.7. The single location having the most prostitutes was 42nd to 49th Streets on Eighth Avenue (table 4-2). The average number of prostitutes per hour observed at this deviant street location was 4.5. The location having the next highest number of prostitutes was the Bowery and Delancey Street (an average per hour of 4.0), then 10th to 14th Streets on Third Avenue (an average per hour of 3.2) and then 32nd Street and Fifth Avenue (an average per hour of 2.5). The locations having the lowest average number of prostitutes per hour were first 44th Street to 50th Street on Lexington Avenue ($\overline{X} = .1$), then 42nd Street and Ninth Avenue ($\overline{X} = .2$), and then 6th Street ($\overline{X} = .4$).

New York's East and West Sides

Contrary to widely held opinion, a greater proportion of prostitutes worked on the East Side of New York (essentially from Delancey Street to East 59th Street, east of Fifth Avenue) rather than the West Side (essentially from West 34th Street to West 59th Street, west of Fifth Avenue). The statistics show that 63.8 percent of the prostitutes observed worked on the East Side, mostly at the Lower East Side, while 36.2 percent worked on the West Side, mostly at Eighth Avenue. The density of prostitutes on the East Side was also greater than for the West Side. Thirty-five prostitutes occupied each city block of deviant street location on the East Side compared to twenty-seven for the West Side.

The proportions of black, white, and Hispanic prostitutes who worked the East and West Sides were similarly divided about 65/35, reflecting the overall ratio of prostitutes for these areas. For example, 67.7 percent of all black prostitutes occupied deviant street locations on the East Side, whereas

Table 4-2
Number, Percent, and Average per Hour of Prostitutes at Thirteen Deviant Street Locations

Deviant Street Locations	Number	Percent	$\bar{X}$
42nd to 49th Streets and Eighth Avenue	253	21.3	4.5
Bowery and Delancey Street	225	18.9	4.0
10th to 14th Streets and Third Avenue	178	15.0	3.2
32nd Street and Fifth Avenue	140	11.8	2.5
38th to 42nd Streets and Eighth Avenue	81	6.8	1.4
Forsythe Street	70	5.9	1.3
25th Street and Lexington Avenue	65	5.5	1.2
46th Street and Ninth Avenue	57	4.8	1.0
26th Street and Park Avenue	54	4.5	1.0
42nd Street and Tenth Avenue	30	2.5	.5
6th Street and Third Avenue	20	1.7	.4
42nd Street and Ninth Avenue	9	.8	.2
44th to 50th Streets and Lexington Avenue	7	.6	.1
Total	1189	100.1	21.3

32.2 percent of the blacks were on the West Side. Considering all the streetwalkers on the East Side, black and white prostitutes were about evenly divided (48.1 and 46.6 percent respectively). However, there was a greater proportion of white prostitutes (54.7 percent) than black prostitutes (40.5 percent) on the West Side. The proportions of Hispanic prostitutes on the East and West Sides were equal (5 percent each). Perhaps more prostitutes occupied the East Side rather than the West Side because New Yorkers from the city's four remaining boroughs, including Queens, Brooklyn, the Bronx, and Richmond (that is, Staten Island) enter Manhattan mainly from its east and not west side. Therefore, East Side prostitutes have easier access to johns.

It was very difficult to obtain a precise count of the number of prostitutes who worked the thirteen deviant street locations because of various combinations of part- and full-time prostitutes who may have worked either during the day or night or both. Full-time prostitutes worked a fairly steady schedule consisting of three, four, or more days a week several hours each tour. On the other hand, part-time prostitutes were sporadic in their habits and worked fewer days and hours.

Several viable typologies could be devised for street prostitutes based on work time (for example, part time, full time), mode of operations (for example, utilizes a car or hotel for business), and style of management (for example, a pimp, a group, or self-management). No attempt was made to prepare operational definitions or a typology for these various groups. In addition to differences in work hours, part-time compared to full-time prostitutes appeared extra cautious. Their tactics for soliciting were more surreptitious and less overt than those of full-time prostitutes.

An attempt was made to estimate the numbers of part-time and full-time prostitutes. These estimates were derived from the overall observational experience and not only from the standardized fifty-six-hour period. At any one time during the early and late evening hours (7:00 p.m. to 7:00 a.m.), the estimated number of street prostitutes ranged between 38 and 165 (table 4-3). On most nights, however, the estimated range was 50 to 70 prostitutes. The estimated size of the pool from which these women came was about 350 to 600 women for a half-year period. This pool consists of full-time prostitutes and does not include part-timers. The estimate is relatively small, but the same women usually worked the same streets over and over again.

The typical number of prostitutes available at any one time at any one location during nighttime falls around the midpoint of the range, shown in table 4-3. Accordingly, the number of prostitutes often observed between 42nd and 49th Streets on Eighth Avenue was about 20, and the number at 6th Street on Third Avenue was approximately 3. At times, at most locations there were not any prostitutes present. During daylight hours the number of prostitutes was reduced to about one-fifth its night average, although this varied substantially by individual street locations. Therefore, the overall range at the thirteen deviant street locations was approximately 7 to 33 prostitutes. Also in snow or rainy weather mainly during the winter months, the overall number of prostitutes was reduced by about 50 percent. Extremely hot weather did not seem to interfere with usual business, but overall incidence decreased by about 25 percent during the cold winter months.

Table 4-3
Estimated Number of Prostitutes during Nighttime at Thirteen Deviant Street Locations

Deviant Street Locations	Minimum	Maximum
42nd to 49th Streets and Eighth Avenue	6	35
Bowery and Delancey Street	5	30
10th to 14th Streets and Third Avenue	4	20
32nd Street and Fifth Avenue	4	15
38th to 42nd Streets and Eighth Avenue	4	13
Forsythe Street	3	12
25th Street and Lexington Avenue	3	10
46th Street and Ninth Avenue	2	7
26th Street and Park Avenue	2	6
42nd Street and Tenth Avenue	2	5
6th Street and Third Avenue	1	5
42nd Street and Ninth Avenue	1	4
44th to 50th Streets and Lexington Avenue	1	3
Total	38	165

Note: Nighttime is 7 p.m. to 7 a.m.

Technological or man-made crises did not appear to affect the overall incidence of street prostitutes. During the blackout in the summer of 1977 in New York City, the number of prostitutes visible in the streets remained about at the same level although the volume of clients was reduced to a trickle. Good street lighting is essential because johns may be reluctant to enter a poorly lit area. Each deviant street location studied had an abundance of street lamps. The week-long New York City transit strike during April 1980 that shut down all city subway and bus lines had only a negligible impact on the volume of street prostitutes and johns in cars although overall the number of johns decreased substantially.

Race

The field counts revealed that 49.6 percent of the street prostitutes were white ($N = 589$), 45.3 percent were black ($N = 539$), and 5.1 percent ($N = 61$) were Hispanic (table 4-4). One Chinese and one Indian prostitute were assigned to the white and black groups respectively.

Individual street networks and locations varied substantially in the mix of black, white, and Hispanic prostitutes, although not a single location was occupied by prostitutes of one race.

The Lower East Side was the only deviant street network with a majority of black prostitutes (51.7 percent). The proportions of black prostitutes for Ninth Avenue, Eighth Avenue, and Park and Fifth Avenues ranged between 40.1 percent and 41.7 percent. Park and Fifth Avenues had a majority of white prostitutes (57.9 percent). The street network having the next highest proportion of white prostitutes was Eighth Avenue (55.7 percent), afterward Ninth Avenue (51 percent), and then the Lower East Side (40.6 percent).

The deviant networks occupied by the largest number of Hispanic prostitutes were the Lower East Side (7.7 percent) and Ninth Avenue (7.3 percent). The proportions of Hispanics for Eighth Avenue was 4.2 percent and Park and Fifth Avenues, only .8 percent.

There were several locations without Hispanic prostitutes. On the East Side these included 32nd Street and Fifth Avenue and 44th to 50th Streets and Lexington Avenue, and on the West Side 38th to 42nd Streets on Eighth Avenue, and 42nd Street and Ninth Avenue. None of these locations were in or near Hispanic neighborhoods. Hispanic prostitutes tended to work neighborhoods of like ethnicity because they blended into the street scene and were less likely to be harassed by the police. The data on Hispanic prostitutes must be interpreted with caution because their overall number is small ($N = 61$).

In nine of ten locations where either black or white prostitutes were in a

Table 4-4
Number and Percent of Prostitutes by Race and Deviant Street Networks

Deviant Street Networks	Black		White		Hispanic		Total	
	Number	Percent	Number	Percent	Number	Percent	Number	Percent
Lower East Side	255	51.7	200	40.6	38	7.7	493	100.0
Ninth Avenue	40	41.7	49	51.0	7	7.3	96	100.0
Eighth Avenue	134	40.1	186	55.7	14	4.2	334	100.0
Park and Fifth Avenues	110	41.4	154	57.9	2	.8	266	100.0
Total	539	45.3	589	49.6	61	5.1	1189	100.0

clear majority at least 70 percent were of one race (table 4-5). Only 10th to 14th Streets had a smaller majority (60.7 percent were white). The locations with a substantial majority of black prostitutes included 26th Street and Park Avenue (90.7 percent), 38th to 42nd Streets (88.9 percent), 42nd Street and Ninth Avenue (88.9 percent), the Bowery and Delancey Street (71.6 percent), and 42nd Street and 10th Avenue (70 percent). White areas included 44th to 50th Streets and Lexington Avenue (85.7 percent), 32nd Street and Fifth Avenue (78.6 percent), 46th Street and Ninth Avenue (71.9 percent), 42nd to 49th Streets and Eighth Avenue (70 percent), and 10th to 14th Streets (60.7 percent).

Forsythe Street (40 percent white and 40 percent black), 6th Street (50 percent white and 45 percent black), and 25th Street and Lexington Avenue (52.3 percent white and 46.2 percent black) had more or less even distributions of white and black prostitutes. The two locations with the highest concentration of Hispanic prostitutes were Forsythe Street (20 percent) and 46th Street and Ninth Avenue (8.8 percent).

Every deviant street network had at least one location with a majority of white or black prostitutes. For example, 32nd Street and Fifth Avenue consisted primarily of white prostitutes (78.6 percent), while 26th Street and Park Avenue which is in the same middle to upper socioeconomic deviant network had a majority of black prostitutes (90.7 percent). However, blacks and Hispanics tended to occupy lower socioeconomic locations even within networks compared to their white counterparts. For example, 44th to 50th Streets and Lexington Avenue is a more expensive and desirable neighborhood than 26th Street and Park Avenue. Similarly, 10th to 14th Streets and Third Avenue lie in a more stable and less decayed neighborhood than the Bowery and Delancey Street. The racial composition for nearly all the deviant street locations remained stable over years. However, the location at 25th Street and Lexington Avenue was mixed during 1977 and 1978, the period of data collection, but by 1980 it tipped in the direction of a black majority. The more recent black prostitutes may be distinguished from their senior counterparts because they are much less attractive and far more aggressive. Also they seem to be independent and not managed by a pimp like the majority of prostitutes at this location. Perhaps the high inflationary times forced the newcomers to work at this lucrative location.

The average number per hour of black and white prostitutes for the Lower East Side was 4.6 and 3.6 respectively (table 4-6). Slightly more white than black prostitutes were observed on Eighth Avenue (average number per hour was 3.3 to 2.4), Ninth Avenue (average number per hour was .9 to .7), and Park and Fifth Avenues (average number per hour was 2.7 to 2.0). The incidence of Hispanic prostitutes was lower at each location than for either blacks or whites. The average number of Hispanic prostitutes per hour for the Lower East Side was .7; for Eighth Avenue, .3; for Ninth

Table 4-5
Number and Percent of Prostitutes by Race and Thirteen Deviant Street Locations Ordered According to Ethnic Majority

Race	Deviant Street Locations	Black Number	Black Percent	White Number	White Percent	Hispanic Number	Hispanic Percent	Total Number	Total Percent
Black	26th Street and Park Avenue	49	90.7	4	7.4	1	1.9	54	100.0
	38th to 42nd Streets and Eighth Avenue	72	88.9	9	11.1	—	—	81	100.0
	42nd Street and Ninth Avenue	8	88.9	1	11.1	—	—	9	100.0
	Bowery and Delancey Street	161	71.6	54	24.0	10	4.4	225	100.0
	42nd Street and Tenth Avenue	21	70.0	7	23.3	2	6.7	30	100.0
White	44th to 50th Streets and Lexington Avenue	1	14.3	6	85.7	—	—	7	100.0
	32nd Street and Fifth Avenue	30	21.4	110	78.6	—	—	140	100.0
	46th Street and Ninth Avenue	11	19.3	41	71.9	5	8.8	57	100.0
	42nd to 49th Streets and Eighth Avenue	62	24.5	177	70.0	14	5.5	253	100.0
	10th to 14th Streets and Third Avenue	57	32.0	108	60.7	13	7.3	178	100.0
Mixed	25th Street and Lexington Avenue	30	46.2	34	52.3	1	1.5	65	100.0
	6th Street and Third Avenue	9	45.0	10	50.0	1	5.0	20	100.0
	Forsythe Street	28	40.0	28	40.0	14	20.0	70	100.0
	Total	539	45.3	589	49.6	61	5.1	1189	100.0

Avenue, .1; and for Park and Fifth Avenues, only .04. The racial composition of prostitutes followed closely an area's socioeconomic status. Whites always were disproportionately overrepresented in higher socioeconomic areas. The rank order among deviant street networks for percentage of white prostitutes corresponds exactly with the socioeconmic rankings of the neighborhoods:

1. Park Avenue and Fifth Avenue
2. Eighth Avenue
3. Ninth Avenue
4. Lower East Side.

Although every one of the thirteen deviant street locations was occupied by white and black prostitutes, the severely skewed pattern in favor of whites indicates that the mixing was token. Apparently the social structure of street prostitution reflects the same discriminatory patterns in legitimate society where routinely blacks are more disadvantaged than their white counterparts.

Time Variations

The number of street prostitutes varied with time of day and night. Few prostitutes worked during morning hours (table 4-7) and there was a steady increase from early morning until late evening. The average number of prostitutes per hour from 7:00 a.m. to 1:00 p.m. was 3.8; from 1:00 p.m. to 7:00 p.m., 13.7; from 7:00 p.m. to 1:00 a.m., 16.2; and from 1:00 a.m. to 7:00 a.m., 32.2. White and black prostitutes closely followed this pattern, but Hispanics worked mainly during afternoon and early evening hours (an

Table 4-6
Average Number of Prostitutes per Hour by Race at Deviant Street Networks

Deviant Street Networks	Black		White		Hispanic		Total	
	Number	$\bar{X}$	Number	$\bar{X}$	Number	$\bar{X}$	Number	$\bar{X}$
Lower East Side	225	4.6	200	3.6	38	.7	493	8.8
Ninth Avenue	40	.7	49	.9	7	.1	96	1.7
Eighth Avenue	134	2.4	186	3.3	14	.3	334	6.0
Park and Fifth Avenues	110	2.0	154	2.7	2	.04	266	4.8
Total	539	9.6	589	10.5	61	1.1	1189	21.3

Table 4-7
Average Number of Prostitutes per Hour by Race and Time Period

Race	Morning		Afternoon		Early Evening		Late Evening		Total	
	Number	$\bar{X}$	Number	$\bar{X}$	Number	$\bar{X}$	Number	$\bar{X}$	Number	$\bar{X}$
Black	10	1.7	60	5.0	101	7.2	368	15.3	539	9.6
White	9	1.5	87	7.3	107	7.6	386	16.1	589	10.5
Hispanic	4	.7	17	1.4	20	1.4	20	.8	61	1.1
Total	23	3.8	164	13.7	228	16.2	774	32.2	1189	21.2

Note: Observation time for the morning period, six hours; afternoon, twelve hours; early evening, fourteen hours; late evening, twenty-four hours; total, fifty-six hours.

average of 1.4 prostitutes per hour). About half this number were observed each hour during late evening hours from 1:00 a.m. to 7:00 a.m. ($\overline{X}$ = .8) and early morning hours from 7:00 a.m. to 1:00 p.m. ($\overline{X}$ = .7). The ethnostatistics confirm that late evening in New York City is the peak activity period for visible female street prostitution.

Time and Location

The Ninth Avenue deviant street network was entirely dormant during the morning and afternoon (table 4-8), but it became active toward evening. An average per hour of .7 prostitutes occupied Ninth Avenue until around 1:00 a.m., and then during later evening (1:00 a.m. to 7:00 a.m.) it increased to 3.6. The Park and Fifth Avenues network also was entirely dormant during morning hours. Also, three of its four deviant locations were inactive from 1:00 p.m. to 7:00 p.m. However, prostitutes were frequently observed in the vicinity of 45th Street and Lexington Avenue from 1:00 p.m. to 7:00 p.m. The relative absence of visible street prostitution during daytime at Ninth Avenue and Park and Fifth Avenues was probably due to neighborhood residents and users who occupied the streets during the day and would not tolerate visible prostituton. After the stores closed and the streets were virtually deserted, visible street deviance surfaced.

The Lower East Side was the most active deviant street network during the day having an average of 2.7 and 9.3 prostitutes per hour respectively from 7:00 a.m. to 1:00 p.m. and 1:00 p.m. to 7:00 p.m. Even the Eighth Avenue network was not as active during daylight hours. The average number of prostitutes per hour for Eighth Avenue between 7:00 a.m. and 1:00 p.m. and 1:00 p.m. and 7:00 p.m., respectively, was 1.2 and 3.8.

During the morning, the most active period was between 7:00 a.m. and 9:00 a.m. when people went to work. Prostitutes who worked these hours usually were a mixture of holdovers from the late evening and women who began work early in the morning. These prostitutes hoped to make up during the morning work rush hour what they were unable or unwilling to earn during the evening when competition for johns is very tough. These women usually were older, less attractive and more poorly dressed than their nocturnal counterparts. They charged less money for services, were more likely to enter a car than a hotel for the sexual transaction, and were willing to risk arrest by roaming far from the protective cover of a hotel or coffee shop. Also these prostitutes tended to be quite bold. Many solicited johns in passing cars from the street rather than the sidewalk. In addition, they generally were more belligerent and hostile toward patrons and passersby than night prostitutes, perhaps because of greater fatigue and frustration.

Most prostitutes who work during the night sleep until early afternoon.

Table 4-8
Average Number of Prostitutes per Hour at Different Times of Day and Night for Deviant Street Networks

Deviant Street Networks	Morning		Afternoon		Early Evening		Late Evening		Total	
	Number	$\bar{X}$	Number	$\bar{X}$	Number	$\bar{X}$	Number	$\bar{X}$	Number	$\bar{X}$
Lower East Side	16	2.7	112	9.3	166	11.9	199	8.3	493	8.8
Ninth Avenue	—	—	—	—	10	.7	86	3.6	96	1.7
Eighth Avenue	7	1.2	46	3.8	6	.4	275	11.5	334	6.0
Park and Fifth Avenues	—	—	6	.5	46	3.3	214	8.9	266	4.8
Total	23	3.8	164	13.6	228	16.3	774	32.3	1189	21.3

Note: Observation time for morning period, six hours; afternoon, twelve hours; early evening, fourteen hours; late evening, twenty-four hours; total, fifty-six hours.

After about 9:00 a.m. even the Lower East Side was dormant. Activity picked up again around noon with the lunch crowd and an increase in passersby. The Eighth Avenue street network was busier in the afternoon (an average of 3.8 prostitutes per hour) than in early evening hours (an average of .4 prostitutes per hour). This was probably because of the dinner and theater crowd that occupied midtown, including parts of Eighth Avenue, between around 7:00 p.m. and 1:00 a.m. Police presence was heavy in the area, with special orders to suppress visible street deviance. Around midnight after most theatergoers left the area, Eighth Avenue escalated into the liveliest place in town. During late evening, an average of 11.5 prostitutes per hour occupied this deviant street network. Activity at other deviant street networks also picked up considerably during evening hours.

During morning hours from 7:00 a.m. to 1:00 p.m. for all street networks, there were no meaningful differences in the incidence of white and black prostitutes. From 1:00 p.m. to 7:00 p.m., however, three white prostitutes for every one black prostitute worked the Lower East Side and Eighth Avenue.

During early evening hours (7:00 p.m. to 1:00 a.m.) the only meaningful differences between black and white prostitutes was for Park and Fifth Avenues. The average number per hour for white prostitutes was 2.0 compared to 1.2 per hour for blacks. Most white prostitutes occupied 32nd and Fifth Avenue (1.2 per hour), while mainly black prostitutes worked 26th Street and Park Avenue (.6 per hour).

Overall the number of black (15.3 per hour) and white prostitutes (16.1 per hour) during late evening (1:00 a.m. to 7:00 a.m.) were nearly equal. However, twice as many black prostitutes (an average per hour of 5.2) as white prostitutes (an average per hour of 2.7) occupied the Lower East Side mainly at the Bowery and Delancey Street. Most prostitutes at Park and Fifth Avenues were white (an average per hour of 5.0) mainly due to the location at 32nd Street and Fifth Avenue. The average number per hour for black prostitutes at Park and Fifth Avenues was 3.8, most of whom worked 26th Street and Park Avenue. Similarly, an average per hour of 6.6 white prostitutes worked on Eighth Avenue compared to an average per hour of 4.7 black prostitutes. Most black prostitutes worked the area from 38th Street to 42nd Street (an average per hour of 2.4), while most white prostitutes worked the strip from 42nd Street to 49th Street (6.4 per hour).

The average per hour of black and white prostitutes from 1:00 a.m. to 7:00 a.m. on Ninth Avenue was equal (1.7). Mostly white prostitutes were observed at 46th Street and Ninth Avenue (an average of 1.4 per hour), while 42nd Street and Ninth Avenue (an average of .3 per hour) and 42nd Street and Tenth Avenue (an average of .9 per hour) had a majority of black prostitutes.

Hispanic prostitutes were observed during morning and afternoon at various locations mostly on the Lower East Side and on Eighth Avenue (an average per hour of 1.2). Slightly fewer Hispanic prostitutes worked during early or late evening hours (an average per hour of 1.0), usually at various locations on the Lower East Side. Except for the Park and Fifth Avenues network, most of the remaining Hispanic prostitutes were about evenly divided during evening hours between the deviant networks on Eighth and Ninth Avenues (an average of .3 prostitutes per hour). The Park Avenue to Fifth Avenue street network had the least number of Hispanics (.04 per hour on average).

The ethnic composition for prostitutes varied at certain deviant street networks by day and night. The shifts were mainly due to certain inactive locations in each network that became active during evening hours after neighborhood shoppers and employees left the area. During daylight hours the Lower East Side was occupied mainly by white prostitutes (51 percent) compared to black prostitutes (39 percent). The ethnic balance shifted with evening hours to a majority of black (56.1 percent) over white prostitutes (37 percent). Eighth Avenue was occupied primarily by white prostitutes both during the day (49 percent) and night (51.0 percent), while Park and Fifth Avenues and Ninth Avenue were inactive during the day but mainly occupied by white prostitutes during nighttime (57.3 percent and 51 percent, respectively).

Age

Information on age was estimated by this researcher and whatever bias exists ought to be constant. In several instances a spot check was made by asking prostitutes their age after I had attempted a guess. In all cases I was never off by more than one or two years. The data on approximate age reported here may not be precise, but they are consistent with information obtained in conversations with prostitutes and also other studies that reported on age of prostitutes and other street actors.[1]

The average approximate age of street prostitutes was 26.8 (table 4-9). Black prostitutes tended to be slightly older than white or Hispanic prostitutes. The average age for black prostitutes was 27.8; white prostitutes, 26.1; and Hispanic prostitutes, 25.6. Younger prostitutes tended to occupy the highest socioeconomic street network of Park and Fifth Avenues. The approximate age for white prostitutes in this network was 25.3 and black prostitutes, 27.2. There was only one Hispanic prostitute observed in this area. Her approximate age was 22.0. The oldest black and white prostitutes worked Ninth Avenue ($\overline{X} = 30.7$ and 27.6, respectively). For Hispanics, the oldest prostitutes were observed on Eighth Avenue ($\overline{X} = 28.0$).

Hispanic prostitutes, unlike their black and white counterparts, tended to work in neighborhoods with a subtantial Hispanic population (that is, the Lower East Side and Ninth Avenue). Apparently Hispanic prostitutes who ventured to Eighth Avenue tended to be older.

Transvestite Prostitutes

Transvestite prostitutes (also known as *drag queens* or *heshes*) are males who dress as females and solicit male customers. Transvestite prostitutes are of particular interest because they engage in behavior similar to female prostitutes, have analogous objectives and goals, and usually occupy areas contiguous with female prostitutes. Transvestite prostitutes were identified utilizing similar techniques as female prostitutes. They occupied specific locations usually during late evening hours when area residents, business people, or shoppers were not present. Also they dressed more flagrantly and outrageously than their female counterparts. When hot pants were in style, transvestite prostitutes almost always wore tighter and more prominent outfits than their female counterparts. When skirts were in style, they were usually clad in the shortest and most daring ones oftentimes with undergarments exposed. Transvestite prostitutes exhibited masculine characteristics. Many were tall and muscular; others had male features such as straight and narrow hips. In general, transvestite prostitutes dressed more scantily and conspicuously than female prostitutes. In addition, they were easily recognized because they nearly always banded together in groups of two to six, where at least some were taller, more bizarre, and masculine than almost any members of a group of female prostitutes.

Transvestite prostitutes were almost always more daring and forceful than female prostitutes. For example, they gesticulated and engaged potential johns more aggressively and noticeably than their female counterparts.

Table 4-9 New York City
Age of Prostitutes by Race and Deviant Street Networks

Deviant Street Networks	Black		White		Hispanic		Total	
	Number	$\overline{X}$	Number	$\overline{X}$	Number	$\overline{X}$	Number	$\overline{X}$
Lower East Side	220	27.4	197	26.0	35	25.1	452	26.6
Ninth Avenue	53	30.7	46	27.6	5	27.6	104	29.2
Eighth Avenue	104	27.8	162	26.5	5	28.0	271	27.0
Park and Fifth Avenues	113	27.2	143	25.3	1	22.0	257	26.1
Total	490	27.8	548	26.1	46	25.6	1084	26.8

Visible Street Deviance

Also they were much less selective. Typically a transvestite prostitute approached a male in a car waiting for a traffic light, opened the door, and immediately got inside besides him. Female prostitutes usually were reluctant to enter a car until they assessed that the driver was *safe*, meaning not a police officer or a dangerous person, mainly through conversation and facial expressions. Sometimes transvestite prostitutes stuck their hands through an open car window on the driver's side and manipulated the driver's genitals to stimulate him and also to provide a sample ("come on") of potential services. Often they propositioned their customers in a loud, harsh, and belligerent tone. Trained listeners easily discerned strong masculine intonations behind the disguised female voice. Unlike female prostitutes, transvestite prostitutes usually contracted potential clients for oral sex rather than intercourse. It was not unusual for transvestite prostitutes to enage passersby by tightly grasping their arms to detain them physically while they propostioned them. They nearly always acted indignant and hostile on rejection by a potential customer, even more so than female prostitutes. Transvestite prostitutes often have transplants or hormonal treatments that provide them with breasts, sometimes more substantial than the most robust female prostitutes. They paraded up and down the blocks with breasts fully exposed, a practice rejected by even the most brazen, courageous, and determined female prostitutes.

In this study a total of 120 transvestite prostitutes were sighted (table 4-10). Over 97 percent were from minority groups; 83.3 percent were black, 14.2 percent were Hispanic, and only 2.5 percent were white. Sixty percent of all transvestites worked the Ninth Avenue network; 30 percent at 41st Street and Ninth Avenue; 24.6 percent at 45th Street and Ninth Avenue; and 5.4 percent at 41st Street and Tenth Avenue. The Lower East Side had the next highest proportion of all transvestite prostitutes (24.2 percent). The area around 7th to 9th Streets on Third Avenue was occupied by 13.3 percent of the transvestite prostitutes, while 10.8 percent were observed between 4th and 6th Streets on Third Avenue. Eighth Avenue was occupied by 13.3 percent of this group, divided about evenly between the two locations below and above 42nd Street.

The Park and Fifth Avenues network had the smallest proportion of female impersonators (2.5 percent). Two of four deviant street locations comprising this network had no transvestite prostitutes (that is, 32nd Street and Fifth Avenue and 25th Street and Lexington Avenue), while only one black transvestite was sighted at 26th Street and Park Avenue, and two at 45th Street and Lexington Avenue (a total of 2.5 percent). Transvestite prostitutes tended to occupy lower socioeconomic locations where they were somewhat tolerated by community and police.

Transvestite prostitutes tended to be older than their female counterparts. The approximate average age of a transvestite prostitute was thirty

Table 4-10
Number and Percent of Transvestite Prostitutes by Race and Deviant Street Networks

Deviant Street Networks	Black		White		Hispanic		Total	
	Number	Percent	Number	Percent	Number	Percent	Number	Percent
Lower East Side	24	24.0	2	66.7	3	17.6	29	24.2
Ninth Avenue	65	65.0	1	33.3	6	35.3	72	60.0
Eighth Avenue	8	8.0	—	—	8	47.1	16	13.3
Park and Fifth Avenues	3	3.0	—	—	—	—	3	2.5
Total	100	100.0	3	100.0	17	100.0	120	100.0

Visible Street Deviance

years compared to around twenty-seven for female prostitutes. No meaningful differences in age existed among transvestite prostitutes at different deviant street locations.

The method of operation for transvestite prostitutes was similar to female prostitutes. The fees for sexual services at given locations were about the same and techniques of prostitution were similar. In the relatively few instances transvestites agreed to perform sexual intercourse, they attempted either to simulate this act or persuade the patron to accept oral sex. This automatically led to greater use of the automobile rather than a hotel room as a place for business.

Visible deviant street locations of transvestite prostitutes were nearly always separated from locations occupied by female prostitutes. Rarely did the two types of deviants mix. Transvestite prostitutes occupied the corner on Ninth Avenue at 45th Street when female prostitutes were absent or while they worked 46th Street and Ninth Avenue. Similarly transvestite prostitutes mainly occupied Third Avenue around 7th to 9th Streets. Only when female prostitutes were absent did they spill over onto 6th and 10th Streets. Generally speaking, transvestite prostitutes occupied less advantageous locations than female prostitutes and they often attempted to imitate female prostitutes by voice, gestures, and walk.

Transvestite prostitutes who worked territories contiguous to the thirteen street locations studied usually catered to male patrons seeking female prostitutes. Male patrons often believed they had obtained the services of female prostitutes and could not discern that their sex partners were actually males posing as females. In situations where the error was discovered either they were too disappointed at that moment to admit it to themselves or violence erupted. Many out-of-town truck drivers entering New York City via the Lincoln Tunnel often encountered transvestite prostitutes at Ninth Avenue in the 40s. One can imagine their surprise on discovering they had had sex with a male impersonating a female.

Transvestite prostitutes preferred being treated like females even when recognized. They became extremely hostile to men who displayed signs of disgust or resentment on discovering the masquerade. Perhaps male customers intentionally seeking transvestite prostitutes visit locations occupied by homosexuals. These include Greenwich Village, 42nd Street between Seventh and Eighth Avenues and the east 50s.

Deviant Managers

A *pimp* is a professional whose primary occupation is managing prostitutes. His duties include their recruitment, selection, training, and supervision. Although pandering techniques vary, a typical pimp in New York City manages a stable of two to eight girls and lives off their earnings. A pimp also controls the proceeds obtained through prostitution by doling out spending money to each prostitute and many times even paying their rents and other fixed expenses.[2]

A key factor distinguishing a *man* from a pimp is that the former works together with one rather than many prostitutes. He may be the prostitute's lover or husband, and he shares the proceeds from prostitution. Or he may simply be a friend or acquaintance of the prostitute and receive monetary payment for his services. The man, like the pimp, performs many services for the prostitute. Unlike the professional pimp, the man also provides immediate on-the-spot protection and supervision. He watches his *woman* constantly, is present where and when she works, and serves as a lookout for the police. He also provides protection for his woman from robbery, assault, or other criminal victimizations by violent persons, devious johns, or competing prostitutes. It is not unusual for a man to make a mental picture of a john, his car, and even its license-plate number as the driver and prostitute leave for the place where the transaction will occur. These actions are sufficiently conspicuous for the john to get the message. Perhaps most prostitutes would have a man were it not that many become overly possessive and resent their woman sleeping with other men even if it is for money rather than love.

A pimp, of course, also provides many of these services, but he cannot easily supervise several woman at once—as closely as a man supervises a single prostitute. A pimp is more likely to establish overall guidelines. He assures that women in his stable work near each other so that they may provide mutual assistance. In one sense, a pimp carries out managerial functions, while a man performs line supervision. A woman works for a pimp, but with a man. A pimp nearly always controls the prostitute, unlike a man who often is controlled by the prostitute.

The man tends to dress in ordinary, often shabby, street clothes rather than bizarre or showy clothing. He endeavors to blend in with the street scene rather than attract attention. A man spends substantial time on the street and seeks not to be noticed by the police, johns, or neighborhood residents. Nevertheless, he frequently carries a visible blunt instrument for protection (for example, stick, umbrella, baseball bat, or handmade walking stick). The pimp rarely is on the street, preferring the safety of the pimpmobile, a bar, or a coffee shop.

A prostitute and her man often both have a heavy drug habit, and much of the proceeds from prostitution are utilized for drug purchases. Several prostitutes, particularly on the lower socioeconomic status areas of the Lower East Side and Ninth Avenue, used drugs enough to warrant the label "drug addict." Prostitutes working in higher socioeconomic status areas (for example, Park and Fifth Avenues) especially under the management of a pimp were less likely to be addicted.

A man and prostitute sometimes lived within a few blocks of the street location where they worked and were familiar with area residents. Prostitutes controlled by a pimp, however, rarely resided in their work area. Only a handful of prostitutes were managed by females who tended to be black, middle-aged, and masculine in dress and appearance.

A total of 97 deviant managers, all male, were identified. Exactly 72.2 percent were black, 20.6 percent were Hispanic, and 7.2 percent were white. Not a single pimp was white or Hispanic; all whites and Hispanics were *men*, although there were also a handful of black men. About 80 percent of the men were Hispanic. Hispanics, like blacks, have encountered blocked and discriminatory opportunity systems. Therefore they were more likely to engage in illegitimate endeavors including prostitution. Perhaps managing a stable requires a facility with the English language because it is an important instrument for controlling many women. Blacks have developed this language facility; Hispanics, whose migration is more recent, may find it more difficult to articulate. Therefore, Hispanic males tended to work with one rather than two or more women.

Most deviant managers (59.8 percent) were sighted on the Lower East Side (table 4-11); next on Eighth Avenue (17.5 percent), then Park and Fifth Avenues (13.4 percent); and the fewest worked Ninth Avenue (9.3 percent). Nearly all deviant managers at Park and Fifth Avenues and Eighth Avenue were pimps, while all at Ninth Avenue were men. Similarly, most managers at three of the four locations on the Lower East Side were men, however, pimps prevailed at the Bowery and Delancey Street.

Pimps appeared to manage prostitutes who worked higher socioeconomic areas at locations used nearly exclusively for purposes of prostitution at least a few set hours each day. Residents, shoppers, sightseers, or theater people did not share these territories. Twenty-Fifth Street and Lexington Avenue, 26th Street and Park Avenue, and 32nd Street and Fifth Avenue were almost exclusively used by prostitutes when conditions were active. Most remaining locations were either occupied by theatergoers, neighborhood residents, or substantial numbers of passersby at least some of the time when conditions were active. Few prostitutes occupied Eighth Avenue during early evening hours when theatergoers were present. Pimps also tended to avoid this area at these hours and instead gathered after 1:00 a.m.

Three of four most active deviant locations including the Bowery and Delancey Street, 32nd Street and Fifth Avenue, and 42nd to 49th Streets had the most pimps. Tenth to 14th Streets on Third Avenue had a substantial proportion of prostitutes (15 percent) but few pimps. Most deviant managers at this location were men, perhaps because like most other locations frequented by men it had a substantial Hispanic community. Men were mainly of this same descent and tended to blend with the local population. Pimps and their prostitutes tended to avoid this location because even

Table 4-11
Number and Percent of Deviant Managers by Race and Deviant Street Networks

Deviant Street Networks	Black		White		Hispanic		Total	
	Number	Percent	Number	Percent	Number	Percent	Number	Percent
Lower East Side	41	58.6	4	57.1	13	65.0	58	59.8
Ninth Avenue	2	2.9	2	28.6	5	25.0	9	9.3
Eighth Avenue	15	21.4	1	14.3	1	5.0	17	17.5
Park and Fifth Avenues	12	17.1	—	—	1	5.0	13	13.4
Total	70	100.0	7	100.0	20	100.0	97	100.0

Visible Street Deviance

when active, it also was used a great deal by passersby. Pimps prefer more deserted locations because they field a large number of prostitutes who work side by side, and they wish to avoid citizen complaints that might lead to police action. The presence of pimps or men was not related to police coverage because both appeared in areas of heavy and light police saturation.

The average approximate age for deviant managers was 33.1 years, (table 4-12). Black managers appeared slightly older, ($\overline{X} = 34.8$) than their white ($\overline{X} = 31.6$) or Hispanic counterparts ($\overline{X} = 29.5$). Perhaps this is because all pimps in this study were black, and pimps tended to be older than men. Overall the majority of managers were in their thirties (about 80 percent) and about 6 percent appeared to be over forty.

Prostitutes controlled by deviant managers tended to be slightly younger than their independent counterparts. The approximate age of managed prostitutes was 25.6 compared to 26.8 for all prostitutes.

The average approximate age differential between deviant managers and prostitutes was about 6.6 years (table 4-13). The difference in age varied by race. Black managers were substantially older than their prostitutes ($\overline{X} = 9.9$ years), but this was due mainly to age differences between black managers and white prostitutes ($\overline{X} = 10.4$). The average age differential for white managers and their prostitutes was 5.4 years and for Hispanic managers, only 2.6 years. The declining age differential for white and Hispanic managers was probably because pimps tended to be older than men, and pimps in this study were black and most men were white and Hispanic. Also, pimps compared to men tended to manage younger prostitutes.

Manager-Prostitute Relationships

More than two-thirds of manager-prostitute relationships were interracial (70.3 percent), while 29.7 percent were intraracial. The majority of managed women were white (73 percent) and most relationships involved a white prostitute and a black manager (40.5 percent; table 4-14). The proportions of white prostitutes with Hispanic managers was 18.9 percent and with

Table 4-12
Average Age of Deviant Managers by Race

Age	N	$\overline{X}$
Black	50	34.8
White	8	31.6
Hispanic	20	29.5
Total	78	33.1

Table 4-13
Estimated Age Differential between Prostitutes and Managers

Race of Manager and Prostitute	Age Differential Number	$\bar{X}$	
Black-white	14	10.4	9.9
Black-Hispanic	1	3.0	
White-white	4	5.0	5.4
White-black	1	7.0	
Hispanic-Hispanic	6	2.5	2.6
Hispanic-white	5	2.8	
Total	31	6.6	

white managers, 13.5 percent. Only 27 percent of the prostitutes with managers were nonwhite. Exactly 16.2 percent of the relationships consisted of a Hispanic manager and a Hispanic prostitute. Only two cases consisted of a white manager and a black or Hispanic prostitute (5.4 percent).

The Patron

A total of thirty-two patrons, for whom background characteristics could be determined during the fifty-six hours of observation, accompanied prostitutes in cars or to hotels. (Actually, more than 32 patrons were observed. However, many johns were in cars and also they constantly tried to shield themselves. These tactics made it difficult to determine personal

Table 4-14
Relationship of Manager and Prostitute by Race

Race of Manager by Race of Prostitute	Number	Percent
Black-white	15	40.5
Black-Hispanic	2	5.4
White-white	5	13.5
White-black	1	2.7
White-Hispanic	1	2.7
Hispanic-Hispanic	6	16.2
Hispanic-white	7	18.9
Total	37	99.9

characteristics. Therefore they were excluded from the analysis.) Three-quarters (75 percent) of these johns were white, 12.5 percent each were black and Hispanic for a total of 25 percent. One Oriental and one Indian were observed among the johns and they were included respectively in the white and black population. The data on patrons must be interpreted with caution because their overall number is small.

The average approximate age for patrons was estimated to be 35.8 years; 36.2 years for white johns and 34.4 for black johns. Younger johns tended to patronize prostitutes at Park and Fifth Avenues ($\bar{X} = 33.3$) especially 32nd Street and Fifth Avenue. A substantial number of slightly older johns patronized prostitutes on the Lower East Side ($\bar{X} = 36.9$). Younger johns tended to patronize younger, more experienced, and more desirable prostitutes.

The approximate age differential between a prostitute and john was twelve years (that is, johns on average were older than prostitutes); about ten years on average for Park and Fifth Avenues, the highest socioeconomic status network; and approximately fourteen years on average for the Lower East Side, the lowest socioeconomic status area studied.

About 56 percent of the contacts between prostitutes and johns were interracial (mainly white prostitutes and white johns), while approximately 44 percent crossed racial lines (black [white] prostitutes with white [black] johns). Of twenty-four white johns, 70.8 percent patronized white prostitutes; 16.7 percent, black prostitutes; and 12.5 percent, Hispanic prostitutes. Accordingly 29.2 percent of the whites crossed racial lines. Of a total of five black johns, three patronized white prostitutes and two, black prostitutes. Three Hispanic johns patronized black prostitutes (75 percent) and one (25 percent), a white prostitute.

The ethnic composition of johns who patronized black prostitutes was 22.2 percent black, 44.4 percent white, and 33.3 percent Hispanic. The ethnic composition of johns patronizing white prostitutes was 85 percent white, 10 percent black, and 5 percent Hispanic. All johns who patronized Hispanic prostitutes were white. White prostitutes were most patronized (62.4 percent), then blacks (27.5 percent), and then Hispanics (9.3 percent).

All but one of eleven contacts for Park and Fifth Avenues were between white prostitutes and white johns (table 4-15). The single exception in the vicinity of 45th Street and Lexington Avenue involved a white prostitute and a black john, who was dressed in expensive but conservative clothes and from his accent might have been a foreign diplomat or businessman.

Five of sixteen contacts for the Lower East Side involved white prostitutes and white patrons (31.3 percent). Only two involved black prostitutes and black patrons (12.5 percent). Among prostitutes who made contact with a john at this street network, seven were white prostitutes, six were black, and three were Hispanic. Ten of the sixteen johns were white (62.5

**Table 4-15
Relationship of Prostitute and Patron by Race and Deviant Street Networks**

Deviant Street Networks	Black Black	Black White	Black Hispanic	White Black	White White	White Hispanic	Hispanic White	Total	Percent Down
Lower East Side	2	2	2	1	5	1	3	16	50.0
Ninth Avenue	—	1	—	1	—	—	—	2	6.2
Eighth Avenue	—	1	1	—	1	—	—	3	9.4
Park and Fifth Avenues	—	—	—	1	10	—	—	11	34.4
Total	2	4	3	3	16	1	3	32	100.0
Percent across	6.2	12.5	9.4	9.4	50.0	3.1	9.4	100.0	

percent), three were black (18.8 percent), and three were Hispanic (18.8 percent). The majority of contacts for the Lower East Side was between prostitutes and johns of different races (56.3 percent).

The single street location having the most contacts between prostitutes and johns was the Bowery and Delancey Street (ten contacts or 31.1 percent of total). Of the ten contacts, five involved black prostitutes; three, white prostitutes; and two, Hispanic prostitutes. Six johns were white, three were Hispanic, and one was black. The location with the next highest number of contacts was 32nd Street and Fifth Avenue ($n = 8$). All eight transactions involved white prostitutes and white johns.

Patrons came by car and foot. The deviant street locations including 10th to 14th Streets, 44th to 50th and Lexington Avenue, 38th to 42nd Streets, and 42nd to 49th Streets drew patrons about evenly by car and on foot. Much of the time, street parking was prohibited or limited in these areas. Also these locations were used least exclusively by prostitutes and had a substantial pedestrian flow. The remaining nine locations including the Bowery and Delancey Street, Forsythe Street, 6th Street, 25th Street and Lexington Avenue, 26th Street and Park Avenue, 32nd Street and Fifth Avenue, 46th Street and Ninth Avenue, 42nd Street and Ninth Avenue, and 42nd Street and Tenth Avenue had mainly an automobile clientele. These locations were used almost exclusively for prostitution during active hours and there was little pedestrian flow. Moreover, ample street parking was available in the vicinity.

Johns in cars (*cruising johns*) usually formed a queue and cruised around and around the corners comprising the blocks where prostitutes were located. This steady flow of cars followed closely the line of prostitutes. The more substantial the presence of prostitutes the greater the number of johns. Typically a john circled the area for ten to thirty minutes before selecting a woman or before he was selected by a prostitute. Cruising johns not satisfied with a location's prostitutes visited other street locations along the circuit until a desirable woman was found. Oftentimes a cruising john blocked traffic when he stopped to talk to a prostitute. Other johns in cars waited patiently and refrained from using their automobile horns. Johns and unengaged prostitutes rarely interfered with an ongoing exchange. An approach by another prostitute or john was likely only after a conversation had ended and the couple disengaged. When ambiguity arose over which prostitute engaged a john, the final selection was left to him. Prostitutes or johns who violated these street rules were repelled by other prostitutes and eventually forced to leave the street location.

Johns had to be extremely cautious because New York City police deploy female decoys. Once a female cop was solicited and the john was placed under arrest by two male back-up officers. Usually the uninitiated were arrested because more experienced johns only engaged prostitutes whom they recognized. This realization was probably one reason that led to the demise of the "John Hour," a program endorsed by New York City's Major Edward Koch where names and addresses of a select group of convicted johns were announced on radio and television and also published in certain city newspapers. The program was aired only once before it was terminated.

Johns and prostitutes employed an informal screening process to determine proof of safety and stability. A short ordinary conversation usually sufficed to convince each other of their mutual integrity, sincerity, and safety. Probing questions always followed suspicious remarks or gestures. Even the most cavalier and frivolous prostitute hesitated to enter an automobile without some form of preliminary screening. External indicators also were used to determine a john's stability or safety, like driving a company truck. Prostitutes frequently entered the cab of all-night, tow-truck operators on duty in the event of automobile collisions. Similarly, johns and prostitutes were reluctant to accompany each other if either was drunk, on drugs, or unable to converse in a coherent manner.

Prostitutes almost never entered a car with more than one occupant. Perhaps this is one reason most johns arrived alone at deviant street locations. Occasionally two prostitutes entered a car with two johns although a single driver was fearful to allow more than one prostitute into his car. On rare occasions two prostitutes were observed in a car with a lone john. They were new to the area and never seen again. I suspect their intent was robbery rather than prostitution.

Most prostitutes glanced in all directions before entering a john's car to determine whether police were in the area. If police were sighted, the prostitute usually waited until they passed before entering the vehicle. Or she asked the driver to meet her at a prearranged destination a short distance away. Oftentimes prostitutes crouched beneath the dashboard to avoid observation by officers in passing radio cars.

A typical business conversation ranged between thirty seconds and five minutes. Most discussions were impersonal and restricted to details of the transaction. However, prostitutes often discussed personal matters with steady johns. Some prostitutes even provided telephone numbers hoping to make arrangements from home.

The prostitute exited the car when an agreement was not reached, usually indifferent but at times hostile. The number of times a prostitute succeeded in engaging a customer that resulted in an actual transaction was small, even when approached first by a potential customer, compared to the volume of actual contacts or conversations. Several dozen contacts usually resulted in only one transaction. A successful encounter depended more on the physical qualities and overall appearance of the prostitute than her level of aggressiveness, including the frequency of verbal and body gestures.

Once an agreement was reached the transaction was likely to be conducted in the car (usually but not exclusively oral sex [*fellatio*]) only a few blocks away in a dark and secluded parking lot or on a poorly lit street. During periods of serious police enforcement, prostitutes often directed the driver to an adjacent precinct where she could not be recognized. This tactic tended to spread prostitution to new neighborhoods.

Sometimes the driver left the vehicle and accompanied the prostitute to a *pros hotel*. Usually they walked together because a prostitute alone was more likely to be harassed or arrested for loitering. Johns without cars (*sidewalk johns*) almost always conducted business in a hotel, although a few found darkened hallways and alleys convenient. In the Park and Fifth Avenues and Eighth Avenue networks most transactions were in hotels, while for Ninth Avenue and the Lower East Side the majority took place in cars. Even in higher socioeconomic status locations, including Park and Fifth Avenues, oral sex was usually carried out in a car. Oral sex does not require the same security measures as sexual intercourse because both partners need not undress. At the same time, transactions involving sexual intercourse at certain locations on the Lower East Side, including the Bowery and Delancey Street, almost always were effectuated in a hotel. Prostitutes managed by pimps were much more likely to utilize hotels than independent prostitutes and those managed by a man. The police rarely bothered johns at the Park and Fifth Avenues and Eighth Avenue street networks, but they persistently harassed patrons on the Lower East Side and Ninth Avenue. Both these areas have a residential community. Cars were stopped constantly, licenses were checked, summonses were issued for various minor traffic violations, and threats of arrest were made and carried out unless the driver immediately left the area. Sidewalk johns on foot also were harassed. The following scenario from my field notes illustrates these patterns.

> On 31 July 1978 at 14th Street and Third Avenue a john and a prostitute were about to enter the hallway of the Oasis Hotel. They were stopped by two police officers from the Ninth Precinct who suddenly crossed 14th Street into the Thirteenth Precinct where the hotel was situated. The patron was a white male, about thirty-five years old, dressed in dungarees, a work shirt, and he wore glasses. He appeared from his clothing to be from the working class. The prostitute was white with auburn hair, very thin, about twenty-five years old and she had worked in the area for several years. The two white police officers aimed their questions at the john and the experienced, street-wise prostitute stood by without uttering a word. One officer menacingly said to the other, "Was he exposed?" It was obvious that the john had not exposed himself, but the police officer wanted to intimidate him. The officers asked the john where he lived, whether he had a car in the area, where it was parked, and whether he was married. The frightened patron answered each question.

One officer asked whether the patron knew the girl. He answered, "I knew her for about a year."

Then the officer asked, "What's her name?"

The patron replied, "I'm not sure."

The officer queried, "Do you want a (desk appearance) summons?"

He answered "No."

Not a single question or remark was directed at the prostitute. The police allowed the john and the prostitute to leave, warning both to stay out of the neighborhood. The prostitute returned to a corner two blocks away on 12th Street and Third Avenue in the neighboring precinct. She continued to solicit passersby in full view. The police followed the john with their eyes until he was out of sight.

Apparently the police officers realized they could do little to intimidate the prostitute so they concentrated on the john. Johns usually have more to lose by an arrest than most prostitutes because many hold steady jobs, have families, and are part of a legitimate community. Also most prostitutes have been arrested previously, whereas a john's arrest may be his first serious encounter with the law.

Hangers-on

Hanger-on is the term utilized in this book for a person who frequented locations of visible street deviance but was not a police officer, john, worker, shopper, or ordinary passerby. A hanger-on simply selected a spot at a visible deviant street location and stood or sat for hours at a time. A typical hanger-on was an unemployed lower-class male. Relatively few hangers-on frequented locations of visible street deviance compared to the number of prostitutes, although nearly 400 were spotted. For every three prostitutes, about one hanger-on was observed. One explanation is that prostitutes tended to discourage individuals especially tough-looking persons from simply standing around deviant street locations because this practice was bad for business. Prostitutes in one location constantly taunted hangers-on yelling "Get the _____ out of here," or "You're going to get into real _____ trouble." Also the police tended to view these suspicious and seedy-looking characters at best as part of the street deviance scene and at worst as suspected felons. They constantly harassed hangers-on and demanded that they leave the area or face charges for loitering.

The majority of hangers-on were black (67.6 percent); the next highest number were white (20.8 percent), and the smallest proportion were Hispanic (11.6 percent). Hangers-on appeared mainly to be in their early thirties regardless of race. Table 4-16 presents the distribution of hangers-

Table 4-16
Number and Percent of Hangers-on by Race and Deviant Street Networks

Deviant Street Networks	Black		White		Hispanic		Total	
	Number	Percent	Number	Percent	Number	Percent	Number	Percent
Lower East Side	84	31.9	24	29.6	28	62.2	136	35.0
Ninth Avenue	59	22.4	21	25.9	9	20.0	89	23.0
Eighth Avenue	99	37.6	22	27.2	8	17.8	129	33.1
Park and Fifth Avenues	21	8.0	14	17.3	—	—	35	9.0
Total	263	99.9	81	100.0	45	100.0	389	100.0

on by race and deviant street networks. The highest proportion of white hangers-on (29.6 percent) occupied the Lower East Side, while the highest incidence of blacks were on Eighth Avenue (37.6 percent). Park and Fifth Avenues contained the fewest white (17.3 percent) or black (8.0 percent) hangers-on and no Hispanics.

Most hangers-on were in groups ranging in size from two to ten persons, the average group consisting of 3.4 persons (table 4-17). The average size was slightly larger for black groups ($X = 3.5$) compared to white ($X = 2.5$) or Hispanic groups ($X = 2.3$). Moreover, most groups were homogeneous with regard to race (77.3 percent). Only 18.6 percent of the groups were ethnically mixed and of these 13.4 percent were comprised of blacks and Hispanics. Only about 5 percent of the groups consisted of whites together with Hispanics and/or blacks. Perhaps hangers-on grouped together because alone they were more vulnerable to harassment by police, pimps, and prostitutes.

This information on hangers-on is limited and not much is known about these interesting street groups. Further research ought to determine the function, role, or aim of these groups; why they hang out at locations where they are not wanted; whether or not they are useful in any way, for example does their presence make the street safer; what are they doing generally at these sites (drinking, stealing, fighting); are they harassed by the police while johns are left alone; are pimps or men drawn from these groups; do they have a relationship with prostitutes or are they equivalent to the virtually homeless men described in *Tally's Corner*.[3] Answers to these questions will expand the knowledge of the underlying processes of deviant street networks.

Table 4-17
Number and Average Size of Groups of Hangers-on by Race

Race	Number	$\bar{X}$
Black	54	3.5
White	20	2.5
Hispanic	5	2.3
Black-Hispanic	13	3.5
Black-white	3	6.3
White-black	1	2.0
White-black-Hispanic	1	6.0
Total	97	3.4

Notes

1. See appendix A and the seminal study by Murray Melbin, "Night as Frontier," *American Sociological Review* 43, no. 1 (February 1978):3-22.

Melbin's study is significant because some of his data from field observations are quantitative, and also his findings raise the thought of viewing victimless crime as a social frontier. One similarity between Melbin's and this book is that background characteristics and behavior patterns for night people and persons involved in street deviance appear to be comparable.

2. Susan Hall and Bob Adelman, *Gentlemen of Leisure* (New York: New American Library, 1972). The prostitute relies on her pimp for assistance, especially in encounters with the police, courts, or corrections. If a prostitute is arrested, the pimp might post bail or pay the fine. A pimp directs his women where and how to work and he resolves disputes between them. He usually allows his women little independence.

3. Elliot Liebow, *Tally's Corner* (Boston: Little, Brown, and Co., 1967).

5 The Police

Police officers on patrol in cars and on foot constantly appeared at the thirteen deviant street locations. New York City Police are allocated to various neighborhoods or *sectors* on the basis of numerous factors including population density, offense type, crime incidence, and number of calls for police service. Therefore, no single uniform pattern was discernible relating police assignments to the distribution of prostitutes.

The police, it has been argued, perform three major functions: law enforcement, order maintenance, and provision of services.[1] Police tactics to control street prostitution do not fit neatly into these three categories. Clearly, the police do not routinely arrest street prostitutes. Therefore they are not engaged in law enforcement. Nor do the police provide services directly for prostitutes as they often do for citizens; for example, helping an elderly woman locked out of her apartment late at night. Nor are police engaged in only routine order maintenance as, for example, when they respond to a family dispute or warn a group of boisterous youths to "keep it low." The police regulate or manage visible street deviance by assuring that it does not expand into neighboring streets or become overly dangerous. This police function can be referred to as *deviance regulation*.

The main tactic or pattern usually followed by the police, regardless of the neighborhood, is to disperse prostitutes. Only rarely do police "sweep" them off the streets by placing them under arrest. This tactic usually occurs during a crackdown when either an important dignitary or group is visiting the city or after a particularly well-publicized violent act, especially one related to prostitution. Then the area police force is strengthened and the police attempt to arrest all women in the street suspected of prostitution. The police often employ vans and special task-force vehicles for this purpose in addition to the regular, precinct police-radio-sector cars. There is little concern for an individual's civil rights. Most prostitutes avoided the location during these special tours.

Usually as the police pass a given location the prostitutes flee or attempt to hide. Sometimes one prostitute serves as lookout to warn others of approaching police. She learns to distinguish among different types of police because officers in certain units, like the Traffic Division and Emergency Service Division, and also the Transit, Housing, and Port Authority Police do not usually interfere with these street activities. New York City's Auxiliary Police Force similarly ignores visible street prostitution. On the other hand, the squad that specializes in the enforcement of laws prohibiting prostitution (referred to as the *pussy posse* by officers and prostitutes alike) are most feared by deviant street actors.

Prostitutes engaged in a game of hide and seek with police in which they appeared to display deference and respect. Abandoning a location momentarily while police passed was a way prostitutes showed that the police really control the streets. Several deviant locations are near precinct boundaries. Prostitutes simply crossed the street into adjacent precincts in order to avoid arrest. Informal organizational mores inhibited police from crossing precinct boundaries except in emergencies. These unspoken rules are part of an internal system of checks and balances that protects police assigned to different precincts from charges of inefficiency. Sometimes police on the street issued court-appearance tickets or arrested prostitutes who remained at a street location.

The police perceive that their safety, security, and status are dependent on complete and unchallenged control of the streets. Hasty departure by prostitutes when police appear symbolizes this control. The police could easily have apprehended and arrested most prostitutes, but because they displayed the proper and expected response there was no need for arrest.

Different reactions occurred depending on the type of police presence. When a radio car passed a given location at a steady pace neither increasing or decreasing its speed the prostitutes casually walked away. As soon as the car was out of sight the prostitutes returned to their former spots. Apparently the women knew that these police did not represent a threat to them in terms of police sanctions. Their reaction in response to the police presence was indicative of a courtesy move to allow the police to believe that they still control the streets. The prostitutes temporarily left the scene and changed locations only when the police slowed or stopped the car or when it rapidly approached a deviant street location. Evidently this signified that the police meant business and would arrest lingerers.

The second type of police presence involved uniformed officers walking on the street. As soon as these officers approached, prostitutes began to half walk and run at a faster pace than when the sector car passed. This appeared to be more than a courtesy move. Police on foot patrol are more likely than officers cruising in sector cars to stop or question a street prostitute, issue a summons, or make an arrest. As soon as the officers were a short distance from the location, the women returned to their previous positions.

The third type of police presence involved an unmarked police car. Often this car was an ordinary automobile painted solid black, grey, or creme, with no trim or chrome and a short radio antenna protruding from its rear fender. Other times it was a taxi cab or other car undiscernible to almost all except the prostitutes. As the unmarked car pulled up to the curb, the women scattered in all directions and ran for cover. The prostitutes obviously recognized the two- or three-man team in the vehicle as plainclothes officers whose main purpose was to control the streets and keep the women on their toes. Many times the teams were racially mixed, which was unusual for groups of potential johns. They represented to the prostitutes a real and imminent threat of arrest. Usually these same teams had made arrests at this location on prior occasions. On balance, dispersal tactics appeared to have the opposite of its intended effects. Instead of decreasing or even containing street deviance, it resulted in its expansion. Uninterrupted police pressure over a substantial period of time usually forced groups of prostitutes to flee a given spot, spread out, and occupy several new locations.

Unlike prostitutes, derelicts rarely if ever made courtesy moves or any other deferential gestures to the police. Usually the police ignored derelicts and instead proceeded directly to a deviant street location occupied by prostitutes. The police usually interfered with derelicts only on a citizen complaint, during a special enforcement campaign, or when there was danger. On several occasions derelicts were unconscious and stretched out on their backs in the middle of heavy traffic. Apparently derelicts do not pose the same security threat to the police as prostitutes.

The fact that the police are unable or unwilling to eliminate easily a deviant street condition indicates that they do not control the streets as much as they perceive.[2] Competing pressures and demands in the field make it virtually impossible for police officers to arrest all street prostitutes. The time required for processing arrested prostitutes would leave few officers available for other tasks including combatting more serious crime, servicing the public, or maintaining order. Moreover, many officers perceive prostitution as a necessary service and not morally wrong even though it is prohibited by law. Also, indifference toward prostitution on behalf of the public and the fact that it may serve certain specialized neighborhood interests, like hotels and restaurants, further impedes attempts by the police to eliminate street prostitution.

Police officers are reluctant to fraternize with prostitutes because they are considered flighty, unstable, and untrustworthy. However, they often bend this policy in the interest of police work. For example, detectives or uniformed officers try to establish rapport with prostitutes in order to gather information on crime. However, in higher socioeconomic areas the police are somewhat more friendly toward prostitutes than in lower-class neighborhoods. On several occasions at street locations in the Park and Fifth Avenues network, uniformed police in radio-motor-patrol cars (RMPs) stopped to converse with prostitutes for substantial periods (for example, one hour). Generally, the police try to maintain an even greater social distance from prostitutes than from ordinary people. However, when police were not responding to a call for service, they spent a disproportionate amount of time patrolling that part of a sector containing street prostitution. This left much of the remaining parts of the precinct less protected. No evidence was found of patterns of extortion by police, although several prostitutes reported isolated encounters where police requested sexual favors in lieu of arresting them.[3]

Police Presence

Police coverage at deviant street locations was determined during the fifty-six hours of standardized field observations described in chapter 4. Approximately equal observation time was spent at each street location. Notations were made each time a police car or an officer on foot passed a deviant street location. These events are called police *sightings*. The ethnostatistics showed that police coverage varied with deviant networks (see table 5-1). The most intensive police coverage was for the Lower East Side (37.2 percent of all police sightings). The next highest number of sightings was for Eighth Avenue or 33.5 percent of the total. The least police coverage was for Ninth Avenue and Park and Fifth Avenues. The proportions of police sightings for these networks were 13.7 percent and 15.6 percent, respectively.

Most police passed in patrol cars (58.7 percent); 116 (91 percent) were radio-motor-patrol cars and 12 (9 percent) were unmarked police vehicles. Only 41.3 percent of the sightings involved officers walking the beat, individually, in pairs, or in groups of three or four. The Lower East Side had the highest proportion of car sightings (34.4 percent), while Ninth Avenue had the lowest (21.1 percent) (table 5-1).

The high incidence of police sightings for the Lower East Side and Eighth Avenue was due primarily to a relatively high proportion of beat officers. Half of all beat officers were observed on Eighth Avenue and 41.1

Table 5-1
Percent of Police on Beat and in Cars by Deviant Street Networks

Deviant Street Networks	Beat		Cars		Total	
	Number	Percent	Number	Percent	Number	Percent
Lower East Side	37	41.1	44	34.4	81	37.2
Ninth Avenue	3	3.3	27	21.1	30	13.7
Eighth Avenue	45	50.0	28	21.9	73	33.5
Park and Fifth Avenues	5	5.6	29	22.7	34	15.6
Total	90	100.0	128	100.1	218	100.0

percent on the Lower East Side. This compared to only 3.3 percent and 5.6 percent, respectively, for Ninth Avenue and Park and Fifth Avenues. The two single locations with the highest police sightings were 42nd Street to 49th Street (28 percent) and 10th to 14th Streets (23.9 percent). Sixth Street and 26th Street at Park Avenue had the least police coverage with slightly less than 1 percent of the sightings.

Unlike 42nd Street and 14th Street, 6th and 26th Streets are not thriving business areas during evening hours, and except for deviant street actors these areas are relatively deserted. Although police coverage is determined by several factors (for example, crime incidence, calls for service, population density), the pattern for police coverage generally followed the incidence for visible street deviance. Beginning with the afternoon from about 1:00 p.m., police coverage tended to increase as did the incidence of street prostitution (table 5-2). The average number per hour of visible prostitutes in the afternoon was 13.7; the average number of police sightings per hour was only 1.9. Both these figures increased during early evening to an average per hour of 16.3 prostitutes and 3.3 police sightings. During late evening the averages per hour increased even more sharply to 32.3 prostitutes and 5.1 police sightings. Morning hours did not follow this overall pattern. During this time there was substantial police coverage due to the early rush hour or an average of 4.5 police sightings per hour, although the incidence of street prostitution was at its lowest ebb (an average of 3.8 per hour). The increase of police visibility at night when deviant street locations were most active is unlikely part of official police-department policy. Instead officers seemed to be drawn to areas where prostitutes were active.

Police coverage by foot patrol was more or less equally distributed throughout the four periods of day and night (average police-beat sightings ranged from 1.4 to 1.7 per hour), but police coverage by car peaked during late evening hours (an average of 3.4 per hour) and was next most active in the early morning (an average of 3.0 per hour). The afternoon hours had the

Table 5-2
Average Number per Hour of Prostitutes and Police by Time of Day and Night

Time of Day and Night	Prostitutes		Police	
	Number	$\overline{X}$	Number	$\overline{X}$
Early morning	23	3.8	27	4.5
Afternoon	164	13.7	23	1.9
Early evening	228	16.3	46	3.3
Late evening	774	32.3	122	5.1
Total	1189	21.2	218	3.9

Note: All fifty-six hours of observation are represented.

least police coverage by car or beat, or an average per hour of .5 police-car sightings and 1.4 police-beat (foot patrol) sightings.

Arrests by Race

Official data on police arrests of prostitutes by race from 59th Street to the tip of Manhattan for most of 1978 were obtained from the New York City Police Department. Data for the months of October and November were also examined and they did not differ meaningfully from the other ten months of the year. These data together with counts of prostitutes acquired are displayed in table 5-3. The data revealed that black and Hispanic prostitutes were arrested proportionally more often than their white counterparts. The proportion of arrests for black prostitutes was 57.5 percent; for Hispanic prostitutes, 11.3 percent; and only 31.2 percent for white prostitutes. This pattern of selective police enforcement occurred in spite of the fact that for the area covered, 49.6 percent of the prostitutes were white, 45.3 percent were black, and 5.1 percent were Hispanic. Although blacks and Hispanics comprised about one-half of all visible street prostitutes (50.4 percent), more than two-thirds of those arrested by the police were black and Hispanic (68.8 percent). Contrariwise, whites comprised about half the deviant street population (49.6 percent) but less than one-third of all police arrests (31.2 percent).

Perhaps the differential police arrest rates for white, black, and Hispanic prostitutes is partially due to a greater concentration of police in areas where black and Hispanic prostitutes prevail. Greater police saturation ought to result in more arrests. One way to examine this hypothesis was to compare the ethnic composition of prostitutes for each deviant location with its level of police. A substantial police presence at deviant street locations with a disproportionately high number of minority members could explain their higher rate of arrest. For this purpose, areas where at least 60 percent of the prostitutes were black or white were termed black and white

Table 5-3
Number and Percent of Prostitutes Arrested by the Police and Identified through Field Counts

Race	Police Arrests		Field Counts	
	Number	Percent	Number	Percent
White	1094	31.2	589	49.6
Black	2017	57.5	539	45.3
Hispanic	397	11.3	61	5.1
Total	3508	100.0	1189	100.0

The Police

ethnic areas, respectively. Three locations had similar proporitons of black and white prostitutes and they were treated as mixed ethnic areas. There were no locations that had a majority of Hispanic prostitutes, but 92 percent of the Hispanic prostitutes worked five deviant street locations including Forsythe Street, 42nd to 49th Streets on Eighth Avenue, 10th to 14th Streets on Third Avenue, the Bowery and Delancey Street, and 46th Streeth and Ninth Avenue.

Table 5-4 shows that the five areas classified as black had very light police coverage. About 20 percent of the police sightings occurred at these five locations. On the other hand, about 70 percent of the police sightings were in those five areas where white prostitutes were a clear majority. Moreover, these white areas had a greater presence of both cars and officers on foot patrol (61.9 percent and 82.2 percent, respectively). If police presence is a determinant of the arrest rate, then a greater proportion of white rather than black prostitutes ought to have been arrested.

Proportionately twice as many Hispanic prostitutes were arrested than their representation on the streets would suggest. Only 5.1 percent of the prostitutes on the street were Hispanic, but they constituted 11.3 percent of all police arrests for street prostitution. Although 73.9 percent of the police sightings were in areas containing 91.9 percent of the Hispanic prostitutes, a similar number of police (70.2 percent) were sighted in those areas occupied by 75 percent of the white prostitutes. Yet white prostitutes made up less than a third of all arrests for prostitution. It appears that the presence of police in an area does not explain the disproportionate number of either blacks or Hispanics arrested for prostitution.

Another explanation why a disproportionate number of black and Hispanic prostitutes were arrested is that they may have occupied the streets during hours of peak police coverage. On the other hand, white prostitutes may have worked the streets when police concentration was relatively light. These patterns could explain the higher proportions of arrests for black and Hispanic prostitutes. Throughout this research from both the ethnostatistics and qualitative observations of field conditions, little evidence emerged to suggest that blacks, Hispanics, or whites differed meaningfully either in the hours engaged in visible street deviance or in exposure to the police.

In order to examine this hypothesis we determined the overlap of police coverage with the extent of activity of visible street deviance for prostitutes of different race by varying time periods and controlling for area ethnicity (that is, as defined by the race of the area's majority of prostitutes). Table 5-5 compares the average number per hour of black, white, and Hispanic prostitutes with the average number per hour of police passes through black, white and mixed areas. The comparison was undertaken at various periods including the morning, afternoon, evening, and night. The data

Table 5-4
Police on Beat and in Cars for Black, White, and Mixed Deviant Street Locations

Areas	Deviant Street Locations	Beat		Cars		Total	
		Number	Percent	Number	Percent	Number	Percent
Black	26th Street and Park Avenue	—	—	2	1.6	2	.9
	38th to 42nd Streets and Eighth Avenue	7	7.8	5	3.9	12	5.5
	42nd Street and Ninth Avenue	—	—	4	3.1	4	1.8
	Bowery and Delancey Street	6	6.7	15	11.7	21	9.6
	42nd Street and 10th Avenue	—	—	5	3.9	5	2.3
	Total	13	14.5	31	24.2	44	20.1
White	44th to 50th Streets and Lexington Avenue	5	5.6	7	5.5	12	5.5
	32nd Street and Fifth Avenue	—	—	7	5.5	7	3.2
	46th Street and Ninth Avenue	3	3.3	18	14.1	21	9.6
	42nd to 49th Streets and Eighth Avenue	38	42.2	23	18.0	61	28.0
	10th to 14th Streets and Third Avenue	28	31.0	24	18.8	52	23.9
	Total	74	82.2	79	61.9	153	70.2
Mixed	Forsythe Street	3	3.3	3	2.3	6	2.8
	Sixth Street and Third Avenue	—	—	2	1.6	2	.9
	25th Street and Lexington Avenue	—	—	13	10.2	13	6.0
	Total	3	3.3	18	14.1	21	9.6
Grand Total		90	100.0	128	100.0	218	100.0

Table 5-5
Average Number per Hour of Prostitutes and Police by Ethnic Areas and Time of Day and Night

Time and Areas	Black Prostitutes Number	$\bar{X}$	White Prostitutes Number	$\bar{X}$	Hispanic Prostitutes Number	$\bar{X}$	Police Number	$\bar{X}$
Morning: 7 a.m. to 1 p.m.								
Black areas	6	1.0	2	.3	1	.2	8	1.3
White areas	3	.5	5	.8	1	.2	16	2.7
Mixed areas	1	.2	2	.3	2	.3	3	.5
Total	10	1.7	9	1.4	4	.7	27	4.5
Afternoon: 1 p.m. to 7 p.m.								
Black areas	42	3.5	24	2.0	2	.1	3	.2
White areas	15	1.2	57	4.8	13	1.1	20	1.7
Mixed areas	3	.3	6	.5	2	.1	—	—
Total	60	5.0	87	7.3	17	1.3	23	1.9
Early evening: 7 p.m. to 1 a.m.								
Black areas	62	4.4	20	1.4	3	.2	13	.9
White areas	21	1.5	67	4.8	10	.7	27	1.9
Mixed areas	18	1.3	20	1.4	7	.5	6	.4
Total	101	7.2	107	7.6	20	1.4	46	3.3
Late evening: 1 a.m. to 7 a.m.								
Black areas	201	8.4	29	1.2	7	.3	20	.8
White areas	123	5.1	313	13.0	9	.4	90	3.8
Mixed areas	44	1.8	44	1.8	4	.2	12	.5
Total	368	15.3	386	16.1	20	.8	122	5.1

Note: Observation time for morning period, six hours; afternoon, twelve hours; early evening, fourteen hours; late evening, twenty-four hours; total, fifty-six hours.

show that the distributions for black and white prostitutes were nearly identical through various times of day and night. For example, the average number per hour of black and white prostitutes working during peak night hours from 1:00 a.m. to 7:00 a.m. were 15.3 and 16.1, respectively. Only Hispanics differed in that proportionately fewer worked during late evening hours (average number per hour was .8) while more worked during the afternoon and early evening hours (average number per hour was 1.4). However, this difference could not explain the higher incidence of arrests for Hispanic prostitutes because overall they worked the streets during hours of low rather than high police saturation.

The data also revealed a greater police presence at deviant street locations occupied primarily by white prostitutes for every one of the four time periods. For example, the average number of police sightings per hour during morning hours from 7:00 a.m. to 1:00 p.m. was 1.3 for black areas, and 2.7 for white areas or about twice as high, table 5-5). Even during late evening from 1:00 a.m. to 7:00 a.m., police coverage for white areas was about four times greater than for black areas (an average number of police sightings per hour of 3.8 and .8 percent, respectively). Similar differences in police coverage existed for the afternoon and early evening. More blacks were arrested even though there were fewer police in black areas. Conversely fewer whites were arrested even though there was at least twice as much police coverage in white areas.

Hispanic prostitutes also were arrested disproportionately even though there were fewer Hispanic than white or black prostitutes working at any time in every area except during the morning hours for mixed locations where the average number per hour, Hispanic and white prostitutes were equal ($\overline{X} = .3$). Hispanic prostitutes tended to work during hours of light police coverage. The heaviest concentration for Hispanic prostitutes was during the afternoon and early evening (an average of 1.4 prostitutes per hour). These periods of day and evening had the lightest police coverage (an average number of police sightings per hour of 1.9 and 3.3, respectively). During morning and late evening hours when police saturation was high (5.0 sightings per hour), few Hispanic prostitutes occupied the streets (an average of .8 per hour).

White prostitutes tended to occupy deviant street networks located in higher socioeconomic areas, and blacks and Hispanics tended to work in more disadvantageous areas. For example, the Lower East Side deviant street network, situated in a relatively low socioeconomic area, proportionately had more black than white prostitutes, although the Park and Fifth Avenues network, part of a middle to upper socioeconomic area, had proportionately more white and black prostitutes. One would expect more arrests of prostitutes regardless of race in higher socioeconomic areas where visible law violations tend not to be tolerated. The police arrest data show that an area's socioeconomic status could not suppress the racial factor. Black and Hispanic prostitutes were arrested disproportionately even though they tended to work lower-class neighborhoods and were less visible most hours of the day (that is, 1:00 p.m. to 7:00 a.m.). The only time blacks were more visible than whites was during the morning hours when the police were busy with traffic control. Furthermore, specialized police units likely to arrest prostitutes usually worked special late-afternoon or evening tours.

The quantitative data in the present study are based solely on street prostitutes at visible deviant street locations. Data on police arrests include prostitutes not on the street or who work in areas where visible street deviance is absent. However, the overwhelming number of arrests involve prostitutes who work in full public view. Moreover, there is no reliable and consistent evidence that the ethnicity of prostitutes who work inside locations differs from those working visible deviant street locations. Most prostitutes work the streets because brothels are expensive, adding considerably to the price of services. This puts inside prostitution beyond the reach of a large number of clients. Also, prostitutes who work in brothels lose a measure of independence, and brothels are easier for the police to control. A brothel is in a fixed place and can be closed, but streetwalkers can simply move to another street corner. The recent closing of massage parlors that fronted for houses of prostitution in New York City forced many women to work on the street where containment and control is much more difficult. Brothels, on the other hand, are generally safer than street work because they provide some protection from police harassment and dangerous johns.

At least 95 percent of all police officers in the field were white. This figure resembles quite closely the overall ethnic composition of the New York City Police Department, which is nearly 90 percent white. Selective harassment of prostitutes from minority groups is yet one more consequence that results from an ethnic and racial imbalance in the composition of the police force.

Discrimination against black suspects by the New York City Police Department will not be eased until at least the department's minority representation reflects more adequately the ethnic composition of the general population. In New York City at least a third of the population is black or Hispanic. This does not mean that an ethnic quota ought to be instituted so that the New York City Police Department reflects the exact composition of the population. It does mean that there should exist a reasonable resemblance between the ethnic composition of a community police force and its general population. There are no hard or fast rules for establishing this goal; it depends on the existing social and community climate. It does mean, however, that a city has not achieved a reasonable balance or approximation when well over a third of its population is black and Hispanic and only about 11 percent of the police force consists of black or Hispanic officers. Efforts over the past ten to fifteen years on the part of New York City's Department of Personnel and Police Department to increase meaningfully the proportion of minority group members has faltered. The proportion of minority representatives in the New York City Police Department remains at around 11.5 percent or only slightly higher than ten years ago when it was 8 percent. Only 4 percent of the officers appointed to the New York Police Department over the last five years were black and 7.6 percent were Hispanic.[4] This should not be tolerated by New York's white, black, or Hispanic communities.

In sum, proportionately more black and Hispanic prostitutes were arrested than their white counterparts even though white prostitutes were present in those areas and at times of greater police coverage. No meaningful differences in the personal or social behavior of black or Hispanic prostitutes might have made them more susceptible to arrest compared to their white counterparts. The data provide strong inferential evidence that race alone and neither the style of prostitution nor socioeconomic status is the key factor in determining who will or will not be arrested. The data support the contention that certain police officers in the field discriminate against black and Hispanic suspects through selective enforcement. Field officers automatically proceed to arrest black prostitutes because in their minds they symbolize the criminal.[5] This strand of discrimination reflects a broader systemic pattern of discrimination against minority members that has operated in police departments and criminal-justice agencies in large urban areas throughout the nation. Much discrimination in New York emanates from the current institutional structure of its police department rather than solely personal motivation and bias on the part of individual officers.

Notes

1. James Q. Wilson, *Varieties of Police Behavior* (Cambridge, Mass.: Harvard University Press, 1968).

2. See Jonathan Rubinstein, *City Police* (New York: Ballantine Books, 1973), especially pp. 267-338.

3. The Knapp Commission confirmed that there were no patterns of corruption in the New York City Police Department (N.Y.P.D.) involving prostitution. *The Knapp Commission Report on Police Corruption* (New York: George Braziller, 1973), ch. 6.

4. *The New York Times*, 19 April 1980, p. 27. Current appointments supercede a decision by Judge Robert Carter of Federal Court based on research by this author prohibiting the N.Y.P.D. from hiring additional officers because of past discriminatory selection procedures. See Jan Chaiken and Bernard Cohen, eds., *Police Civil Service Selection Procedures in New York City: An Ethnic Comparison* (Santa Monica, Calif.: The Rand Corporation, 1973). More recently the United States Court of Appeals for the Second Circuit ordered that one-third of all new recruits must be black or Hispanic. The Federal Appeals Court found that the New York City Police Department's hiring procedures discriminate against minority applicants, although not deliberately. See *The New York Times*, 3 August 1980, section 4, p. 6E.

5. See Jerome Skolnick, *Justice Without Trial: Law Enforcement in Democratic Society* (New York: John Wiley and Sons, 1966).

6 The Division of Deviance

With virtually no information on visible deviant street locations, my initial concern was to determine geographic relationships. Initially interest focused on the spatial relationships and interactional patterns between female street prostitution and nearby locations of other forms of street deviance. The map (figure 6-1) highlights the spatial distribution for locations of female street prostitution and adjacent locations of other visible street deviance from the southern tip of Manhattan to 59th Street. In addition to the thirteen street locations with female prostitutions, nearby there were four fixed locations of prostitution by transvestites, three of prostitution by males, and three for drunkenness. I refer to small areas that contain many different forms of deviance adjacent to each other as *deviant street clusters*. These territorial entities may be more difficult for the police to control than deviant street networks not only because of the heterogeneity of different deviant groups but also because of complex enforcement policies and varying legal issues associated with each form of deviance.

Spatial Distribution of Street Deviance

One interesting feature is that street deviance was widespread and not limited to only a few types of neighborhoods. For example, male prostitutes occupied the vicinity of 53rd Street and Third Avenue, a middle to upper socioeconomic area, while derelicts occupied the Bowery, a lower socioeconomic area. Moreover, the same forms of visible deviance were situated in many different types of neighborhoods of varying land use and socioeconomic status. Accordingly, female prostitutes congregated at the Bowery and Delancey Street, a lower socioeconomic business area; on 25th Street and Lexington Avenue, a middle-class business and residential area; on Park Avenue and 26th Street, an upper-middle-class residential area; and on 46th Street and Ninth Avenue, a lower-income residential area. Therefore, visible deviant street locations were distributed throughout the city and not linked with any single type of neighborhood. Deviant street locations in New York City do not resemble "delinquency areas" in Chicago, as described by Shaw and McKay where they were clustered or concentrated in a few well-defined areas.[1] Unlike delinquency areas in Chicago, deviant street locations in New York City are not necessarily situ-

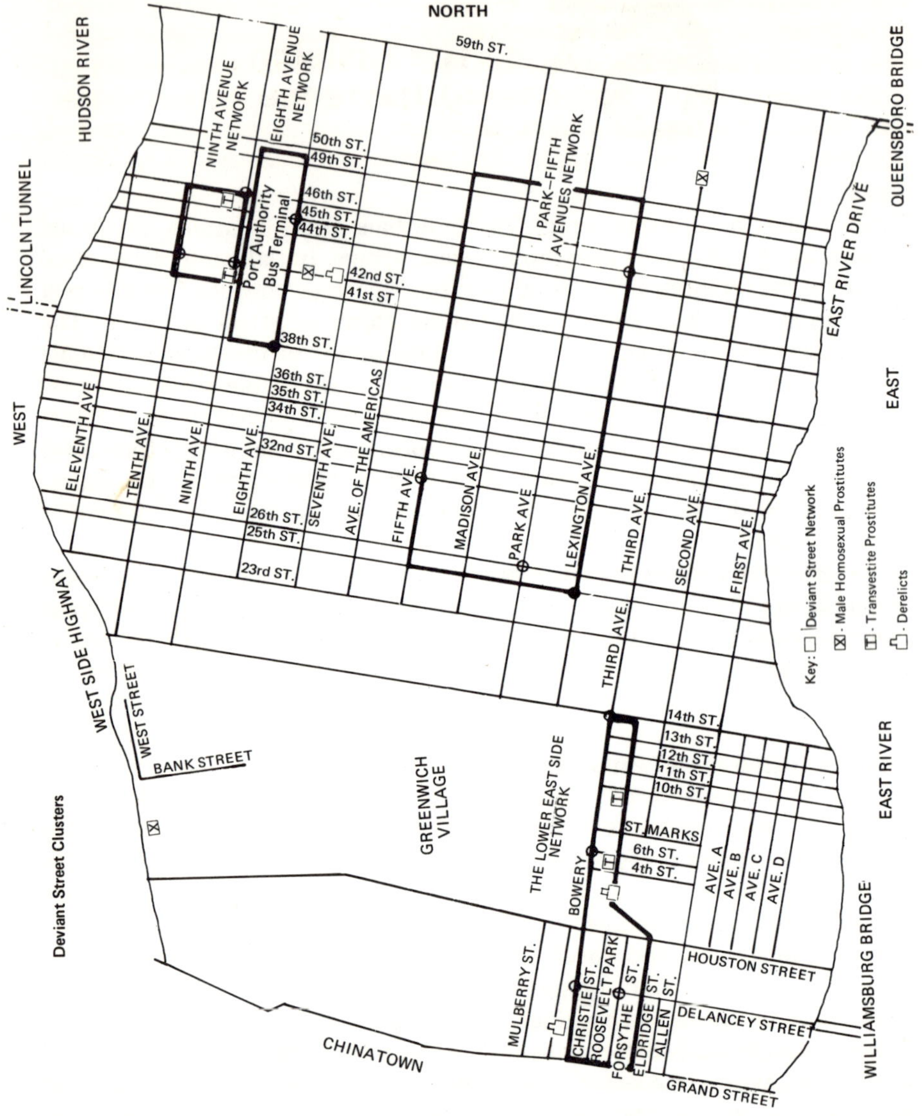

Figure 6-1. Deviant Street Clusters

The Division of Deviance

ated in congested, disorganized, twilight, interstitial, or transitional zones of factories and railroads or in unstable communities on the edge of respectable neighborhoods. The data show that visible street deviance, perhaps unlike street crime (for example, murder, rape, robbery, aggravated assault and battery, burglary, and auto theft), is concentrated in a variety of neighborhoods, including upper- and lower-class business and residential areas.

Deviance Segregation

Another salient finding is that visible public street deviance like ordinary social behavior is differentiated, specialized, and territorially segregated. Different forms of deviance rarely surfaced at the same locations. Even in the Times Square area where varying forms of deviance appeared to mix, alcoholics, female prostitutes, male prostitutes, gamblers, and drug addicts were spatially separated on the immediate work territory even if only by a short distance.

At the Bowery, alcoholics were confined mainly to an area stretching several blocks from the north side of Delancey Street to Fourth Street. Individuals frequently strayed beyond these boundaries, but they were the exception rather than the rule. Nor did this wanderlust result in the formation of permanent deviant street locations. Stragglers were repelled and sometimes even assaulted by deviants already in control of particular street locations. Numerous incidents were observed where prostitutes injured derelicts who attempted to share their turf. In one incident at 47th Street and Eighth Avenue, a prostitute pushed an annoying derelict through the large, glass, display window of a coffee shop. On the other hand, female prostitutes virtually never occupied the same Bowery streets appropriated by derelicts, and the latter avoided entirely the nearby southeast corner of Delancey Street and the Bowery where prostitutes worked. Deviance, like oil and water, appears immiscible.

One block south of Delancey at Broome Street and the Bowery, street bums established a location on the opposite side of the street from female prostitutes. Men in automobiles continuously circled the square block shopping for prostitutes. The derelicts begged for money and cigarettes in exchange for cleaning windshields, while drivers waited for the traffic light to change. Most drivers kept their car windows and doors tightly secured but a few doled out nickels, dimes, and quarters. The bums and prostitutes never worked the same side of the street, and the derelicts usually approached cars only when the prostitutes were not present. The overwhelming majority of panhandlers were male, but two female bums were observed among a group of male derelicts begging for change on the Bowery at Houston Street.

A similar scene occurred at 14th Street and Third Avenue, although Broome Street and The Bowery was the only location where a single pool of customers routinely were solicited by prostitutes and derelicts. Female prostitutes occupied the east side of the street while derelicts milled around its west side. At 12th Street and Third Avenue, a flight of steps off a permanently sealed doorway served as a sitting place for female prostitutes and their men. Derelicts, male prostitutes, and transvestite prostitutes almost never occupied them. Male prostitutes frequented the victinity of 53rd Street and Third Avenue, but virtually no female prostitutes, derelicts, drug addicts, or gamblers were visible at this location. Transvestite prostitutes formed separate groups and worked streets and corners not usually appropriated by female prostitutes. Although locations occupied by transvestite prostitutes were adjacent to territories used by female prostitutes, they nevertheless were separated from each other even if only by part of a city block. This was illustrated by the territory surrounding the Port Authority Bus Terminal between Eighth and Ninth Avenues. Female prostitutes occupied 42nd Street and Tenth Avenue and 42nd Street and Ninth Avenue, while transvestites remained primarily at 41st Street and Ninth Avenue. These two forms of deviance did not mix even though they were separated by only a short distance. Similarly, female prostitutes dominated Third Avenue between 10th and 14th Streets, while transvestite prostitutes occupied the area between St. Mark's Place and 9th Street.

Transvestite prostitutes who shared neighboring locations with female prostitutes seemed to have developed a parisitic relationship. They depended on johns who were drawn to the area by female prostitutes and through a process of mimicry hoped to attract them. Transvestite prostitutes worked a separate turf because female prostitutes resented their intrusion. Structurally, the deviant cluster consisted of a central location of female prostitutes with peripheral nodes occupied by transvestite prostitutes. Transvestites who catered exclusively to males seeking female impersonators usually worked territories far from female prostitution. Several locations were observed in Greenwich Village. A similar parisitic structure was developed by alcoholics. As previously noted, prostitutes occupied a central location at the Bowery and Delancey Street and attracted johns to the area. Alcoholics, one block away at Broome Street, begged for money and cigarettes from those johns.

The Typicality of Deviance

The spatial division, specialization and territorial segregation of visible street deviance in one sense parallels closely patterned orders of legitimate, normative, and ordinary behavior for large cities described by the early Chicago Urban School, including Park, Burgess, and Wirth.[2,3] Deviance and normative behavior are both ordered in similar ways, although the determinants for these orders may differ. The Chicago School applied Durkheim's principles for the division of labor to cities.[4] They pointed out that a city's large population, heterogeneity, and moral density led to division, differentiation, and specialization.

Wirth pointed out that certain factors selected and distributed individuals into separate and distinct areas or neighborhoods including nature of work, income, racial and ethnic characteristics, custom, habit, taste, and prejudice.[5] The diverse population elements generally found in large cities, Wirth argued, tended to separate from each other to the degree that their activities, mode of life, sentiments, and requirements were incompatible. Moreover, persons with similar traits and interests unwittingly gravitated toward each other, consciously elected to be together, and were forced by certain pressures to live in the same area. Once these areas were defined they tended to attract persons of similar socioeconomic status, age, race, ethnicity, and family status. This is the way different neighborhoods and parts of a city acquired specialized functions.

Similar factors may also explain the division of deviance. Substantial deviant concentrations, coupled together with a city's anonymity and population density produced differentiated and specialized forms of deviant behavior. The selection, distribution, and division of deviance among different neighborhoods resulted from sociodemographic factors, cultural factors, the degree of homogeneity of a specific form of deviance, competition, mutual security, and community expectations. Deviant occupations like other types of work or ways of life had its own needs and prerequisites; therefore, these amassed in different neighborhoods.

Deviant Sorting

I refer to this process of territorial segregation of different forms of deviance as *deviant sorting*. The sorting process divides different types of deviant groups into mutually exclusive affiliations. There are little if any face-to-face relations. The different types of deviant groups occupy mutually exclusive territories. Deviant sorting occurs among groups of individuals where negative judgmental consequences and potential for conflict and competition are greatest. Sorting keeps these different groups apart by designating them to certain territories.

By confining similar deviant types to the same location, shared expectations and standards are developed and recognized; conflict is minimized. People can read each others intentions and thoughts. This introduces social control and relatively peaceful social relations.[6] Short-run opportunism is dangerous because the opportunist must continue to live with his victims.[7] Members are held accountable for their actions. The enduring character of the group allows everyone to learn each others abilities, character, strengths, and weaknesses.

Deviant groups participate in the sorting process by constructing their own independent strategies for staking out various territories. The police and community also assist in this process. Three factors are particularly important for understanding how these groups contribute to territorial segregation or sorting; competition, mutual security, and community expectations.

Competition

A significant determinant for deviant division and territorial sorting is competition. Different deviant groups may compete with one another for customers, territory, shelter, and business places.

Customers for male, female, and transvestite street prostitution are primarily lower- and middle-class white males between twenty and fifty years old. Conflict between different deviant groups would be inevitable if they shared the same territory. One can picture a scenario in which tranvestite prostitutes and female prostitutes solicit and argue over the same customers. Moreover, imagine the chagrin, bewilderment, and embarrassment of johns seeking female prostitutes only to discover they had unknowingly participated in sexual acts with males posing as females. Similarly, it is easy to perceive the discomfort and annoyance of customers seeking either male or female prostitutes who are subjected to harassment by derelicts.

Suppose male prostitutes, transvestite prostitutes, female prostitutes, derelicts, drug addicts, and gamblers shared the same territory. Each competing street group would vie for the most advantageous positions. This interactional process would result in constant conflict and violence. Customers, of course, would find this very distasteful and probably avoid the area. Also, the police would be called to suppress the conflict by increasing the number of arrests. On the other hand, a certain optimum number of female prostitutes who work together at the same location attracts customers because it assures them of a choice. Once a territory is staked out and developed for heterosexual prostitution it is important to keep it homogeneous.

In addition to economic competition, different types of deviant street groups may possess competing deviant value systems. A particular deviant value system once rooted in a neighborhood tends to repress most other forms of deviant values. The deviant occupiers tend to repel invading deviants. For example, male homosexual prostitutes may exclude derelicts or female prostitutes from their turf because their activities are degrading to them.

The Division of Deviance

Mutual Security

Another factor contributing to the division and territorial sorting of deviance is mutual security. Persons sharing the same occupation work together, have common problems, and get to trust and protect one another. Accordingly, female prostitutes occupy the same territory, provide similar services, have common needs, and tend to aid each other. On the other hand, persons who perform different deviant services do not share identical goals and need not occupy the same territory. Prostitutes have few interests in common with derelicts, drug addicts, and gamblers; there scarcely is any incentive for mutual aid.

Several incidents from the field data illustrated how female prostitutes provided mutual aid to each other. One incident occurred at 32nd Street and Fifth Avenue.

> A group of seven or eight tough young girls around seventeen to twenty years appeared on the street at 11:30 p.m. and began harassing several prostitutes who worked this location. The young girls cursed and yelled epithets. Next, one obese, strong-looking girl assaulted a prostitute and a fight ensued. Other prostitutes immediately came to their companion's aid. They kicked the young girl and hit her with sticks and umbrella handles in front of her shocked and startled companions. One sanguinary prostitute dug the heel of her shoe into the girl's head and eyes. By the time the police arrived and arrested the intruders, the young woman was bleeding from the head and other parts of her body. Several prostitutes accompanied the officers to the stationhouse to make out a complaint.

Another incident occurred at the corner of 12th Street and Third Avenue.

> The police were about to arrest a group of prostitutes for loitering. A member of the group informed them that one of the women was not a prostitute but an innocent bystander. The police arrested all the women except the bystander. It turned out that the selfless prostitute was several months pregnant. The prostitute whom she had successfully shielded from the police was the mother of young children. Apparently, the mother-to-be empathized with the parent and took steps to protect her. The prostitute who was not arrested, in appreciation, promised to give her friend twenty dollars upon her release from jail.

Numerous other incidents occurred where street prostitutes provided mutual aid. This usually took the form of alerting each other about the presence of police, driving away a troublesome bystander or hanger-on, and providing assistance during an assault.

Community Expectations

Another significant factor in the division of deviance is community expectations. People who reside or work in a particular area, including the police, develop certain expectations about their neighborhood. Many neighborhoods occupied by female prostitutes do not welcome other deviant types including drug addicts, derelicts, gamblers, transvestite prostitutes, and male prostitutes. When members from these groups attempt to enter the area they are driven away.

The police contribute to this process by selectively arresting intruders. In other words, the community and its police may accept a certain type of deviant value system but exclude others. A given community may tolerate illicit straight sex, that is, prostitution, but may condemn sexual acts that are perceived as unnatural including male homosexual prostitution and transvestite prostitution. Derelicts were driven by the police from the Park and Fifth Avenues network whereas prostitutes were left relatively free so long as they worked within the boundaries of the deviant street location. On the other hand, derelicts were permitted almost complete freedom on the Bowery where prostitutes were continuously harassed.

Stratified Street Order

Not only were different forms of visible street deviance differentiated and territorially sorted, but they were also stratified or hierarchically ordered. Usually male prostitutes appropriated prime socioeconomic areas like Third Avenue in the 50s and Greenwich Village. In general, prostitutes preferred to work in higher socioeconomic neighborhoods because they were more safe, quiet, and clean than lower socioeconomic areas. Also they offered higher paying clientele and generally less police harassment. Even on 42nd Street between Seventh and Eighth Avenues, male prostitutes appeared to have seized choice spots. Female prostitutes occupied the next most desirable locations in several key business and residential districts. Transvestite prostitutes established conditions on fringe territories bordering areas occupied by female prostitutes. These territories were usually less advantageous than even the more run-down locations utilized by many female prostitutes. Derelicts tended to occupy some of the city's most disagreeable and lower socioeconomic areas characterized by flea-bag hotels, deteriorated buildings, and cheap stores.

Not surprisingly, ranking deviant groups raises the same problems as ranking ordinary societal groups. Depending on the criteria used, a group may place high or low. Rarely does consistency prevail. Generally, however, each of the determinants for social order are linked together and may be

The Division of Deviance

used in combination to reflect the rank of any particular group.[8] The stratified order among different types of deviant groups is due to several factors; power, economic assets, social status, and function. The rank of a deviant group will depend upon the extent it possesses certain attributes, qualities or characteristics valued by society.

Power

One determinant of a stratified order among differentiated and specialized forms of deviance is power. In this context *power* refers to the extent a group can control, shape, and direct its own destiny.[9] One form of power is political might. Male homosexual prostitutes are part of the broader homosexual movement in America (gay liberation). This movement has developed into a politically powerful organization that seeks for its members civil rights and political clout. One reason male homosexual prostitutes occupy higher socioeconomic areas may be because they possess more political might than most other deviant street groups.

Female prostitutes also have begun to organize politically. Aside from the impetus and at times hindrance from the National Organization of Women, they have formed their own organizations. A main aim of these organizations is to secure civil rights for their members (for example, one New York group is known as Scapegoat; another PONY, Prostitutes of New York; Coyote, an acronym for "Call Off Your Old Tired Ethics," is a national organization).[10] But female prostitutes have yet to ascend the level of political organization and power achieved by male homosexuals. Female prostitutes, therefore, tend to occupy the next most desirable work areas.

Transvestite prostitutes are not organized politically, perhaps because they are few in number. However, they do share strong internal group ties. Thus they occupy less desirable fringe areas adjacent to female and male prostitutes.

Finally, derelicts are the least powerful group. They scarcely have political power and are disorganized within their own ranks. Thus they occupy the most disadvantageous locations and street positions.

Physical might plays only a small part in determining this order. Homosexual, female, and transvestite prostitutes have access to weapons or outside assistance from pimps. Perhaps physical power is significant in ordering derelicts because they usually are old, sick, or in a state of intoxication and cannot pose a serious physical threat.

Economic Hierarchy

Another principle that determines the stratified order among deviants is economic advantage. Groups having the greatest wealth, money, and resources ought to occupy prime locations. Although additional research is required to determine precisely the earning power of each deviant street group, the field observations suggest that male and female prostitutes earned more money than transvestite prostitutes with male prostitutes having a slight edge over female prostitutes. In addition, transvestite prostitutes who cater to males seeking women depend heavily on female prostitutes to attract customers. It is certain, however, that all types of street prostitutes, including transvestites, earned more money from illicit sexual activities than did derelicts from panhandling.

Social Status

Social status is another significant determinant for a stratified order of deviance. Important here are social esteem, position, honor, and prestige bestowed by society. Homosexual street prostitutes in New York City at locations of visible deviance are male and predominantly white. Much of their status derives from membership in the dominant ethnic and sex groups. About half the female street prostitutes studied were white and half were black and Hispanic. On the other hand, the majority of street transvestites and derelicts were black. Apparently, ethnicity was more important than sex in determining positions in the social order; therefore, female prostitutes occupied more desirable areas than either transvestites or derelicts.

Function

Society's ordinary social groups are assessed on the basis of function and performance. These partially determine the worth of each group and its rank on a social scale. Deviant groups are similarly evaluated. Male and female prostitutes provide services mainly to white males. Transvestite prostitutes who work nearby locations of female street prostitutes also provide services primarily to white males, but the transaction often involves deception. The male client usually believes he has hired the services of a female when in fact the prostitute is a male posing as a female. Nevertheless, transvestite prostitutes are in the business of providing certain sexual services. In contrast, derelicts are parasitic and provide no apparent direct service. Therefore, they occupy the least desirable territories of the four groups, while transvestites are close follow-ups.[11]

Notes

1. See Clifford Robe Shaw and Henry D. McKay, *Juvenile Delinquency and Urban Areas* (Chicago: University of Chicago Press, 1942), pp. 45, 166.
2. See Edwin M. Schur, *Interpreting Deviance* (New York: Harper & Row, 1979), ch. 2.
3. See Louis Wirth, "Urbanism as a Way of Life," *American Journal of Sociology* 44, no. 1 (July 1938):1-24.
4. Emile Durkheim, *The Division of Labor in Society* (New York: The Free Press, 1964).
5. Wirth, "Urbanism as a Way of Life," p. 15.
6. Gerald D. Suttles, *The Social Construction of Communities* (Chicago: The University of Chicago Press, 1972), p. 162.
7. Ibid.
8. Roland Mousnier, *Social Hierarchies: 1450 to the Present* (New York: Schocken Books, 1969), part I.
9. For a thorough discussion of power see Talcott Parsons, ed., *Max Weber, The Theory of Social and Economic Organization* (Glencoe, Ill.: The Free Press, 1947), pp. 152, 324-336; and Robert Dahl, *Modern Political Analysis* (Englewood Cliffs, N.J.: Prentice-Hall, 1963).
10. Jennifer James, Jean Withers, Marilyn Haft, Sara Theiss, and Mary Owen, *The Politics of Prostitution* (Washington: University of Washington, November 1975).
11. The highly structured and stratified order for those four deviant groups was different from the "segmental order" for four major ethnic groups in a Chicago slum described by Gerald Suttles. (See Gerald Suttles, *The Social Order of the Slum* [Chicago: University of Chicago Press, 1968].) The ethnic groups were ordered in four neighborhoods geographically juxtaposed to one another within the same slum and they were much less stratified. Moreover, these ethnic groups were dependent to some extent on each other for security. Derelicts, female prostitutes, and male prostitutes are highly stratified and they occupy territories near but not necessarily juxtaposed to each other. Also, they are much less dependent on one another for security than the different slum groups described by Suttles.

7 Deviant Street Network Stratification

The four street networks of female prostitution were definitely arranged according to a neighborhood's socioeconomic class. The four networks ordered from high to low socioeconomic status are: (1) Park and Fifth Avenues; (2) Eighth Avenue; (3) Ninth Avenue, and (4) The Lower East Side. In general, more desirable prostitutes were found in areas of high socioeconomic status, which usually were safer, cleaner, and more prestigious than lower socioeconomic areas. Also, prostitutes in better neighborhoods experienced less harassment by police and tended to charge higher prices for services. These more desirable entrepreneurs included younger, better dressed, more attractive, and higher-priced prostitutes. Less desirable prostitutes occupied lower socioeconomic areas.

Female Prostitutes

Age

The deviant street network between Park and Fifth Avenues on Manhattan's East Side, covering the area from around 23rd to 53rd Streets, is situated in one of the city's higher socioeconomic areas. Prostitutes in this area were generally younger and more attractive than prostitutes from other locations. Older and less desirable prostitutes tended to work Ninth Avenue, a lower socioeconomic area. The estimated average age of white and black prostitutes, respectively, on Ninth Avenue was twenty-eight and thirty-one. This compared to an average of twenty-six for white prostitutes and twenty-seven for black prostitutes at Park and Fifth Avenues. Eighth Avenue was occupied by white and black prostitutes, respectively, with estimated average ages of twenty-seven and twenty-eight years. The average age of prostitutes regardless of race for Ninth Avenue was twenty-nine; Eighth Avenue, twenty-seven; and Park and Fifth Avenues, twenty-six.

Only the Lower East Side did not conform to this pattern relating socioeconomic status and age. The average age for all prostitutes at this deviant street network was twenty-six and one-half; twenty-seven for blacks, twenty-six for whites, and twenty-five for Hispanics. Although Eighth Avenue is a somewhat more desirable neighborhood than the Lower East Side, its prostitutes tended to be slightly older. The overall average age for prostitutes on the Lower East Side was deflated by several groups of prostitutes managed by pimps. Professionally managed women tended to be younger than independents. Most prostitutes who worked Park and Fifth Avenues also were managed by pimps.

Rating of Desirability

More attractive, better dressed, and generally desirable prostitutes tended to occupy higher socioeconomic networks.[1] The ethnostatistics showed that prostitutes on the Lower East Side and Ninth Avenue, respectively, had the weakest ratings of desirability ($\bar{X} = 2.7$ each), whereas prostitutes on Eighth Avenue, a slightly higher socioeconomic area, had a somewhat higher average rating ($\bar{X} = 3.1$). Park and Fifth Avenues had the highest average rating of desirability (5.0). In general, prostitutes who worked higher socioeconomic neighborhoods were better and more conservatively dressed than their lower socioeconomic class counterparts. Women at the Bowery and Delancey Street, for example, tended to dress in loud and cheap clothes. These socioeconomic patterns persisted regardless of a prostitute's race.

Race

A greater proportion of white prostitutes than black or Hispanic prostitutes occupied higher socioeconomic areas. Accordingly, the proportions of white, black, and Hispanic prostitutes in the Park and Fifth Avenues network were 57.9 percent, 41.3 percent, and .75 percent respectively. On the other hand, 40.6 percent of the prostitutes on the Lower East Side were white, 51.7 percent were black, and 7.1 percent were Hispanic.[2]

Cost and Operations

Prostitutes in more advantageous neighborhoods compared to lesser areas charged higher prices for services. Routine sexual services included intercourse and oral sex (*a French* in street argot). Anal sex and kissing were rare, the former because it was deemed too painful, the latter because it was considered a sign of intimacy.

Prices charged by prostitutes for sexual intercourse at locations in the Park and Fifth Avenues street network, including 25th Street and Lexington Avenue, 26th Street and Park Avenue, 32nd Street and Fifth Avenue, and 44th Street and Lexington Avenue, during 1977 and 1978 averaged $20 to

$30. This range compared to $10 to $20 in less desirable networks like the Lower East Side including Forsythe Street, the Bowery and Delancey Street, 6th Street, and 10th to 14th Streets.

The price for oral sex also varied from one location to another. The going price for the lowest socioeconomic street networks, including the Lower East Side and Ninth Avenue, was approximately $10. In higher socioeconomic networks the price for this act ranged from $10 to $20. Moreover the fee for oral sex and intercourse together (frequently referred to as *half and half* in street jargon) was usually $5 to $10 higher than intercourse alone.

Bargaining for slightly reduced rates was frequent, especially in slow, cold, and rainy periods, but prostitutes almost never accepted less than a few dollars below the original asking price. Prostitutes were especially offended by a john who drove to a deserted location and then offered a ridiculously low price like $5. This gesture was communicated to the area's prostitutes who from then on avoided the frugal john.

Hotel rooms in higher socioeconomic areas averaged $10 to $12, which was considerably more than the $5 to $8 range for hotels in neighborhoods of lower socioeconomic status. Incidentally, hotel rates and fees for prostitution were not exempt from inflation. A recent survey of street conditions revealed that prices for hotels and sexual services had risen from 20 to 25 percent over a one-year period.

The method of operation for prostitution varied also by a neighborhood's socioeconomic level. For example, prostitutes in the Park and Fifth Avenues network did not usually risk sexual intercourse in an automobile, preferring the relative safety and protection of a hotel. It is more difficult for police to gather evidence from a hotel room than a parked automobile. Also a hotel room provides more security and protection for the prostitute because business is conducted on familiar ground and the client is screened by the hotel clerk and even prostitutes who frequent the hotel. Prostitutes and johns are aware that assistance may be available in an emergency. Sexual activities conducted in a patron's car increase the risk of harm. In addition, a hotel room is more comfortable than a car. The patron and prostitute may feel less inhibited and totally undress. The advantages of conducting activities in a car for johns, although it is more conspicuous, include savings on hotel costs, greater anonymity, not signing in, and for some a more exciting and adventurous experience. Generally the balance of power and control shifts slightly in a car from prostitute to client. From the point of view of the prostitute, control and power must always be in her favor in order to survive.

Only a handful of street prostitutes rented private rooms by the week or month. This tended to be cheaper than hotel rooms and the savings could be passed on to the customer. Moreover, a rented room provides greater safety from the police because it is more obscure and not used by large numbers of prostitutes. Its disadvantage is that it does not offer the protection of a hotel. Johns tend to fear accompanying a prostitute to a rented room. Oftentimes tough looking youth hang out in the hallways of buildings where these rooms are situated. For several years one attractive white prostitute about twenty-six years old positioned herself on Third Avenue at 11th Street and brought johns to a rented room in an old, deteriorated building three blocks away in a lower socioeconomic residential neighborhood. Youth frequently congregated in the building. Her man was a middle-aged black who, like herself, was hooked on drugs. Street prostitutes rarely took customers to their private residence.

Sexual intercourse or oral sex alone or together were likely to take place in cars in the two deviant street networks located in lesser neighborhoods, including the Lower East Side and Ninth Avenue, because clients were often unwilling or unable to provide extra money for a hotel. Moreover, hotels used for prostitution in lower socioeconomic networks were less attractive and more seedy than similar hotels in higher socioeconomic areas. However, even in more affluent neighborhoods, oral sex often was conducted in an automobile. In general, less attractive and older prostitutes from lower socioeconomic networks tended to take greater risks than their more desirable and younger counterparts from higher socioeconomic networks including soliciting by standing in the street rather than on the sidewalk and making conspicuous, overt gestures. More cautious prostitutes stood with their backs against the building line and were selective. They waited for johns to signal or solicit them rather than initiate the encounter themselves.

Temporal Patterns

Three of four street locations in the Park and Fifth Avenues network were active only during evening (7:00 p.m. to 1:00 a.m.) and late evening (1:00 a.m. to 7:00 a.m.). However, street deviance at 44th Street and Lexington Avenue was active albeit slight during daytime. Deviant activities at this location increased substantially during evening. Street deviance was dormant during daylight in the lower socioeconomic area as well. Visible street prostitution surfaced at each of three locations comprising the Ninth Avenue network only during early and late evening with much or all activity receding during daytime. Visible street prostitution at Eighth Avenue and the Lower East Side was active twenty-four hours a day. Apparently, temporal patterns were unrelated to a neighborhood's socioeconomic status.

Incidence

The incidence of prostitutes was approximately the same for areas of varying socioeconomic status, although they were more concentrated in lower socioeconomic areas. Together the Lower East Side and Ninth Avenue was occupied by 589 or 49.5 percent of the 1189 prostitutes compared to 600 or 50.5 percent for Park and Fifth Avenues and Eighth Avenue. However, there were 37 prostitutes per city block of deviant street location for the Lower East Side and Ninth Avenue compared to 27 prostitutes for Park and Fifth Avenues and Eighth Avenue. Utilizing this measure of density, the number of prostitutes per block of deviant street location for the Lower East Side was 45; Ninth Avenue, 19; Eighth Avenue, 30; and Park and Fifth Avenues, 24. The number of prostitutes per block was 27 for the West Side and 35 for the East Side.

Volume

Volume, or the number of separate business transactions, fluctuated with individual prostitutes, but it also varied with a neighborhood's socioeconomic status. Volume was substantially higher for the Lower East Side and Ninth Avenue compared to Park and Fifth Avenues and Eighth Avenue.

A very rough estimate of the average number of contacts per prostitute for the Lower East Side and Ninth Avenue, two lower socioeconomic areas, was one per hour compared to .5 per hour for Fifth and Park Avenues and Eighth Avenue. Apparently, the different prices in varying socioeconomic areas helped regulate the level of business. These rates allow an estimate of average earnings of prostitutes by deviant street networks. Of course income also varies according to the age, attractiveness, and enterprise of individual prostitutes. The following income estimates refer to steady, hardworking, diligent prostitutes who *hustle* six nights a week for eight hours.

	The Lower East Side and Ninth Avenue	*Park and Fifth Avenues and Eighth Avenue*
Nightly	$120	$100
Weekly	720	600
Monthly	2,880	2,400
Yearly	34,560	28,800

These rough approximations show that prostitutes in lower-class neighborhoods earn on average about 20 percent more than their upper-class counterparts, although they have to work twice as hard as measured by the number of contacts.

The duration or amount of contact time between prostitutes and clients was longer in lower than higher socioeconomic areas. Also it varied depending on whether a hotel or car was utilized for activities. The average time elapsed from when a couple entered a hotel to departure was approximately twenty-five minutes for the Lower East Side compared to about twenty minutes for Park and Fifth Avenues. Sex in cars, mostly of the oral variety, took an average of ten minutes for Park and Fifth Avenues compared to fifteen minutes for the Lower East Side. Evidently safety, prestige, cleanliness, and a lighter work load associated with higher socioeconomic areas compensates for lower income. Additional research is needed to test the reliability of these tentative findings.

Male Transvestite Prostitution

Visible, male, transvestite street prostitution surfaced primarily in the two lowest socioeconomic areas, but usually not in the two highest ones, and was observed on the Lower East Side and on Ninth Avenue. Sixty percent of all transvestites occupied Ninth Avenue and 24.2 percent were on the Lower East Side. Only 13.3 percent were observed on Eighth Avenue and even fewer (2.5 percent) on Park and Fifth Avenues. Transvestites occupied these two higher socioeconomic areas only occasionally and usually they were on the move. In general, transvestite prostitutes appeared more mobile and less stationary than female prostitutes. One explanation might be that they depend on deceit to gain clients. Most clients who discover this subterfuge tend to avoid them. Moving aggregates do not constitute permanent, stable street deviance. For a short period of time a group consisting of four to five transvestite prostitutes occupied the corner of Eighth Avenue and 45th Street but eventually they dispersed.

Apparently transvestite prostitutes do not easily form stable, visible street conditions in high socioeconomic areas. This may be due to more intense competition between prostitutes for clients in more desirable neighborhoods. Also, it may be that the community and police combine efforts to exclude transvestites from higher socioeconomic neighborhoods. These communities may tolerate female prostitution but they are unwilling to accept visible prostitution by male transvestites.

The most established condition of transvestite prostitution was at 41st Street and Ninth Avenue (30.0 percent); the next most extensive condition was at 45th Street and Ninth Avenue (24.2 percent); then between Seventh and 10th Streets and Third Avenue (13.3 percent); and the least extensive condition was between 4th and 6th Streets on Third Avenue (10.8 percent). Although near the core of visible female street prostitution, transvestite prostitutes operated almost exclusively out of separate locations and they did not regularly mix with female prostitutes.

Transvestite prostitutes, like female prostitutes, were ordered according to the socioeconomic status of the territories they occupied. For example, transvestites at 45th Street and Ninth Avenue tended to ask higher prices for services than those around Fourth Street. Also, they appeared to be better dressed than their Lower East Side counterparts. Fees for services were similar to those for female prostitutes, although transvestites had a lower volume of business transactions.

Deviant Management

The two major forms of control over prostitutes were management by agent and self-management. *Management* by agent included either a pimp or a man, and *self-management* was effected through independent groups or the prostitute herself. The form of deviant management varied with an area's socioeconomic status. Prostitutes in lower socioeconomic areas tended either to be independent or managed by men. Management by pimp was more frequent in higher socioeconomic areas; self-management was less likely. Pimps seemed to avoid lower priced and less prestigious neighborhoods. Men, more than pimps, operated in lower socioeconomic areas like the Lower East Side. Except for the Bowery and Delancey Street, pimps rarely frequented other street locations in this lower socioeconomic network. A substantial number of prostitutes on the Lower East Side were *independents* (that is, not managed by a pimp or a man) either working individually or in groups. Many prostitutes working the Ninth Avenue complex were independent, but those who were managed worked with a man and not for a pimp. The majority of men were Hispanic and they tended to blend in with the local Hispanic communities on Ninth Avenue and the Lower East Side. Hispanics were more likely to be men than pimps perhaps because of a language handicap.

The majority of prostitutes in the Park and Fifth Avenues network were managed by pimps, although a small number of these women were independent. Few women working this desirable area were managed by a man. The Eighth Avenue network had a mixture of independent and managed women. Most of the nonindependents were managed by pimps and a few were supervised by a man.

The failure to make the important distinction between a pimp and a man has led certain police authorities and the public to conclude that all or most prostitution is organized. In fact, more prostitutes appeared to be managed by men than pimps. Still, less than half the prostitutes studied appeared to be managed by deviant agents. I was unable to identify links between organized crime and street prostitution. This is in accord with previous findings that street prostitution in New York City is not controlled by elements of organized crime.[3]

Johns

One of the most striking differences among neighborhoods of varying socioeconomic status was the type of individual who patronized different street networks. Visible street prostitution in more desirable neighborhoods attracted johns of higher socioeconomic status than similar conditions in lesser neighborhoods. For example, johns who frequented prostitutes at Park and Fifth Avenues often were clean shaven and wore business suits and neckties. Several carried attaché cases and appeared to be junior, middle, or even upper-level corporate executives. Moreover, many johns cruised in high-priced-late-model cars including Cadillacs, Lincoln Continentals, or expensive sports cars. Several patrons spoke with a foreign accent and dressed immaculately, some wore thick gold chains and watches. Apparently these individuals were either well-to-do tourists, foreign businessmen, or diplomats. Except perhaps foreign diplomats, the overwhelming majority of patrons at Park and Fifth Avenues were white.

An entirely different type of john frequented the Lower East Side. Most were dressed in dungarees; work clothes; cheap, soiled, open shirts; and old shoes. They tended to drive older autos in the low-to middle-price range. Many johns arrived in trucks and vans which often served as surrogate hotels. The patrons in this network certainly were not from the same social and occupational classes as persons who patronized prostitutes further uptown, especially Park and Fifth Avenues. Nevertheless, the majority of johns were white (71.6 percent).

Hangers-on

Hangers-on as explained in chapter 4 do not participate directly in the process and control of prostitution, (for example, patrons, pimps, prostitutes, or police) nor do they usually work or shop in the area. Instead they spend substantial time hanging around a visible deviant street location.

The incidence of hangers-on tended to be higher in lower socioeconomic neighborhoods. The Lower East Side was occupied by a disproportionate number of hangers-on (35 percent), while the upper socioeconomic area of

Park and Fifth Avenues had the least hangers-on (9 percent). The proportion of hangers-on was substantial at Eighth Avenue and Ninth Avenue (33.1 percent and 23.0 percent, respectively). The Park and Fifth Avenues network had the greatest proportion of prostitutes managed by pimps who tended to discourage the presence of hangers-on. Moreover, hangers-on were least expected and tolerated in this deviant street network by the community and the police because it was a higher socioeconomic area. Park and Fifth Avenues include mostly white, well-dressed residents and business persons, and anyone not conforming to their dress code, appearance, or life style stands out.

On the other hand, the Lower East Side network consists of heterogeneous neighborhoods with varying ethnic and immigrant groups who dress in different styles and inexpensive clothing. This area also included the Bowery with its derelicts and bums who often drift into other nearby neighborhoods. Groups of young, unemployed, male residents usually hang out in these neighborhoods. Hangers-on blend in very well with these persons and the cultural and social fabric of the neighborhood. This might explain the ethnic background of hangers-on at specific deviant locations. Black hangers-on were found mainly in areas occupied by black prostitutes, white hangers-on occupied areas with a high proportion of white prostitutes, and Hispanic hangers-on were found in neighborhoods with a substantial Spanish population. For example, at 32nd Street and Fifth Avenue, a location occupied mainly by white prostitutes, nearly twice as many hangers-on were white as Black (64.7 percent to 35.3 percent). There were no Hispanic hangers-on in this neighborhood. The two locations with the most Hispanic hangers-on were 10th to 14th Streets (42.2 percent) and Ninth Avenue and 46th Street (20.0 percent), areas with a substantial population of Hispanics. Even at these locations, however, the majority of hangers-on were black (63.5 percent).

Deviant Spacing

Deviant spacing is the process of stratification that orders different locations occupied by the same types of deviants. This process is similar to deviant sorting, but it is not as rigid. Unlike deviant sorting, deviant spacing occurs within a stratified system where there is some mobility and fluidity between various levels. The major functions of deviant spacing are to reduce competition, provide mechanisms for mutual protection, and produce small enough groups to allow face-to-face recognition so that persons can work together with some degree of control and responsibility. Naturally this process allocates similar persons to the same areas. A major difference between spacing and sorting is that spacing allows a certain measure of mobility between deviant locations whereas sorting results in nearly complete territorial segregation and exclusion.

Order within Deviant Street Networks

Not only were each of the four deviant street networks of female prostitution hierarchically ordered according to socioeconomic status, but the *sets* of locations within each network were also similarly stratified (table 7-1). Generally, they tended to decrease in socioeconomic status from midtown to downtown, a trend characterizing most Manhattan neighborhoods although differences between nearby locations might be extremely small. For example, on Eighth Avenue, 42nd Street to 49th Street is a more desirable location than 38th Street to 42nd Street. However, differences between 26th Street and Park Avenue and 25th Street and Lexington Avenue are negligible. These deviant sets followed the same patterns found between networks. The higher the socioeconomic status of a location within a single network the more likely that it was occupied by younger, more desirable prostitutes who obtained higher fees from more sophisticated and advantaged patrons. Moreover, prostitutes in more desirable locations tended to utilize hotels for transactions rather than automobiles, spend less time with johns, and be

**Table 7-1
Approximate Order of Locations from High to Low Socioeconomic Status within Deviant Street Networks**

Deviant Street Networks

Park and Fifth Avenues
1. 44th to 50th Streets and Lexington Avenue
2. 32nd Street and Fifth Avenue
3. 26th Street and Park Avenue
4. 25th Street and Lexington Avenue

Eighth Avenue
1. 42nd to 49th Streets and Eighth Avenue
2. 38th to 42nd Streets and Eighth Avenue

Ninth Avenue
1. 46th Street and Ninth Avenue
2. 42nd Street and Ninth Avenue
3. 42nd Street and Tenth Avenue

The Lower East Side
1. 10th to 14th Streets and Third Avenue
2. 6th Street and Third Avenue
3. Bowery and Delancey Street
4. Forsythe Street

under the management of pimps. Generally differences among street locations within a network were not as sharp as differences in locations between networks.

Order within Deviant Street Location

In addition to the stratified order among different deviant street locations is the distinct hierarchical order within each locations's core to its external boundary. The thirteen locations of female prostitution ranged in size between one and seven city blocks though a typical condition was spread over one to four blocks (table 7-2)

Each deviant street location covered a well-defined and circumscribed territory with a core and an invisible, unmarked, but nevertheless known, delineated, outside boundary. Most prostitutes worked at or near the core because it usually was situated by a doorway, a hotel, a coffee shop, or other building used as a place of business or for hiding from the police. Moreover, the core usually provided the most propitious vantage point for soliciting business and surveillance. In general, the greater the distance from the core the less advantageous the position. Younger, more attractive and senior prostitutes tended to position themselves at or near the core while older, less desirable women with little *time in trade* took up positions somewhere between the core and its outside boundary. Moreover, white prostitutes were more likely than black or Hispanic prostitutes to occupy positions at or near the core.

The most disadvantaged women occupied positions at or near the condi-

**Table 7-2
Approximate Area Covered by Each Deviant Street Location**

Deviant Street Locations	*City Blocks*
42nd to 49th Streets and Eighth Avenue	7
44th to 50th Streets and Lexington Avenue	6
10th to 14th Streets and Third Avenue	4
Bowery and Delancey Street	4
38th to 42nd Streets and Eighth Avenue	4
46th Street and Ninth Avenue	3
32nd Street and Fifth Avenue	2
26th Street and Park Avenue	2
Forsythe Street	2
42nd Street and Tenth Avenue	1
42nd Street and Ninth Avenue	1
25th Street and Lexington Avenue	1
6th Street and Third Avenue	1
Total	38

tion's outer boundary and these included drug addicts, obese individuals, and unattractive older women. These prostitutes also were less likely to remain stationary and instead continuously changed street positions. Although fees for services did not vary as much within as between different deviant street locations, prices were generally higher for prostitutes stationed at or near the core. As one proceeded from the core to the outer boundary fees usually decreased by 10 to 15 percent.

The methods of operation for prostitution also varied with territorial position. Prostitutes near the core tended to conduct business in hotels rather than automobiles. As noted previously, a hotel compared to an automobile provides greater safety and protection from the police and dangerous johns. *Core prostitutes* were less likely to perform oral sex in a car than prostitutes positioned away from the core.

A condition's core tended to be more active than other territorial positions. Only after positions at or near the core were activated did other positions along the condition become alive. Several conditions were active during daylight hours and then expanded from the core with evening. The volume of contacts also usually was greater for prostitutes positioned at the core.

Johns who patronized core prostitutes tended to be of higher socioeconomic status than those who patronized prostitutes away from the core. They were better dressed and drove more expensive cars. One advantage of engaging a prostitute near or at the core was that it reduced the time that the john and prostitute were visible together on the street thereby decreasing the risk that the transaction would be discovered. Prostitutes always led johns quickly and directly from the street pick-up point to the hotel. The amount of time spent with a customer did not differ for core and noncore prostitutes.

Males who hung around locations of visible street deviance usually stationed themselves away from the core near a condition's external boundary. Males observed around the core usually were deviant managers. These were men rather than pimps because the latter tended to maintain a physical distance from the street condition.

Transvestite prostitutes almost never shared a core with female prostitutes. Occasionally, however, when a condition's core was vacant, usually during early morning hours, it was occupied by transvestites.

The further away from the core the higher the risk of harassment and arrest because prostitutes have a greater distance to traverse in order to reach a place of safety. Prostitutes who ventured too far from the core posed a threat for the police because it raised doubts about who actually was in control of the streets. The police tended to overreact and arrest a disproportionate number of these prostitutes.[4]

The condition of female prostitution at the Bowery and Delancey Street highlighted the different patterns between core and noncore prostitutes. The core consisted of the territory in front of the hotel and the adjacent coffee shop on the southeast corner of the Bowery and Delancey Street. Desirable, young, white and black prostitutes who worked this area over a long period and spent many hours at this location almost always clung to the core. Women managed by pimps, who charged higher prices, nearly always utilized the hotel. Core prostitutes tended to do a greater volume of business and attracted more advantaged clients. The core was active even during the day and as evening approached the condition expanded around the entire square block. Hangers-on almost never utilized the core. Instead they stood around a nearby park or at a corner a short distance from the core. Similarly, transvestite prostitutes almost never occupied the core, but were sometimes positioned at a corner two blocks east of it. The police did not concentrate on prostitutes positioned at or near the hotel or coffee shop preferring, instead, to stalk prostitutes further up the block or around the corner.

Determinants of Core Positions

Seniority, perseverance, appearance, and management are important factors for determining the hierarchical order among prostitutes within a single location. The same prostitutes almost always worked the same locations remaining well within its boundaries. The greater a prostitute's seniority at a particular location, the greater the likelihood that she was situated near the core. Prostitutes with the least work time tended to be positioned near or at a condition's outside boundary.

A second factor significant in structuring the order of prostitutes at a particular location is perseverance. The more days and hours a prostitute had worked at a particular location, the more likely she occupied a position close to the core. Most regular prostitutes worked four to eight hours a day, between five and six days a week. Several worked ten to twelve hours daily, but almost none worked seven days a week, many taking off on Sunday.

Appearance also is significant for determining a deviant actor's position. The more attractive prostitutes tended to congregate near the core while less desirable prostitutes were closer to the core's external boundary.

A fourth determinant of position, everything else being equal, is the degree and form of management, organization, and independence of a prostitute. Prostitutes managed by pimps usually occupied positions at or close to the core, whereas prostitutes protected by a man were positioned a bit further from the core. Independent prostitutes in pairs or larger groups were situated even further from the core and loners frequently occupied positions near a condition's outer boundary.

Seniority, perseverance, and appearance seemed to be more important than the degree of management or independence for determining street positions. This was illustrated by the experience of an independent prostitute who for several years occupied the core position on the northeast corner at 12th Street and Third Avenue. This was an excellent location for street prostitution because deserted doorways, dark alleys, and nearby poorly lit parking lots provided protection and refuge from the police. This corner had been occupied for four or five years by a young, attractive prostitute who worked six days a week from about 8:00 p.m. to 4:00 a.m. Other prostitutes in the area had not succeeded in displacing her. In fact, four newly arrived prostitutes managed by a pimp were forced to work across from this corner at much greater risk of arrest. Eventually, they moved to another corner near a pizza parlor on the side of the street where the condition already was established and they attempted to develop a second core. The pizza parlor was utilized by the four prostitutes as a place of refuge. Even though the lone prostitute was independent, she still occupied the condition's core because she was attractive, persistent, and senior to other prostitutes on the street. Eventually she became pregnant but she continued to work at this location for at least the first six months of pregnancy. Although her condition caused a decrease in business, several faithful customers returned for her services.

Deviant Distancing

Deviant distancing is the main process characterizing the internal order of a single deviant location. Unlike the processes of deviant sorting or spacing that result in physical segregation, deviant distancing involves face-to-face contact. Distancing allows different gradations or levels of association and a series of stages along which an individual can move to progressive affiliation.[5] Moreover, distancing provides a range of alternatives for individuals who intereact with one another. There is a choice for persons to move between levels of intimacy without creating conflict. The distancing process provides means of interaction between individuals through a wide variety of spatial signals that serve as communicative devices. These alert people to the gradations of interaction and extent of interpersonal affiliations.[6] For example, the prostitute and john use the same kind of early warning system to assess the safety involved in the interaction context. Each feels their way into the situation with varying degrees of care and apprehension utilizing walk, stance, eye movements, gestures, and conversation. These are signs that inform each of the assumed trust.[7] Of course, the mere presence of a prostitute at a deviant street location is the first signal informing the john, police, and other street users who she is and her immediate intentions.

The social processes of spacing, sorting, and distancing are crucial for understanding street deviance. Each process fulfills a highly specialized function. Deviant sorting is a significant mechanism in the geographical division of different forms of deviance and it operates on the macrosocial level. Once sorting occurs the participants almost never come into contact with each other. Deviant spacing facilitates arrangements among similar forms of deviance by ordering participants and assuring the day-to-day smooth conduct of business. It is on an intermediate social level because it deals with multiple aggregates but not with a variety of deviant forms. The process of distancing facilitates personal interaction between individuals who may come into physical contact. It involves behavior on the microlevel.

Notes

1. A crude scale of desirability was developed based on overall dress and attractiveness. The scale ranged from 1 for undesirable to 10 for most desirable. Each prostitute was rated by this researcher and whatever bias arose hopefully remained constant throughout the rating. Similar estimates including age were undertaken with success by Murray Melbin, in "Night as Frontier," *American Sociological Review*, no. 43-1 (February 1978): 3-22.
2. These socioeconomic patterns were not sufficient to explain the higher arrest rates for black and Hispanic prostitutes compared to their white counterparts.
3. *The Knapp Commission Report on Police Corruption* (New York: George Braziller, 1973), ch. 6.
4. However, these practices could not explain why a disproportionate overrepresentation of black and Hispanic prostitutes compared to white prostitutes were arrested by the police.
5. Gerald D. Suttles, *The Social Construction of Communities* (Chicago: University of Chicago Press, 1972).
6. Ibid. p. 156.
7. Ibid.

8 Determinants of Deviant Street Locations

Determinants imply facilitative factors or conditions rather than causes of street deviance. The theoretical roots and probable determinants for deviance in large cities were described by Simmel, Tönnies, Durkheim, and Weber.[1] The Chicago Urban School (Park, Burgess, and Wirth) borrowed their ideas including *Gemeinschaft*, *Gesellschaft*, mechanical and organic solidarity, rationalization, sensory stimulation, and impersonality and broke them down into separate and more concrete elements, which helped to explain why deviance was likely to surface in cities rather than in small towns.[2] Wirth, for example, explained that high population density accounted for individual variation and that a relative absence of intimate or personal relationships, segmentalization of human interaction, anonymity, heterogeneity, superficiality, and the transitory nature of the city were a perfect milieu for variant life styles.[3] Under these circumstances it is understandable why most visible street deviance emerged in large urban centers and not primarily in small towns, or rural and suburban areas. But these writers did not explain why street deviance surfaced in certain areas and neighborhoods on specific blocks and certain sides of the street at particular intersections and corners during certain hours of the day or night.

This chapter provides tentative answers to these questions utilizing information gathered mainly from field observation. The present aim is to determine why and under what conditions visible female street prostitution emerged in specific neighborhoods on certain sides of the street at particular times of the day or night at the thirteen Manhattan street locations studied. Community acceptance and resistance, neighborhoods that do or do not tolerate inroads of deviant street conditions, and competition between groups of deviants who always are probing and testing new locations are crucial for understanding the spatial distribution of visible street deviance. These social determinants together with other facilitative correlates, including ecological, demographic, and economic factors, form a rough conceptual model for explaining where visible street deviance is likely to surface. This information suggests numerous strategies for increasing a community's ability to control or eliminate street deviance.

Ecological Factors

Two key elements for determining the approximate location of visible female street prostitution are the presence of a place for business and a place for sanctuary. A place to conduct business usually included small, run-down, seedy hotels and poorly lit, outdoor parking lots and to a lesser extent inconspicuous service-station lots and massage parlors. Each deviant street network was near several hotels and parking lots used by prostitutes for illicit sexual transactions. Massage parlors were utilized almost exclusively by street prostitutes on Eighth Avenue. In most locations the core of a condition for female street prostitution was established on the street on the side where the hotel was located.

Sometimes business was conducted in a parked car in the street, but many prostitutes were reluctant to utilize this mode of operation because it was conspicuous and they feared police on patrol or even passersby. Other times a prostitute accompanied a john to a small local hotel where several rooms on the second and third floors were reserved for prostitution. A typical hotel had a stairway leading up to the main desk on the second floor. The ground floor was occupied by stores. A clerk assigned a room for a $5 to $12 fee (depending on the location) after the john signed the hotel card, usually as man and wife, and provided a false name and address. The majority of hotel desk clerks were black. In several hotels the desk clerk was in an enclosure protected by steel bars or an iron screen. In most hotels the desk clerk gave the prostitute and john a towel and soap. The couple then proceeded to conduct business in a room that usually was on the same floor. Most pros hotels specifically set aside certain rooms for short visits by prostitutes and johns. Other rooms were occupied mostly by single males, transients, and persons on public assistance.

Frequently the couple proceeded to an outdoor parking lot closed for the evening. The enclosed lot offered greater protection than a street especially one near the spot where contact had been made because that was where police-patrol activities tended to concentrate. The parking lot was nearly always only a few blocks from where contact had been made between prostitute and john. In this way, traveling time to and from the place of business was minimized, and the prostitutes remained on familiar ground. An attempt was made to park between or behind other unoccupied parked cars, usually by backing the auto against the wall or fence of the parking lot so that approaching cars, especially the police could be observed. Other times even an active parking lot was used. The prostitute and john drove up in a car, paid the regular parking fee, and proceeded to park. In parking lots where the attendant worked in collusion with the prostitute, the parking fee was usually less than the prescribed fee for ordinary customers and no parking ticket or receipt was issued. If an indoor parking lot was used the car's occupants drove to an upper level, searched for an isolated or desolate spot and then parked. Frequently a parking lot was occupied at the same time by several automobiles, each with a john and a prostitute. The sexual transaction began only after the car doors were locked and the front seat was moved far back from the driving wheel to allow maximum space. Most prostitutes considered a car's rear seat risky.

In addition to a hotel, a combination or cluster of coffee shops, delicatessens, bars, and parks open sometimes for twenty-four hours, were always accessible when a condition was active. These were used by prostitutes mainly for sanctuary or escape from the police but also to relax, have a cup of coffee, and talk. Pimps often patronized the coffee shops, especially on the East Side, at the Bowery and Delancey Street, and at 32nd Street and Fifth Avenue. Each of the thirteen locations of female street prostitution had facilitative places for refuge or escape. The visible deviant street conditions usually were situated on the same side of the street as the places of sanctuary and business. Seven deviant street locations had sites for business and refuge; four locations had places of refuge, primarily relying on cars or nearby hotels for business; and two locations used a hotel as a place of business and refuge.

Most discussions of business (for example, fees, amount of time, nature, and place for services) were held in the street or in the john's car but usually not in the place of sanctuary. In only one instance was the place of escape used for business. On 42nd Street and 10th Avenue the men's room of a coffee shop was used by two prostitutes to perform sexual services, apparently without the proprietor's knowledge.

The side of the street, the particular corner or intersection, and the core of the visible deviant street location were determined first by the place of business and then the place of escape. The deviant condition nearly always was situated in front of or near either of these two sites.

Street Locations

Favor was given to a specific corner or side of a street which was oriented in such a way to facilitate routine solicitations to passersby, ease of discussion, some degree of concealment and escape from the police. Prostitutes usually occupied the corner or side of a one-way street on an automobile's driving side. The prostitute and john could then discuss business without requiring the prostitute to walk around to the driver's side or have the john stretch and open the passenger window. The latter arrangement makes the police's task easier because the prostitute usually has to traverse a greater distance to reach the place of sanctuary and the john is less able to detect passing police by looking through the rear or sideview mirrors. Four-corner intersections have many positive work features including the most advantageous lookout positions, the point of greatest traffic, and numerous directions for escape rather than only two that are available for prostitutes standing in the middle of the block. This may be one explanation why prostitutes tend to stand at intersections instead of working the middle of a block.

Another factor associated with the majority of public sites for female prostitution are accessible curbside areas where cars can easily approach and temporarily park. Overcrowded parking conditions interfere with business negotiations. Therefore, female prostitution is also likely to surface on streets that prohibit or restrict parking and at curbs reserved for bus stops. The driver then can easily approach curbside and speak with a prostitute. Abandoned or closed buildings or ones where few persons walk in and out provide excellent settings for street solicitations because neither prostitutes nor ordinary occupants interfere with one another.

Transportation Networks

Another ecological factor that determines the location of visible street deviance is a primary transportation network including tunnels, bridges, subways, and major bus depots. Traffic flow stemming from major transportation conduits not only provides clients but also tends to weaken nearby communities. The Lower East Side, particularly locations at the Bowery and Delancey Street and at Forsythe Street are very well situated for providing services to vehicular traffic from the Williamsburg Bridge. This bridge is one of the main thoroughfares for traffic from and to Manhattan, Brooklyn, Queens, and Long Island. The Park and Fifth Avenues complex is also conveniently located near the 34th Street Midtown Tunnel which is a heavily used link connecting Queens to Manhattan.

Eighth and Ninth Avenues are located near New York City's Port Authority Bus Terminal and the Lincoln Tunnel, which connects New Jersey and New York. Two locations of visible street prostitution, 38th to 42nd Streets on Eighth Avenue and 42nd Street on Ninth Avenue, are almost directly across from various entrances of the New York Port Authority Bus Terminal. Other street locations on Ninth and Tenth Avenues are near service roads to the Lincoln Tunnel or have access to the main body of traffic leading to and from the tunnel.

Each deviant street network and its individual locations are near bus and subway stops and thus are accesible to people living in the five boroughs of New York City and in the surrounding metropolitan area who do not depend on automobiles for transportation.

Economic Base

Another key determinant for locations of visible street deviance is the existence of a sufficient business base to sustain prostitution. The street locations studied had heavy vehicular traffic and pedestrian flows that generated enough customers to sustain a high volume of business.

Sociodemographic Factors

Visible female street prostitution emerged in neighborhoods and on streets with a highly selective sociodemographic profile. Important characteristics included age, sex, household composition, and socioeconomic status. In New York City, as in other large cities, the sociodemographic composition for contiguous blocks in the same neighborhood may differ radically from one another. Therefore, data from community planning districts (CPD) and the census are not refined enough to provide an accurate and precise picture of the sociodemographic characteristics for locations of visible female street prostitution.[4] These data focus on residents rather than actual street users. Therefore, whenever feasible an attempt was made to determine sociodemographic characteristics of deviant street locations from field observation.

Age

The vast majority of persons visible at each location of street prostitution (well over 80 percent) were adults estimated to be between twenty-five and fifty-five years of age. Children, teenagers, young adults in their early twenties, and persons over fifty-five, especially senior citizens, rarely were observed at these locations.

Sex

Another demographic factor that apparently operates to eliminate certain segments of the population is sex. The street locations when active were nearly devoid of females except for prostitutes. Young girls and even teenagers were absent from areas occupied by prostitutes. On rare occasions a woman alone or perhaps accompanied by a male either hurriedly walked through the area, waited nervously for a bus, or attempted anxiously to hail a taxi. The only women observed using the area for a substantial time were prostitutes. Most other women, including neighborhood residents, avoided these areas.[5]

Race

Not only are areas of visible street prostitution stratified on the basis of age and sex, but also they are composed of a specific ethnic mix. Most locations are either nearly all white or have a majority of white persons with a mix of blacks or Hispanics. Johns tend to fear neighborhoods heavily populated with blacks or Hispanics. One exception was Forsythe Street between Delancey and Grand Streets where the population was primarily Hispanic. Also females and elderly persons were more likely to be present at this street location than the other twelve locations. Another exception was around 38th to 42nd Streets on Eighth Avenue where substantial numbers of black males were present.

Household Composition

The age, race, and sex of street users were estimated through field observation. Household composition was determined from census-tract data. The overwhelming majority of households in census tracts containing conditions of visible street prostitution were composed of primary individuals, unrelated persons, or single people.[6] For example, the proportion of primary individuals (essentially singles) for the census tracts covering 10th to 14th Streets, 32nd Street and Fifth Avenue, and 42nd to 49th Streets on Eighth Avenue and Ninth Avenue, respectively were 64 percent, 82 percent, and 90 percent. Few families headed either by a husband and wife or even a single parent resided in these areas. Only 15 percent of the households in census tracts covering 32nd Street and Fifth Avenue, for example, consisted of husband-wife families, and only .6 percent were comprised of single parent families. The family composition for all Manhattan was 51.6 percent. Single individuals are more likely to possess a less rigid set of moral standards than married couples with children.

The census data, therefore, support the ethnostatistics that areas of visible female street prostitution were nearly devoid of families, teenagers, and young adults. Except for Forsythe Street, no families were observed using locations of visible female street prostitution for strolls, leisure, or recreation. Although the eastern side of Forsythe Street was inhabited by families, children or young mothers rarely used the streets for recreation. However, several male groups in their twenties and thirties utilized the corners and park for leisure activities.

Socioeconomic Areas

I determined from observations of individual streets, buildings, and residents, and from census data that the majority of visible female street prostitution locations were in stable lower-, and middle-, or upper-class neighborhoods. Several street conditions were located in better neighborhoods on the East Side at Park and Fifth Avenues, whereas others were on the Lower East Side, a relatively depressed area. All thirteen conditions of female street prostitution were on or immediately next to business thoroughfares and most were in neighborhoods with decent housing. None of the locations of visible female street prostitution were in slum neighborhoods (for example, parts of Avenues A, B, C, and D on the Lower East Side between Houston and 14th Streets) characterized by deteriorated housing, abandoned buildings, garbage-strewn streets, people in shabby clothes, and unsupervised groups of children.

This finding was confirmed by census data. For example, the 1970 mean income for census tracts with visible street prostitution was $11,920 compared to $14,202 for the borough of Manhattan. Moreover, the mean income for locations of deviance in census tracts on the Lower East Side (the lowest socioeconomic network in this study) was $8,324 compared to $6,944 for census tracts in Avenues A, B, C, and D, a partially deteriorated area between Houston and 14th Streets also on the Lower East Side.

Community Tolerance

A city's population density, anonymity, heterogeneity, and rapidly changing mores provide a propitious setting for the development of visible street deviance. Nevertheless, even in large cities visible street deviance is likely to develop only in certain neighborhoods. Female street prostitution is likely to surface on certain streets and even specific street corners characterized by special sociodemographic, economic, and ecological factors. These factors provide strong clues about blocks and even side of streets that are particularly vulnerable for visible street deviance. The degree of community consciousness, however, is a key factor in determining the initial emergence or suppression of visible street deviance. Visible street prostitution rarely emerges in neighborhoods with strong sentiments and norms against this type of behavior. It is more likely to surface in neighborhoods where either community consensus is weak or where there is little or no community resistance. This is one reason street deviance is concentrated in Manhattan and not the remaining boroughs of the city which are primarily residential. Many of Manhattan's neighborhoods are characterized by anonymity and an absence of a sense of community. Nor will visible street deviance surface where there are competing legitimate or illegitimate interests. The development of a deviant street location will be hastened where certain business interests benefit from deviance.

Neighborhoods in New York City differ dramatically from block to block in levels of community cohesiveness and tolerance. It is likely, therefore, that visible street prostitution will be tolerated in a one- or two-block area but will meet resistance when it overflows into adjacent neighborhoods with strong, coordinated, community opponents.

Weak community sentiment toward visible female street prostitution, the absence of competing interests, and the presence of interests that benefit from street prostitution characterize the thirteen street locations studied. This is evident for Eighth Avenue between 38th Street and 49th Street, an area with a long history of visible street prostitution. It is a transient, highly mobile community mainly of unattached male adults. This area is peppered with cheap, seedy, transient hotels; fast-food restaurants; bars; massage parlors; and X-rated movie houses. Many of these businesses are likely to profit from street prostitution. Families, children, young adults, elderly persons, and women are noticeably missing from this area. There is little community force which might repress the area's visible street prostitution. After a period of time the history of prostitution in an area becomes a determinant of the weakness of community resistance among residents. Families and other opposed groups will not move into the neighborhood. Eventually most residents will be unattached males and transients.

The absence of community opposition and presence of business interests that benefit from street deviance (for example, run-down hotels, coffee chops) also characterized the Lower East Side and Ninth Avenue, at least on those streets where visible female prostitution was present. However, when visible street prostitution in these two networks spilled over into neighboring streets, it was met by strong community resistance. For example, prostitutes initially populated the north and south corners of Forsythe Street between Grand and Delancey Streets. After some time the condition expanded and spilled into adjacent blocks, including Eldridge Street, which is populated primarily by a cohesive Hispanic community and a substantial number of Chinese people. Concerted action was taken to eliminate the condition. The reaction was further fueled by the murder of a little child in the neighborhood park. Though unrelated to the area's street prostitution (the young girl presumably was murdered by a dishwasher from a nearby restaurant), this incident further galvanized the community into action against those conditions thought to have created a social milieu for crime. Banners were strung across adjacent streets stating "PIMPS-WHORES-JOHNS STAY OFF OUR STREETS." The word was out that the personal safety and even lives of pimps, prostitutes, and johns were in danger. The Hispanic community held meetings with its nearby Italian neighbors and reported that it was going to introduce methods used by the Italians to repress visible street prostitution.

The banners were not placed on Forsythe Street itself where the local visible street deviance originated and had its core but were strung across Eldridge Street, one block east of Forsythe. Both sides of Eldridge Street are heavily lined with tenements and there is a critical mass of families that generate strong community opposition against visible street deviance. Moreover, Eldridge Street concealed a substantial illegal drug industry. These illegitimate interests, although behind locked apartment doors and not visible from the street, tended to repel prostitution. On the other hand, only the east side of Forsythe Street is lined with tenements. A city park is on its west side. It is substantially less populated than Eldridge Street and viewed as an extension of the Bowery and Delancey Street. The tenements on the east side of Forsythe Street formed the perimeter for the Hispanic community, which extends east toward the Williamsburg Bridge. Somehow, the small number of residents on Forsythe Street learned to coexist with the prostitutes. Each group left the other alone and seemed to perceive each other as nonpersons who could be safely ignored.[7]

With the assistance of the police the community temporarily succeeded in reducing, although not eliminating, the area's visible street deviance by confining most prostitutes to its cores on the north and south corners of Forsythe Street. Prostitutes, their male associates, and johns were reluctant to parade or cruise back and forth between cores or even station themselves in the middle of the block as had been the custom. Several prostitutes left the area and were observed at other locations.

Forty-sixth Street and Ninth Avenue street deviants had a similar experience. Originally, visible street prostitution had stabilized on Ninth Avenue between 45th and 46th Streets, the commercial section of the neighborhood. Its core was established in front of a bar on the southwest corner of 46th Street and Ninth Avenue. Then it spread through the entire block between Ninth and Tenth Avenues on 46th Street. The presence of prostitutes on 46th Street, a quiet, stable, and fairly well-maintained residential neighborhood aroused the indignation of the community. A long and vigorous campaign was waged, led by St. Clement's, a Protestant church on 46th Street, to eliminate the visible street prostitution. The police increased foot and motorized patrols and they stopped and questioned drivers who repeatedly circled 45th and 46th Streets. Community residents threatened to photograph automobiles and determine the identity of the potential johns from license plates. Then they intended to embarrass them by contacting wives and families and publicizing this information in newspapers. The residents succeeded in reducing the condition substantially at least in the middle of the block and restricting it to the two corners on 46th Street at Ninth and Tenth Avenues.

The intensity of community sentiment may vary with time of day. For example, a strong consensus exists during the day when business is active at 32nd Street between Fifth and Park Avenues. The business community will not tolerate visible street prostitution during business hours because it interferes with commerce. The deviant street condition surfaces only at night when businesses are closed, disappearing early each morning with the arrival of workers and shoppers.

Likewise, visible female street prostitution on Park Avenue at 26th Street, Lexington Avenue at 25th Street, and on Ninth Avenue are active primarily during early and late evening hours because business and residential communities will not tolerate street prostitution during the day. As evening approaches and daytime street users recede, conditions are activated. All-night people include street-repair crews, tow-truck operators, sanitation workers, service-station attendants, cab drivers, and young men on bicycles and skateboards.

Although visible female street prostitution is not likely to emerge on streets where there is organized community resistance or strong competing interests, nevertheless each location of visible street deviance studied was in a stable commercial or residential area where crime is moderate. Also many deviant conditions were in stylish commercial neighborhoods where side streets are lined with very expensive and well-kept town houses. Forsythe Street, came closest to a marginal neighborhood but even it is bounded by a park on one side and on the other a poor, but more or less stable community.

Street deviance will be tolerated only in a neighborhood where the sense of community is weak or fragmented but not so disorganized that customers are reluctant to enter the area. Sociodemographic factors, transportation networks, and an economic base are central in determining the general location where deviant street networks are likely to be situated. A place of business, a place of refuge, the orientation of a building and to a lesser extent accessible curbside areas determine where street deviance will be located within these general areas. Community tolerance or resistance is central in both cases, however, and overall probably is the most salient determinant of visible deviant street conditions.

Apparently, unlike juvenile or gang delinquency and street crime, visible street deviance involving prostitution is not as likely to emerge and persist in deteriorated, transient, and slum neighborhoods. Poor, unsavory conditions, including the presence of crime, repress visible street prostitution, especially the type that attracts clients city-wide, because it intimidates clients and prostitutes, who are anxious about their personal safety. Also, clientele fear minority neighborhoods. These neighborhoods have a heavy police presence, which represses visible street prostitution too. This is another reason why stable conditions of female street prostitution do not usually develop on streets where drug sales or muggings are prevalent.

When prostitution does surface in slum areas, it borders on stable commercial areas.

The Bowery and Delancey Street

Figure 8-1 shows a map of the area around Delancey Street and the Bowery, a typical deviant street location. This location illustrates the determinants or facilitative conditions for street deviance. The hotel located at the southeast corner was used for prostitution. Next door, an all-night luncheonette and an enclosed neighborhood park served as places of escape from the police. The park was not usually used for business transactions because neighborhood residents and children constantly played, walked, and sat in it. Oftentimes the subway entrance in front of the hotel was used to hide from the police. Alleys, doorways, and parked cars were also utilized for the same purpose, but prostitutes feel most secure in privately owned coffee shops where police authority is limited. Sometimes streets parallel to the park were used to conduct business. Usually the prostitute and john selected a parking spot away from street lights so that privacy might be further assured. Parking between two parked cars was preferred over parking in front or at the back of a line of cars because it afforded greater concealment. Also, relatively empty streets with few parked cars were avoided because then the john's car was more noticeable.

Street prostitution at the Bowery and Delancey also is highly accessible. Much traffic to and from the Williamsburg Bridge, traveled heavily by residents of Queens and Long Island, proceeds to Delancey Street, past the visible deviant street condition. It is most convenient that the condition was primarily located on the south instead of the north side of the street because after-work traffic returned on that side to Queens and Long Island. Visits to prostitutes may be more likely during early evening than early morning when potential customers are hurrying to their jobs. After the corner luncheonette closed, however, an all-night, fried-chicken restaurant opened across the street, and part of the deviant street condition transferred to that side. Evidently a place of sanctuary is more important in determining street deviance than traffic or work patterns.

The immediate area surrounding the deviant location at Delancey Street between the Bowery and Christie Street is sparsely populated. Roosevelt Park takes up much of the area and the entire square block where visible street prostitution is most prominent consists of a lightly traveled commercial area. Except for numerous stores on the Bowery, mainly selling light fixtures, the majority of businesses on the remaining three sides of the square block are wholesalers. Few shoppers or customers are seen on the streets. Many stores have gone out of business. Visible street deviance recedes

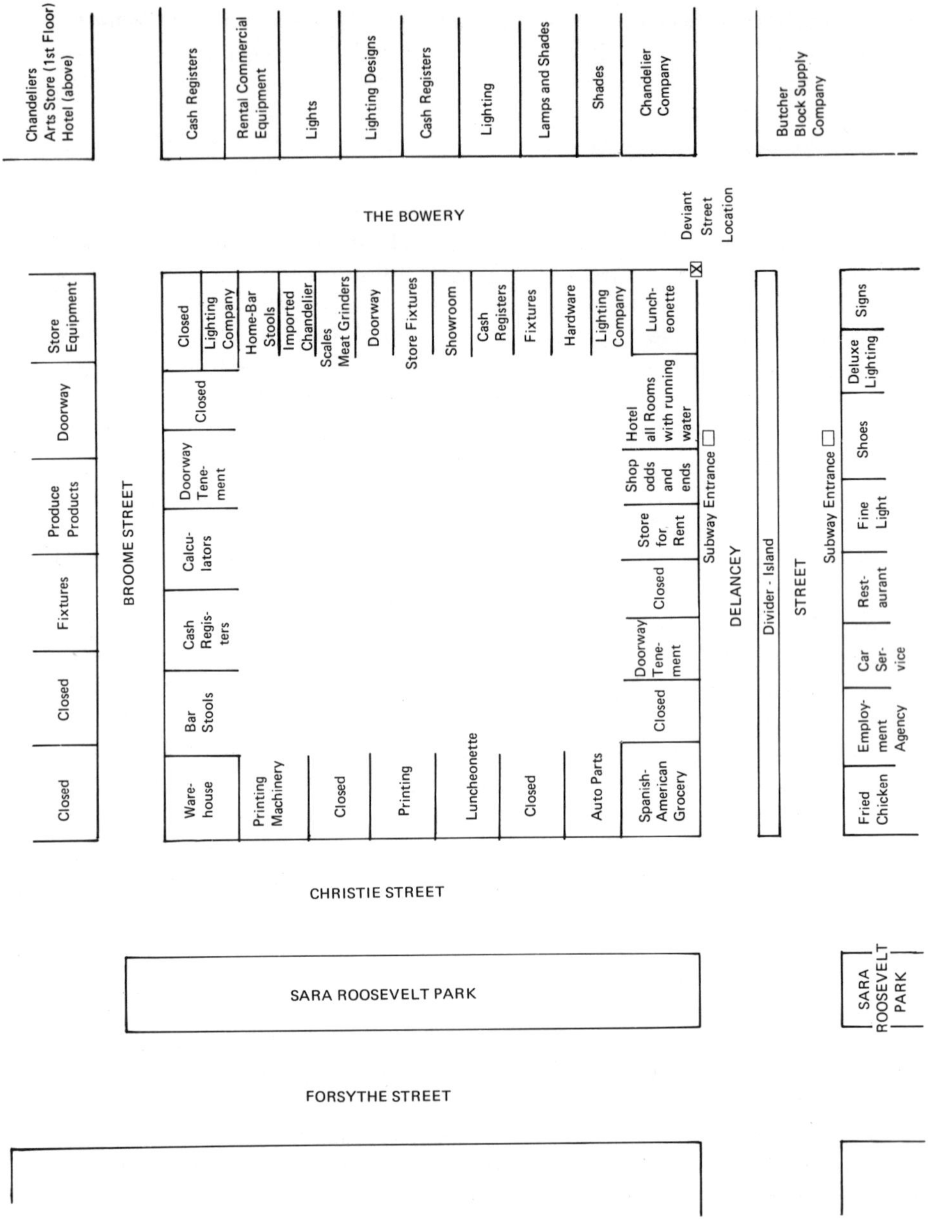

Figure 8-1. The Bowery and Delancey Street

dramatically during the day on the west side of the square block when stores selling light fixtures are open and patronized by shoppers. At night, however, after the stores close, this block is transformed into an active part of the visible deviant street condition.

Scarcely any people reside on this square block. Few pedestrians use either side of Delancey Street. Persons are prevented from crossing Delancey's six lanes, except at corners, because of a divider in the middle of the road. This divider doubles as a barrier that conceals illegal behavior and also prevents the police from surprise sorties by suddenly crossing the street.

The south side of Delancey Street where the bulk of visible street prostitution is located is used predominantly by prostitutes, johns, and pimps. Nonparticipants in street deviance, especially women, seem to avoid this block, although a few passersby were observed from time to time usually just before and after working hours. The street was almost never utilized for play by children or teenagers, although at one time several children of a local gypsy fortune-teller hung around at all hours of day and night.

Prostitutes primarily positioned themselves at the condition's core, situated directly in front of the hotel and the adjacent coffee shop. The condition extended around the entire square block, but the number of prostitutes usually diminished the further the distance from the core. More attractive, desirable, better-dressed, and higher-priced prostitutes were positioned closer to the core. The same was true for prostitutes who belonged to a stable managed by a pimp. Prostitutes who ventured further from the core were more likely than core prostitutes to conduct business in a car.

Another small hotel situated at the corner of Houston and Allen Streets only a few blocks from Delancey Street also was used by prostitutes for business, but a condition of visible female prostitution did not surface on that corner. This location could not compete with the Bowery and Delancey perhaps because there was not sufficient traffic to sustain a healthy business. Another hotel, less than a block away from the core at the Bowery and Delancey situated on the west side of the Bowery (see figure 8-1) was not converted into a deviance workplace because it was part of an Italian residential neighborhood (Little Italy) with a strong sense of community. Moreover, traffic off the Williamsburg Bridge diminished substantially by this point, having first passed the location at the Bowery and Delancey Street.

10th to 14th Streets

Heavy vehicular traffic from the Williamsburg Bridge passes Forsythe Street, then feeds into the Bowery, and it is likely to proceed north on Third

Avenue past 6th Street toward 14th Street. (The Bowery runs into Third Avenue). The Bowery at Houston to 4th Street on Third Avenue is heavily populated with derelicts and 7th to 9th Streets are occupied by male transvestites, but relatively few prostitutes work these streets. (A few fleabag prostitutes on the Bowery work inside bars.)

The condition of female prostitution between 10th and 14th Streets on Third Avenue exhibited many features present at the Bowery and Delancey Street. First, at 14th Street a subway entrance, pizza shop, and cigar store were utilized by prostitutes as places for sanctuary. Second, a small, old, deteriorated, walk-up hotel near the northeast corner was utilized for prostitution. A similar hotel on 13th Street was used for the same purpose although not as frequently as the one on 14th Street. The 13th Street hotel was more selective; only prostitutes known to the desk clerk and a more respectable clientele were allowed on its premises.

The entire area is lined with parking lots that stretch for almost three blocks on the east side between 9th and 12th Streets. An important feature of this business-residential thoroughfare is its sociodemographic composition. There is nearly a complete absence of families, young children, teenagers, young adults, ordinary females, and elderly men and women. The streets are populated primarily by black, white, and Hispanic males twenty-five to fifty-five years of age. Third Avenue is a busy vehicular and pedestrian thoroughfare. The major condition of prostitution is on the east side of the street where smoke shops, pizza parlors, hotels, and parking lots abound. The entire street condition, although primarily confined to Third Avenue, is embedded in the midst of a stable, mixed, middle- and lower-class residential neighborhood consisting of neat and well-maintained town houses and small apartment buildings. Residents stick closely to residential blocks and the shops on Second Avenue. They rarely promenade on Third Avenue between 10th and 14th Streets.

Several interesting features characterize street prostitution on the Lower East Side. First, the four locations of visible street deviance including the Bowery and Delancey street, Forsythe Street, 6th Street, and 10th to 14th Streets are geographically connected and nearly contiguous. They lie in the same community planning district and exhibit similar demographic and social characteristics. Many prostitutes at the four separate locations know or recognize each other. These locations draw on the same pool of clients who have established cruising-john routes or mini-deviant street circuits that conveniently pass the cores of the four locations. Most traffic coming from the Williamsburg Bridge passes Forsythe Street then continues one block west to the corner of Delancey Street and the Bowery. Afterwards substantial traffic proceeds north on Third Avenue to 6th Street and then to 14th Street. This john route takes about five minutes in light traffic and eight minutes in heavy traffic.

Although the overwhelming majority of prostitutes generally stuck to a specified territory at a particular location, a few worked several locations but nearly always within the same street network. On several occasions the same prostitutes worked 6th Street and also the Bowery and Delancey Street. In one unusual instance, however, several prostitutes moved temporarily from one street network to another because of a police crackdown. Prostitutes who usually occupied the Bowery and Delancey Street were observed at 32nd Street and Fifth Avenue after a young child was murdered in the neighborhood park and additional police were assigned to the area. Eventually they returned to the Bowery and Delancey Street.

Forsythe Street is a satellite of the Bowery and Delancey Street. Prostitutes from these two locations often used the same hotel, coffee shop, and park. They frequently competed for the same customers and were policed by the same officers. The main difference between Forsythe Street and the Bowery and Delancey was the mode of operation. Most Bowery and Delancey prostitutes used the corner hotel for sexual intercourse, although oral sex was frequently conducted in automobiles. However, prostitutes at Forsythe Street conducted most transactions in automobiles and rarely used the hotel. This difference may be explained partially by varying types of deviant management. Many prostitutes who worked near the hotel were managed by pimps, unlike Forsythe Street where they were either managed by men or were independents. Prostitutes working for a pimp are taught to take advantage of the safety provided by a hotel. They are reluctant to enter a car, leave the area, and increase their risk of assault and arrest.

The location at 6th Street and Third Avenue is a spinoff of 10th to 14th Streets. Spinoffs rarely develop as fully as the initial location. Thus fewer, less desirable, and less experienced prostitutes occupied 6th Street. Prostitutes who worked satellite locations also were more likely to be harassed by the police.

When the core of a location is cut off or altered (for example, a hotel or a coffee shop is closed) the prostitutes usually move to nearby locations. Several years ago the condition on Third Avenue was situated on the west side of 12th Street instead on its east side as at present. A hotel and a coffee shop located on the street's west side formed a core. The hotel was closed and afterward the coffee shop went out of business, incidentally, displaying its dependence on the deviant economy. The condition shifted across the street near two other hotels and extended from 10th to 14th Streets. Likewise, a hotel used for prostitutes on 6th Street was closed several years ago. Sixth Street prostitutes moved most of their business to a hotel two blocks north on St. Mark's Place, but the condition's core remained on 6th Street. Other prostitutes simply conducted business in the john's car.

32nd Street and Madison Avenue

The present condition of female prostitution at 32nd Street between Fifth and Park Avenues initially surfaced in front of two adjacent welfare hotels on 32nd Street between Fifth and Madison Avenues. The hotels were subsequently converted into apartments. The core for this street condition eventually shifted to the front of a nearby, coffee shop on the corner of Fifth Avenue, and the local prostitutes were forced to conduct business at three hotels on east 36th Street. Eventually a nearby welfare hotel on 32nd Street near Park Avenue, about 100 yards east of the condition's core, allowed prostitutes to use its premises. The three hotels on 36th Street soon were forced to close due to low occupancy. The all-night coffee shop and hotel were used as places of refuge. Apparently the conversion of the two original welfare hotels to respectable apartments resulted in displacing and spreading the condition to two nearby susceptible locations. Thirty-second Street between Fifth and Madison Avenues still remained an active part of the condition except now it extended on 32nd Street beyond Madison to Park Avenue, a two-block stretch instead of the original one-block area. The condition originated on 32nd Street between Fifth and Madison Avenues mainly because of the presence of run-down hotels suitable for prostitution and a coffee shop ideally situated for escape and refuge. The area also boasts several poorly lit, desolate, parking lots and alleyways suitable for shielding prostitutes and customers during evening and late evening hours.

Another facilitative element that may have contributed to the emergence of street deviance at 32nd Street is that it is an important conduit to the Queens Midtown Tunnel connecting Manhattan and the borough of Queens. Thirty-second Street runs one way from west to east and bears much of the crosstown traffic including heavy flows to the Midtown Tunnel. Thus an adequate business base exists for prostitution.

Patrons can easily pull their cars to curbside and hold discussions with prostitutes because during evening hours, after day people leave the area, few vehicles are parked on 32nd Street. Prostitutes mainly line the south side of the street where the hotel and coffee shop are situated. They must approach a car from the passenger side. Positions near the hotel and coffee shop are more important than convenient access to a driver. Convenience is significant only when it does not meaningfully alter the time to the place of refuge as when prostitutes roam so far that from a safety point of view the few extra feet due to standing near the driver's side do not matter.

A heavy vehicular flow continues throughout early and late evening. At this time pedestrian traffic is light, except for participants in street deviance including prostitutes, pimps, patrons, and a few area hangers-on. The only places of business open late at night are the hotel and coffee shop. Both benefit financially from the deviant economy. Most other businesses are closed by 8:00 p.m. During the day the entire area is heavily populated with workers but few persons reside on these blocks. This area is a very busy, respectable, and desirable commercial district with a mixture of small retail shops, large office buildings, and wholesale businesses. The eastern boundary for the deviant street condition is Park Avenue at 32nd Street, a highly desirable middle- to upper-income residential area.

A comparison of two sets of neighboring and parallel streets between Fifth and Park Avenues highlights those elements that tend to make 32nd Street more than 33rd to 35th Streets vulnerable to visible street deviance. Table 8-1 shows that 32nd Street between Fifth and Park Avenues had two deteriorated, welfare hotels compared to none between 33rd and 35th Streets. About 19 percent of the retail establishments on 32nd Street were restaurants, including two all-night coffee shops, compared to 13 percent for 33rd to 35th Streets. There were no all-night coffee shops on these streets. Furthermore, about 9 percent of the entrances on 32nd Street led to open alleyways, compared to about 5 percent for 33rd to 35th Streets. The run-down hotels on 32nd Street provided ideal places for business. The preponderance of alleyways and restaurants offered a means of escape from the police and even surrogate business settings. Thirty-second Street is primarily a business area, while 33rd to 35th Streets include a substantial residential community. This is evident by the absence of apartment houses

Table 8-1
Comparison of Structures on 32nd Street and 33rd to 35th Streets

Type of Structure	33rd to 35th Streets Fifth and Park Avenues		32nd Street Fifth and Park Avenues	
	Number	Percent	Number	Percent
Stores	25	27.2	9	20.9
Alleys	5	5.4	4	9.3
Restaurants	12	13.0	8	18.6
Welfare hotels	—	—	2	4.7
Entrance to lofts and offices	7	7.6	9	20.9
Empty buildings	2	2.2	1	2.3
Subways	5	5.4	3	7.0
Stores with better merchandise	21	22.8	2	4.7
High-rise apartments	13	14.1	—	—
Churches	2	2.2	—	—
Freight receiving	—	—	5	11.6
Total	92	99.9	43	100.0

and churches on 32nd Street, whereas high-rises and churches constitute 16 percent of the structures between 33rd and 35th Streets.

Neighborhood residents with a strong sense of community usually will not tolerate visible street deviance in their immediate residential area. Also, about 21 percent of the building entrances on 32nd Street led to lofts, offices and freight receiving, compared to only 8 percent for 33rd to 35th Streets. These data suggest that 32nd Street was utilized more by persons who work in the area than a mixture of workers, shoppers, and residents which tend to repress visible street deviance. Thirty-second Street stores generally displayed less expensive merchandise than stores between 33rd and 35th Streets, further suggesting that a higher-class clientele patronized these businesses. The presence of upper-class shoppers, especially women, might tend to repress visible street deviance. None of these sociodemographic factors alone explain the absence or presence of visible street deviance but taken together they strongly suggest why 32nd Street was susceptible to female street prostitution whereas 33rd to 35th Streets were not.

A similar comparison was undertaken between 38th and 49th Streets, the Eighth Avenue deviant network with its northern extension 50th to 59th Streets on Eighth Avenue. It was found that the deviant network on Eighth Avenue compared to 50th to 59th Streets proportionately has more porno shops, bars, adult theaters showing X-rated films, peep shows, massage parlors, cheap welfare-type hotels, stores selling junk merchandise, and fast-food stores. In addition, part of the New York Coliseum (where major business and cultural exhibits are shown) and the New York Cultural Center (which administers the city's budget to the arts) are located at the northern stretch of Eighth Avenue. The social, cultural, and business interests represented by these organizations suppress overt deviance. It should be emphasized that it is not the type of structure or building alone that determines where street deviance will emerge but the combination of interests and sense of community associated with buildings providing certain functions. Structures alone facilitate but do not cause street deviance.

Notes

1. See Alan S. Berger, *The City* (Iowa: C. Brown, 1978), ch. 6.
2. Ibid.
3. Louis Wirth, "Urbanism as a Way of Life," *American Journal of Sociology* 44 (July 1938):1-24.
4. *New York City Planning Commission Community Planning District Profiles* (New York, 1973).

5. The age, sex, and other selected personal characteristics of persons who do and do not frequent deviant street locations cannot help but recall the types of persons who are most likely to be out during nighttime, which has been referred to as the "last frontier in America." See, Murray Melbin, "Night as Frontier," *American Sociological Review*, 43 no. 1 (February 1978):3-22.

6. *Census Tracts New York, N.Y., Standard Statistical Area, 1970, Census Population and Housing, Parts I, II, III* (Washington, D.C.: U.S. Department of Commerce, Bureau of the Census, 1970), pp. 99-117, 603, 698-717, 801, 835-843.

7. The perceptions neighborhood people and prostitutes have for each other should be determined by future research. One excellent study that deals with a similar problem, the perceptions of neighborhood people to different residential settings, is by Robert E. Kapsis, "Black Street-corner Districts," *Social Forces* 57, no. 4 (June 1979):1212-1228.

The Deviant Street Location Cycle

This chapter addresses problems on how deviant street locations originate, develop, and finally dissolve. By definition, a deviant street location endures for substantial periods of time. I was not able to follow each separate stage in the overall life cycle for any single deviant street location. However, I was able to observe each distinct phase at several different deviant locations.

The life cycle of a deviant street location consists of four stages: emergence, expansion, equilibrium, and dissolution. Additional research focusing on these distinct processes, especially following each stage in one deviant street location, most certainly will shed further light on this development process. There may even be other distinct phases in the life cycle of a deviant street location. Until this study is more complete the ideas set forth in this chapter must be viewed as tentative and exploratory.

Emergence

It was not possible to observe the process of *emergence* for the thirteen deviant street locations because they were in existence at the outset of this study. However, during the course of this research I observed the genesis of several additional deviant street locations that were newly established since 1977. These include the locations at 16th Street and Third Avenue, 34th Street on Eighth Avenue, and 37th Street on Ninth Avenue. The *birth* process also was encountered at 48th Street on Tenth Avenue, but this condition never stabilized.

The process of deviant emergence deals with the birth or origin of a deviant street location. Its major interrelated components are *site selection* and *deviance street testing*. The process of site selection precedes deviance testing and usually occurs by accident or by forced displacement. A typical example of this process is when a prostitute moves to a rather inexpensive dilapidated hotel and accidentally discovers opportunities for business merely by standing on the street in front of the hotel or on a nearby corner. Or a prostitute or deviant manager by happenstance may have passed a neighborhood and sensed its suitability for a successful business of street prostitution. The second way a site may be discovered is through forced displacement. This may occur when police crack down on a particular

131

deviant street corner location or when a city agency forces closing of an unseemly hotel used for prostitution. The prostitutes must then search for another street location to continue their illicit activities. Usually they try a nearby street location; several sites may be tested before one is selected for a permanent base of operations. Except for instances of forced displacement, little if any structured or planned canvassing is undertaken.

Deviance street testing is the second phase of this process. A prostitute arrives at a location to determine whether it is safe and lucrative. She will soon learn to what extent the community and the police tolerate activities of prostitution, whether there exists suitable places for business and refuge, and whether the street location generates adequate income. A steady and sufficient supply of customers is crucial for establishing a permanent street location. Suppose the prostitute is constantly harassed and arrested or cannot earn a satisfactory income. Then she will be forced to leave the area without a deviant street location having been established. On the other hand, if the prostitute can work and achieve a satisfactory level of business, she would then be likely to remain at that street location. Eventually through either word of mouth or happenstance, other prostitutes, especially friends, may be drawn to the test site. Increased visibility constitutes a further test of the area. Prostitutes may encounter substantial resistance from the community and the police or too little business, and the street location will disintegrate. Or they will find the area comfortable and lucrative, in which case the deviant street location will take root, endure, and prepare for the next stage in its development. The emergence phase is likely to last from several months to a year.

Each emerging deviant street location developed at night when activities of prostitution did not interfere with daytime street users, including business people and neighborhood residents. The deviant street location at 16th Street and Third Avenue, a middle- to upper-socioeconomic residential area, still is in its initial testing phase. One white, *pioneer* prostitute about twenty-five years old spends several hours four or five nights a week near the corner bus shelter soliciting customers. Occasionally she is joined by one or perhaps two other prostitutes but because of constant police pressure the street condition has not stabilized and still is in its testing phase. The absence of an immediate place for business or refuge also serves to depress the emergence of a deviant street condition at this location. The lone prostitute in collusion with a doorman often hides from the police in the lobby of a nearby high-rise apartment building.

The deviant street location at 34th Street on Eighth Avenue is a busy commercial district during the day, but at night the area is relatively deserted. Each evening, approximately three to five white and black prostitutes take up positions in front of a typical pros hotel and an adjacent cheap bar. This street condition is at best sporadic due to strenuous police enforcement and is still in the testing phase. Interested bystanders can easily see prostitutes disappear into the hotel or bar when the police pass by in cars or on foot.

The deviant street location at 37th Street and Ninth Avenue has been in existence since 1977. It is part of a neighborhood consisting of dilapidated buildings, cheap bars, unfenced parking lots deserted in the evening, and all-night fruit stands. The prostitutes catch the traffic proceeding either to the Lincoln Tunnel or downtown. At first, two or three black prostitutes tested this location; there are now some four to six prostitutes, almost all black, and the location appears to have stabilized.

Deviance street testing also occurred at the corner of Tenth Avenue and 48th Street. One young, white prostitute began soliciting potential spillover customers cruising the area of 46th Street and Ninth Avenue. The block at 48th Street between Ninth and Tenth Avenues is residential; there are few places for hiding and none for business. Most sexual activities must be conducted in the john's automobile. After a few months attempts to establish a permanent deviant street location failed; the prostitute no longer appeared on this street corner.

During normal diffusion when community and police pressures were absent, I was unable to discern distinctive personal characteristics between all prostitutes and pioneer prostitutes who carved out new locations and seemed to play a key role in the division of deviance. Many pioneer prostitutes were loners (that is, independents) and others were managed by a pimp or a man. However, prostitutes that developed new territories because of forced displacement appeared younger, more attractive, and more senior than their counterparts. But no differences were discerned in the style of management.

Expansion

Expansion of a deviant street location follows a successful testing phase and it may extend over a period of several years. This stage includes *initial expansion* and *renewed expansion*. Initial expansion involves a small increase in the number of prostitutes and only a negligible extension in the physical size of the location. Pioneer prostitutes, usually joined by others, work the location on a steady basis. Neighborhood residents, storekeepers, shoppers, and police gradually begin to perceive conditions as inevitable. At this stage of development the police strive to control and contain rather than eliminate street deviance.

As a condition stabilizes, *neighborhood typing* takes place; the location is fixed in the minds of neighborhood users and the police as a deviant street location. Now the mere presence of a person at that location in itself may impose a deviant label. The location attracts deviants from outside the area and expectations develop that encourage deviant behavior. The deviant expectations now associated with the location influence police attitudes and behavior. Police often approach men in parked cars and in hostile tones demand an explanation for their presence. Nearly every explanation triggers a similar police response, "Unless you get the _____ out of here, you will be arrested for picking up prostitutes."

A neighborhood likely to be susceptible to street prostitution is one where there are no strong competing legitimate or criminal interests. Often there is little sense of community or an insufficient degree of neighborhood cohesion capable of mounting opposition to the intrusion.[1] No single group appears to have sufficient power to coax or encourage action by the police. This type of neighborhood usually is characterized by substantial anonymity and scarce use of neighborhood sidewalks. Also it is a neighborhood where special interests are likely to benefit and profit from the deviant street condition. These interests include cheap hotels, unseemly restaurants, fast-food-take-out places, cheap bars, massage parlors, and pornographic shops. These businesses have a stake in perpetuating the deviant street location, and sometimes an alliance is formed to assure that their interests are served. This business alliance may easily overwhelm other local interests and combat any influence they may have on the police to drive out undesirables.[2] So long as the deviance is proscribed and limited to a small, circumscribed area residents and police will not expend the effort to correct the condition. But as soon as the condition spills over and threatens certain interests or results in unacceptable violence, then the community joined by the police will attempt to eradicate it.

The deviant street location on Christie Street at the corner of Stanton Street on the Lower East Side illustrates this process of initial expansion. It is bounded on its east side by Roosevelt Park, on its northern side by a parking lot, and is situated in an area of run-down tenements and few businesses. Scarcely any interests, legitimate or illegitimate, exist to oppose the formation of a deviant condition. After the initial testing phase by one white and two black prostitutes, several other white and black prostitutes joined the corner. The street condition has stabilized, and prostitutes are visible at this street location on a steady nightly schedule.

Renewed Expansion

Renewed expansion usually succeeds initial expansion. The process of renewed expansion involves a substantial increase in steady, part-, or full-time prostitutes and a sizeable extension in the physical area of the deviant street location. Prostitutes may begin to wander from the core and take up positions around the entire block. For example, the deviant condition at the Bowery and Delancey Street now extends around the square block, although originally it was confined primarily to the core area immediately in front of the hotel. Similarly, the condition at 26th Street and Park Avenue originated at the northeast corner in front of the hotel. After a while it stabilized and expanded on Park Avenue, one block in both directions. Renewed expansion depends on numerous factors that regulate the size of a deviant street location including community tolerance, police visibility, and availability of clientele.

During various stages in the life cycle of a deviant street location very little conflict occurred between prostitutes who were part of a stable, those who had a man, and loners. Knife and fist fights over position and customers were rare. This suggests that the need for mutual defense against common enemies is very strong and the supply of prostitutes never seriously exceeds demand. Competition, stigma, police harassment, risk of assault, and numerous other street threats regulate the supply of prostitutes. During the first half of 1980, two prostitutes in separate incidents were found in hotel rooms murdered, mutilated, and decapitated.[3] Although rare, these violent occurrences frighten prostitutes and underscore the ever-present dangers of street life.

Equilibrium

Following deviant expansion, a street condition enters a state of *equilibrium*, neither increasing or decreasing in size. Equilibrium is maintained by several competing cross-pressures. The personal needs of johns, economic requirements of prostitutes, and certain local business interests produce pressures that encourage deviant street conditions while supply and demand, business competition, community opposition and police resistance check and regulate these forces. At a certain point the equilibrium provides the best fit for maximizing each group's interests, given a certain set of constraints. A deviant street condition that falls below a certain minimum level attracts more prostitutes and johns. A deviant street condition that increases beyond the point of tolerance encounters community and police resistance. Conflict may also arise among competing prostitutes. These actions serve community interests by isolating deviance and also those of prostitutes by reducing unwanted competition. In this way the deviant street condition maintains itself. The state of equilibrium usually lasts for several years and sometimes for decades. The majority of the thirteen deviant street locations have completed deviant expansion and currently are in a state of equilibrium.

Dissolution

The final stage in the life cycle of a deviant street location is *dissolution*. One determinant for dissolution is area redevelopment accompanied by an underlying shift in community expectations and attitudes. In this situation a critical mass develops in opposition to street deviance and it garners sufficient power to overwhelm deviant interests. Dissolution is relatively rapid and usually coterminous with the time of redevelopment. The dissolution process was encountered at two deviant street locations that had persisted for several years, both on Eighth Avenue in the Chelsea district, one at 30th Street and the other at 23rd Street. The development of a new site for Madison Square Garden on Eighth Avenue between 31st and 33rd Streets was accompanied by overall area redevelopment. Old decayed town houses and tenements formerly occupied mainly by lower-class welfare recipients between Eighth and Ninth Avenues on 29th and 30th Streets were renovated and occupied by middle-class tenants. Also, a massive, middle-income, cooperative apartment complex for the International Ladies Garment Workers Union was constructed between 26th and 29th Streets. Although no similar construction event occurred at 23rd Street and Eighth Avenue as the erection of a tremendous sports stadium, many buildings were renovated and middle-class persons took over apartments formerly occupied by lower-class, unemployed, welfare recipients. In both these neighborhoods a sense of community developed and prostitutes were isolated and opposed by a coalition of residents, storekeepers, restaurant owners, and city agencies. A vigorous and steady enforcement campaign by the police suppressed the deviant street conditions. Many prostitutes who formerly occupied these areas simply moved further uptown to deviant street locations on Eighth and Ninth Avenues.

Two additional deviant locations at 42nd Street on Ninth and Tenth Avenues are in the midst of disintegration for a similar reason. A massive, middle-income apartment complex known as Manhattan Plaza has recently been completed and occupied by middle- to upper-income residents. Moreover, several abandoned, dilapidated buildings formerly housing massage parlors have been renovated and converted into small attractive theaters. The block on 42nd Street between Ninth and Tenth Avenues is now referred to as Theater Row. The deviant street conditions at this location have diminished substantially.

Another determinant for the dissolution of a deviant street location is the occurrence of certain dramatic or shock events. These events occurred during the middle to late 1970s in Chinatown in the vicinity of Chatham Square where a substantial deviant street condition endured for years, consisting of ten to twenty white, black, and Hispanic prostitutes who catered primarily to the area's Chinese workers. A series of Chinese youth gang

The Deviant Street Location Cycle

shootings unrelated to the area's prostitution resulted in several deaths including that of an innocent passerby. These events led to a successful campaign to clean up the area's street prostitution. The prostitutes moved about ten blocks north to deviant street locations at the Bowery and Delancey Street and Forsythe Street.[4]

A similar event, involving the murder of a young girl in Sara Roosevelt Park situated between two deviant locations on Forsythe Street and the Bowery and Delancey Streets, led to a two-year joint community and police effort to eliminate the conditions of street prostitution. It seemed for a while in the early part of the campaign when police enforcement was particularly strong and community interest high that the deviant conditions would be suppressed. However, this does not appear to be the case because two years later street prostitution was about at the same level as prior to the incident. Perhaps the difference between success in suppressing the deviant street location in Chinatown and the failure to eliminate the two Lower East Side locations is that the Chinatown site was situated in a thriving business area that attracts tourists from the entire city and outlying metropolitan area. The conditions of prostitution interfered with this business and a sustained, vocal, and organized community demanded its suppression. On the other hand, the deviant conditions at Forsythe Street and the Bowery and Delancey are in neighborhoods nearly devoid of residences, businesses, and shoppers. Advocates for suppression were unable to mount a meaningful, organized, and powerful campaign capable of overwhelming the deviant interests including prostitutes, pimps, and even business people who benefit from deviance. However, residents one block east on Eldridge Street, a more densely populated neighborhood with an established sense of community, succeeded in preventing the condition from expanding into their immediate neighborhood, thanks to the assistance of heavy illegal drug interests situated inside apartment houses on those blocks (see chapter 8).

A similar campaign to suppress street prostitution in the vicinity of 46th Street and Ninth Avenue has met with little permanent success as evidenced by the ever increasing incidence of prostitutes working in the area. Apparently the community was unable to rally sufficient support needed to overwhelm the interests of those groups benefiting from deviance.

Events like closing a hotel or a commercial establishment used for prostitution usually displaces the condition to several nearby locations, but it does not eliminate it. In this sense, such actions by public agencies may increase rather than decrease street prostitution because opportunities for prostitution expand with the number of deviant locations. Deviant locations tended to expand and the number of prostitutes usually increased with the closing of hotels used for prostitution at 32nd Street between Fifth and Madison Avenues, and East 6th, 12th and 13th Streets on Third Avenue.

A hotel used for prostitution on 55th Street and Eighth Avenue finally was closed, forcing the prostitutes to relocate ten blocks south to the vicinity of 46th Street and Eighth Avenue.

Notes

1. Gerald D. Suttles, *The Social Construction of Communities* (Chicago: University of Chicago Press, 1972).
2. Ibid., p. 240.
3. See *The New York Times*, 7 June 1980, p. 22.
4. An excellent discussion of this dissolution process may be found in a study by Ivan Light and Charles Choy Wong, "Protest or Work: Dilemmas of the Tourist Industry in American Chinatowns," *American Journal of Sociology* 80, no. 6 (May 1975):1342-1368. Light and Wong show how the reliance of New York City's Chinatown on tourism and the attraction of clientele forced residents to suppress visible street deviance and other manifestations of social unrest. Tourism and street crime are competing and conflicting value sytsems; they cannot coexist.

10 Maintaining Deviance

There are several critical processes that explain the persistence of deviant street locations that are concerned with:

1. How female street prostitution remains stable at the same deviant street location usually for periods of several years.
2. How a deviant location retains its segregated status and withstands outside invasions.
3. How a deviant location maintains internal cohesion and control over its own members.

Four key processes explain the perpetuation and maintenance of deviant street locations. These are an economic-social model, the theory of normative succession, the territorial exclusivity of deviance, and deviance stratification.

Economic-Social Model

The persistence of street deviance can be partially explained by an *economic-social model*.[1] Street prostitution, for example, involves an open-market transaction where services are exchanged for cash. The supply-and-demand aspects governing prostitution therefore must be fully understood within the context of the marketplace. Community tolerance is another critical element in street prostitution; it is the social dimension of this model. The three main components comprising this economic-social model include:

1. Factors that determine the supply of prostitutes.
2. Factors that influence the demand for prostitution, in particular the supply of johns.
3. Factors that influence community tolerance and resistance toward prostitution.

Only a rough and tentative outline for an economic-social model is presented here. Invariably it raises more questions than solutions.

Supply

A steady and adequate supply of prostitutes is essential for maintaining deviance at a particular location. However, this supply must not be so large that conflict arises due to intense competition and community opposition. It may be that different deviant street locations have different recruitment mechanisms. For example, the main mechanism for the Minnesota Strip (42nd to 49th Streets on Eighth Avenue) may be recruitment by pimps of runaway teenagers and other kinds of importation from outside New York. Similarly, women may be placed by pimps at desirable locations, for example 44th to 50th Streets on Lexington Avenue and 32nd Street and Fifth Avenue. The main methods of recruitment at less desirable offbeat areas, such as Forsythe Street, Ninth Avenue, and 6th Street on Third Avenue, may be personal observation and newspaper accounts about a specific location (that is, self-recruitment) or from friends who have already worked at that location. It is crucial for research to explore what factors might affect the aggregate supply of street prostitutes over time including economic conditions (for example, upturns and downturns in the economic cycle), political suppression, and community denial of places for business.

Demand

A second significant factor in the maintenance of street prostitution is the supply of clientele. Given that many potential customers come in cars and by public transportation from other parts of the city, a market situation exists with a potential for extreme volatility. Johns have access to other locations and can be extremely fickle as indeed the deviant street circuits studied suggest. However, it is my impression from the fieldwork that despite high mobility a large percentage of johns tend to be quite faithful to particular prostitutes.

Several factors explain the fidelity of customers including trust, danger, threat, habit, and the personal nature of the service. Given the illegal nature of the transaction, the chance of being rolled or even beaten-up and the risk of contracting venereal disease, most johns usually prefer to stick with familiar locations and prostitutes. In many instances after repeated encounters a bond of trust is established between a john and a prostitute. Both become confident that each will carry out his or her part of the bargain. Rarely are they disappointed. Also, johns are a bit less apprehensive about the threat of police harassment in familiar neighborhoods where prostitution is tolerated than in outlying locations where the risk of arrest is greater. In most established locations of street prostitution the police rarely arrest johns or prostitutes found together unless they are caught in the act. Repeated encounters with the same small group of prostitutes probably does much to maintain the stability and persistence of a given location. It would be extremely useful to know in this regard the proportion of clientele that are regulars, one-timers, or sporadic customers.

Habit also contributes to the stability of a location. A certain behavior pattern stemming from encounters with the same prostitute is acquired through repetition. A marketplace for sex is established. It increases business and makes for efficient transactions by attracting more johns who are assured a larger choice of women. Moreover, it is easier for johns and prostitutes to locate each other. If streetwalkers simply wandered through the city, it would be difficult for johns to find them. Consequently, prostitutes could not establish a steady flow of clientele.

The private nature of the service is another important factor that might explain why johns seek out the same prostitutes. This is a business in which clients undoubtedly continue to prefer the corner store. It is conceivable that prostitution could be run by major corporations but then it would be necessary to preserve the elements of personal service and contact for a large section of the clientele.

Traffic layout and patterns together with other facilitative factors, such as places for business and refuge, are significant for the establishment of a street location but they also play an important role in maintaining street deviance. Generally speaking, traffic patterns and other facilitative conditions remain fairly constant over a long period of time. Therefore, once a location of street prostitution is established, the same facilitative factors present during its emergence help to sustain it over time. During the 1980 New York City transit strike for example, public transportation was partially disrupted and fewer johns were observed at most deviant street locations.

In sum, a number of factors from the demand-and-supply sides exist that favor market stability. These factors are the same sort of determinants that favor stability of clientele in any small local business operation. Clients and sellers have to agree on a fixed place at which they can regularly find each other and conduct business in a familiar setting of trust.

Community Resistance

Persistence of neighborhood tolerance or at least apathy toward prostitution are extremely crucial for maintaining street deviance. Community resistance or tolerance are major sociological variables that in effect represent a distortion of pure market forces. Deviant street locations can exist only in a neighborhood stable enough to attract a clientele and yet not so cohesive that prostitution is suppressed. Weak but stable lower-, middle- and upper-class residential communities and commercial streets best fit this description, although like other communities they run a wide gamut on the continuum of community tolerance.

Maintenance of deviance is buttressed where certain individuals or organizations in the community actually benefit from prostitution. Massage parlors, porno houses, all-night restaurants, and seedy hotels may depend on business generated by the area's street prostitution. Evidence is needed to determine whether these establishments actively participate in deviance maintenance or whether they simply look the other way. Business owners may not attempt to bribe the police or other public officials because the costs of exposure are extremely high (for example, imprisonment, unwanted publicity, stigma in their home neighborhoods), whereas the risk of being closed down is not that great. The establishments might simply reopen or find new locations. Many businesses, however, allow prostitutes to use their premises to hide or escape from the police.

After a while, residents, business people, and other users of deviant street locations develop a feeling of powerlessness. These people have probably come to believe that the police are being paid off, municipal authorities are in on the deal, and change is not possible. A systematic survey of neighborhood residents most likely could determine the attitudes and feelings of potential or real users of deviant street locations.

A unique neighborhood selection mechanism maintains deviance at locations of street prostitution. People in neighborhoods in which prostitution has continued for a long time come to be selected for tolerance. Individuals and families who move into these neighborhoods tend to be those who are likely to tolerate street deviance. Persons who are unwilling to endure conditions of prostitution avoid the area and move to more desirable communities.

A deviant street condition always has an element of business risk. A shock or stigmatizing event such as a murder, a child molestation, an exceptionally violent or sadistic assault, or a seemingly positive event such as a major construction project usually result in an attempt to suppress prostitution. Few locations would be able to survive these occurrences and all of them would have a precarious existence. The murder of a young girl on the Lower East Side, for example, resulted in increased police presence at Forsythe Street and the Bowery and Delancey and placed these locations in jeopardy for several years. It is far from certain whether these deviant locations will survive in the future, although it appears from recent visits by this writer that as the police ease patrol activities and become less visible business is returning to its previous level.

Many issues remain concerning the tentative market-community model presented here. One major question is whether the current level of prostitution at the thirteen deviant street locations reflects business fairly and accurately. Is the demand for prostitution basically fixed or is it at the present time severely repressed by the absence of favorable locations in which to do business? If prostitution were permitted and tolerated more widely would this result in a substantial increase in the number of johns and prostitutes? Would there be an epidemic of new deviant street locations? If the demand for prostitution is fixed, it would appear that further repression is unnecessary.

The alternative view suggests that demand has been repressed by social norms, community resistance, police visibility, and perhaps other factors (a *repressive model*). If prostitutes are denied places to work, street prostitution will be correspondingly curtailed. The evidence presented in chapter 8 shows that when prostitution is suppressed in one place it tends to surface in another, a sort of *social-hydraulic model*. For example, when the communiuty and the police attempted to suppress prostitution on Forsythe Street and the Bowery and Delancey it simply emerged at other locations. Similarly the renovation of two old hotels used for prostitution on 32nd Street led to an expansion of a deviant street location in which two new core positions developed and replaced the older one.

Community tolerance is a significant element in the stabilization of street prostitution. Together with pure market forces, it provides a logical model for explaining the persistence of this phenomenon.

Normative Succession Theory

Visible street prostitution in New York City, like crime, remains concentrated in the same neighborhoods on the same streets month after month, year after year. Neighborhood entrenchment of crime, as well as street prostitution, in the nation's large cities have been traditionally explained in terms of "cultural transmission."[2] This view asserts that for a particular neighborhood the techniques, norms, and values of crime are transmitted from generation to generation through age-graded levels. Cohorts of older criminals transmit criminal norms, techniques, and values to younger persons within the context of a neighborhood usually characterized by extreme deterioration and poverty.[3] Deviant street locations of female prostitution as distinguished from crime or delinquent areas do not fit neatly into this theoretical perspective. First, female street prostitution, unlike much predatory street crime, occurs in stable lower-, middle- and upper-class areas and not primarily in extremely deteriorated and poverty stricken neighborhoods. Second, the cultural transmission of deviant norms for *implementation* of prostitution does not appear to take place exclusively or even primarily in the context of the neighborhood where it occurs. Most prostitutes probably learn the techniques of deviance from other prostitutes outside a neighborhood of street prostitution. The majority of prostitutes do not reside in the work neighborhood and there is little within-neighborhood recruitment. Yet the same neighborhood year after year maintains stable conditions of prostitution. How is this stability accomplished?

Apparently, norms of *acceptance* and *tolerance* for street prostitution, as distinct from norms of implementation, are transmitted from one generation to another primarily through legitimate ordinary neighborhood residents, merchants, and police, and not mainly through pimps or prostitutes. Long-term neighborhood occupants and veteran police transmit to newcomers norms of tolerance and acceptance for prostitution. In this way, tolerance and acceptance of deviant values become part of a community's collective conscience. These norms are location specific; they are associated with specific neighborhood streets and corners. Once those norms are rooted in a specific location, a set of deviant expectations develop that attracts more prostitutes.

At the same time, the legitimate community rejects norms of implementation of street prostitution. Society is probably more against the status of the prostitute, especially a career prostitute, than the act of prostitution. This probably is one reason why prostitutes more than johns are condemned by the community. There are no career johns in the same sense that there are career prostitutes, (although there are chronic or steady johns). The primary work activity of most johns, unlike most street prostitutes, falls well within society's legitimate opportunity structure. The community strives to prevent its own members from assuming the role of a prostitute because of its intense stigma, but it tolerates prostitutes who arrive from outside. At the same time these outsiders nearly always conceal their identity by using pseudonyms and they claim that family and friends are unaware of their illicit activities. Typical street pseudonyms include "Sugar," "Violet," "Kim," "Peaches," "Dawn," "Candy," and other nicknames. Crime, on the other hand, may be perceived by certain communities as a route to upward mobility and the transmission of norms of implementation as well as those of tolerance and acceptance may occur through its own members inside the community.

We refer to the process where one generation of ordinary citizens transmits to another norms and values tolerating if not supporting the persistence of deviance as *normative succession. Cultural transmission* connotes the transmission of cultural values including their implementation from one criminal group to another where the recipients internalize and implement these values. Normative succession denotes how norms are perpetuated in a neighborhood through the collective conscience of ordinary citizens. In this way certain locations continue year after year to perpetuate prostitution and attract prostitutes even though they may exhibit a moderate or even low incidence of crime.

Maintaining Deviance

Norm Violations and Violators

The distinction between the status of a prostitute and the condition of prostitution implicit in the theory of normative succession suggests a sociological rather than a strictly legal approach for differentiating between crime and deviance (see table 10-1). According to the present conceptualization, crime involves both an act of norm violation and a status of norm violator. A *norm violation* involves the commission of a reprehensible act resulting in real or potential physical, fiduciary, or social harm. The actual or potential harm must be tangible or concrete.

A *norm violator* is a rational and culpable person who assumes a status or role that is stigmatized or condemned by society. For an act to be a crime according to this normative definition, it must include both real or potential harm and a rational and culpable perpetrator who has assumed a condemned status. Robbery, for example, involves loss of money or property and also it is usually committed by a rational and culpable person who assumes a certain negative status.

Deviance involves either a norm violator or a norm violation but not both. A norm violator emerges in absence of a norm violation when a rational and culpable person engages in behavior deemed negative or wrong but which does not result in a tangible, physical, financial, or social injury. The individual is a violator by virtue of a specific status rather than by the commission of a specific act that results in a tangible, physical, financial, or social injury. These statuses include prostitutes, transvestites, homosexuals, gamblers, adulterers, and pornographers. The acts associated with these statuses are disapproved primarily because of a moral or political imperative and not because they are physically, financially, or even socially harmful. The actors are disvalued more than the acts; the status of prostitute is denounced and not the harmless act of prostitution. (However, certain aspects of prostitution like visible street solicitations may be harmful.)

Deviance involving a norm violator but not a norm violation is *intrinsic deviance*. This is deviance intrinsic or internal to the status of the actor but not harmful to others. The status associated with the deviant act is castigated and not necessarily the act itself.

Table 10-1
Patterns of Human Behavior

Behavior	Norm Violator	Norm Violation
Crime	+	+
Intrinsic deviance	+	—
Extrinsic deviance	—	+
Legitimate behavior	—	—

The second form of deviance involves a norm violation but not a norm violator. This is an act that is condemned because it is harmful to an individual or to a community and not because a negative status has been established. This type of act usually is one where the actor is not considered responsible or culpable. Mental illness, also referred to as *residual deviance* precisely because a negative status is absent, often fits this description.[4] The actor may commit a harmful act (that is, a norm violation), but he or she is not held responsible and, therefore, not considered a criminal (that is, a norm violator). The external consequences of the act are harmful to society, but they do not feed back on the actor. Therefore, these norm violations are referred to as *external deviance*. According to this reasoning, accidents may be viewed as deviant behavior. An individual who accidently burns down a house that results in the death of one or more persons is not a norm violator, but a norm violation has occurred. The person is stigmatized for the accident and not for a specific assumed status.

Finally, table 10-1 shows that legitimate behavior involves normative conforming acts that do not result in either norm violators or norm violations. The present approach defines legitimate, criminal, and deviant behavior in terms of the act, actor, and audience involved in the event.

Territorial Exclusivity of Street Deviance

Different types of deviants tend to be territorially segregated. Female prostitutes, male homosexual prostitutes, transvestite prostitutes, alcoholics, and even street-gang members appropriate and utilize separate territories. They do not routinely occupy the same locations. Territorial exclusivity of street deviance is extremely localized and occurs primarily in the immediate work area. Considering the law-violating climate at deviant street locations, very little street crime or deviance appeared other than prostitution. For example, few drug sales, muggings, larcenies, or assaults were observed or reported at locations of street prostitution, contrary to popular belief that areas of prostitution breed crime and violence. Even hangers-on were at a minimum, and youth gangs were virtually absent from deviant street locations. Based on these findings the following proposition can be formulated:

> *An inverse relationship exists between specific forms of deviance and crime in certain neighborhoods. When the incidence is high for a specific form of crime or deviance the incidence is low for other specified forms of crime and deviance.*

For this book the proposition suggests that in a given neighborhood the greater the presence of visible female street prostitution, the lower the incidence of most other forms of deviance or crime. In other words, female

Maintaining Deviance

street prostitution tends to suppress on its immediate work territory many other forms of norm-violating behavior including gambling, drug abuse, and alcoholism. Conversely, the presence of these acts (such as drug abuse and alcoholism) tend to suppress visible female prostitution.

Another proposition related to the previous one may be formulated.

Certain forms of deviance and crime will surface only in neighborhoods relatively free from other forms of illegitimate behavior.

An area appropriated by a certain form of street crime, gang delinquency for example, tends to exclude street prostitution because these two forms of illegitimate behavior are incompatible. Youth-gang members create an atmosphere of fear and intimidation that repels patrons and prostitutes. They also embody a value system at odds with prostitutes. In other words, the mixing of gang delinquency with prostitution in the same immediate area would result in a conflict between illegitimate interests.

These propositions are referred to as the *progression-regression hypothesis* because as certain illegitimate acts *progress* or increase (for example, prostitution), other forms of illegal acts *regress* or decrease (for example, drug abuse, gang delinquency).[5] This does not necessarily mean that the presence in a neighborhood of a specific form of deviance or crime automatically represses every other form. Certain forms of deviance and crime at a single location may or may not be correlated. For example, robbery and homicide or assault and alcoholism may recur at a single location. Moreover, there may be certain cases of complementarity among different forms of deviance even though they may be territorially segregated, at least for the immediate work area. Relationships between heterosexual and transvestite prostitution may be parasitic but also they are complementary; they divide and diffuse community efforts to rid them from the area and together they attract a larger number of clients. Seemingly, street crimes involving property-theft or violence tend to occur together whereas illegitimate covert economies are incompatible with these as well as most other forms of crime and deviance. One task for future research is to determine how and why different forms of deviance and crime are related.

In this context, female street prostitution is a stable, money-making enterprise. It involves a covert economy that not only nourishes itself but also feeds into the legitimate economy. Street deviance may even contribute to the economic stability of a community. Street actors do not conduct business in a vacuum. Prostitutes, johns, and other street actors patronize hotels, parking lots, bars, pizza parlors, coffee shops, and luncheonettes. The survival of an enterprise may depend on business generated by street actors. Therefore, it is in the interests of prostitutes, patrons, pimps, passersby, proprietors, and police to assure neighborhood stability. In other words, there is a vested interest for street actors who share a common purpose to cooperate in order to exclude from an area unrelated forms of deviance and crime, especially those that might undermine the covert economy and the community's sense of security. Street crime, for instance, often results in highly visible victims and citizen complaints. These lead to police action aimed at eliminating or containing the area's illegitimate behavior, including female street prostitution.

Another aspect of this problem is that the presence of different forms of illegitimate behavior (for example, male homosexual prostitution, alcoholism, mugging), at locations of female street prostitution, create fear, confusion, and increased competition. Patrons seeking female prostitutes might well be solicited, accosted, or robbed by the male prostitutes, alcoholics, and muggers. Fighting requiring police action would likely erupt between the deviants and johns. The net product would be less income, increased trouble, and perhaps even dissolution of the location, all events that the street actors hope to avoid.

The exclusion of selective forms of deviance by one already entrenched in a neighborhood not only involves economic competition but also entails competing and conflicting, deviant value systems. Impinging deviant systems create conflict where either intruders must be repelled or they must prevail over the occupiers. Many prostitutes are parsimonious, business-like, utilitarian, and persevering. They value hard work and budgeting of time; they subscribe to a value system rooted in economics. This value system invariably clashes with certain classes of street actors who might be hedonistic, negativistic, nonutilitarian, and uninterested in business and economic gain (for example, certain delinquent gangs, rapists, and so forth).[6] Also many female prostitutes limit activities to straight sex, and condemn variant sex styles. Certain sexual acts may be perceived as unnatural including male homosexual prostitution and transvestite prostitution. Moreover, female prostitutes generally are tendentious toward derelicts and drug addicts because they are parasitic rather than providers of useful services. Deviance, like legitimate social systems, is multifaceted embodying several different value systems; it is not monolithic consisting of one overall value orientation. Some deviant value systems cannot coexist, while others exist in harmony.

Deviance Stratification

Solicitations for prostitution in full public view is not a randomly scattered set of events composed of pockets of prostitutes sociologically unrelated; instead it is hierarchically ordered. This system of *deviance stratification* is crucial for the maintenance and persistence of visible street prostitution because it provides a mechanism for control and order on the street where these elements routinely do not exist. The process of street stratification accomplishes these objectives by automatically selecting and distributing prostitutes to the most suitable locations. An old, unattractive, and unenergetic prostitute cannot operate successfully in the Park and Fifth Avenues network because she is unable to compete with more desirable, young, and energetic prostitutes. Any attempt to substantially lower the usual fee will be opposed, sometimes violently, by area prostitutes. Invariably she will be diverted to a location of deviance in a lower socioeconomic area with less competition.

Movement in an upward direction may occur soon after a prostitute first enters the street. This was illustrated by the case of a young, attractive prostitute who began her New York City street career accompanying johns in cars on Forsythe Street, a lower socioeconomic area. After several weeks, she realized an error in initial site selection had been made and that she could command higher prices than average for Forsythe Street. She shifted activities to 25th Street and Lexington Avenue, a more desirable location. She refused to enter automobiles, unlike prostitutes on Forsythe Street, preferring the safety and security of the corner hotel. Similarly, johns tend to stratify themselves. Johns from the middle and upper classes who can afford relatively high fees may patronize prostitutes located at Park and Fifth Avenues. Those unable to pay high fees are more likely to end up on the Lower East Side.

The process of stratification also explains the relative absence of mobility among prostitutes (except that which occurs at the outset as a result of an error in initial site selection) between and even within deviant street networks. Prostitutes gravitate to an appropriate location and remain locked in. They virtually always work the same territory and do not float from one location to another. Therefore, each deviant street location has its unique population of prostitutes and several locations are not formed by a single roving band. The main reasons for this pattern of single and exclusive territorial affiliation are security and economic advantage. Prostitutes make friends with one another and also with other street actors by working a single territory for a substantial period. Moreover, they develop relationships with hotel clerks, storekeepers, and police. In addition, the prostitute becomes thoroughly familiar with neighborhood places for hiding and escape, which are an integral part of survival. Not only are prostitutes more comfortable and secure at the particular deviant street location where they work, but also they are assured that steady customers know where to find them.

Territorial affiliation can be so fierce that prostitutes over-identify with a particular street location and come to believe they have proprietary rights.

This often leads to hostile and aggressive statements and even violent acts against persons who remain at a street location for more than a reasonable amount of time. Thus, prostitutes often become angry and yell epithets at potential johns who continuously cruise the neighborhood but do not *go out*. Also they dislike hangers-on or bystanders whose mere presence is perceived as a violation of their right of ownership.

Territorial changes are more likely among nearby locations within a single deviant street network than between separate networks. These changes generally involve horizontal rather than vertical mobility. Shifting prostitutes usually remain in locations of similar socioeconomic status. Moreover, these shifts tend to be temporary and usually involve prostitutes who desire to test a nearby deviant street location because their permanent location is slow. These *floaters* usually return to their original location after a short time.

The process of stratification explains the lack of vertical mobility in both an upward and downward direction. A prostitute who is suitable for a lower socioeconomic status deviant street location at the outset of her career certainly is not expected to climb to a more desirable location. Prostitutes, like all people, tire, weaken, and grow older with time. Nor does downward mobility occur. The average working life for the vast majority of street prostitutes ranges from a few months to six or seven years. Most prostitutes leave street life after two or three years. This relatively short work period at the thirteen deviant street locations is due to many dangers, hardships, and difficulties encountered by prostitutes. Before a prostitute is ready to move to a less desirable deviant location most likely she will have exited from street life.

Prostitutes who survive for long periods usually are not violent; do not steal; get along well with street peers; follow street rules; show proper deference to the police; maintain an air of calm, coolness, and respectability; have pleasant personalities; do not abuse drugs; and know how to control the business encounter. One cool and level-headed prostitute remarked that harassment by the police and violent encounters with johns, experiences that tend to promote viciousness, hate, and resentment among prostitutes, "go with the territory." She added, "It's sort of like insurance. If you can't pay the premiums get out of the life." This prostitute refused to carry a weapon although many prostitutes conceal razors, knives, stick pins, and mace. Others rely on umbrellas or handbags with long shoulder straps for protection. She was very well versed, however, in the techniques for controlling an encounter with a john including acting firm, curt, and detached, speaking in a friendly but determined, resolute tone, providing directions where to go, and asking for payment before providing the service. Some prostitutes wore jeans rather than dresses, not only for comfort but also to display a semblance of authority and control.

Violent, dishonest, aggressive, arrogant, and bumptious prostitutes and also drug addicts tend to clash with other prostitutes, johns, and the police. Some prostitutes simply do not deliver what they promise; others attempt robbery. Still others are brazen when confronted by the police. Eventually these prostitutes become known to johns, as dangerous johns become known to prostitutes, and the johns refuse to go out with them. As a result they are unable to earn enough money to survive. At worst, these prostitutes are injured or even killed by other street actors or they are arrested by the police and ultimately sentenced to prison for substantial periods. Full- and even part-timers are unlikely to be included among the ranks of more miscreant prostitutes. Usually this group consists of independents who work on rare occasions and for one reason or another disappear from the street scene. Overall few prostitutes or johns are robbed or injured considering the high volume of contacts although nearly every prostitute and chronic john can relate experiences of dangerous and threatening encounters. During the course of this project only a handful of homicides and robberies were attributed to street encounters. Most steady street prostitutes appeared honest and hardworking; they more or less delivered on their agreements with johns.

One-Sex Peer Group

The relative absence of formal social controls at deviant street locations establishes the need for a control mechanism that will assure the maintenance of order on the street itself. The segregation and stratification systems that *sort, space,* and *distance* different types and classes of deviants supply such a mechanism for control. The sorting process assures that different deviant types whose close physical interaction generate conflict remain far apart, including female prostitutes, male prostitutes, derelicts, and drug abusers. Similarly, spacing a process that occurs within the same form of deviance assures that deviant persons of varying social classes stay physically apart and do not come into conflict, such as the desirable, young, persevering female prostitute who caters to upper-class clientele and the less desirable, older prostitute who provides sexual services primarily for working-class customers. Deviant distancing accomplishes similar objectives at a single deviant street location. The sorting process serves as a high-pass social filter to screen out persons with dissimilar needs and interests like prostitutes, drug addicts, and derelicts. The spacing system serves as an intermediate-range social filter for ordering persons who engage in the same form of deviance, but who operate on different class levels. Deviant distancing is a low-pass social filter for ordering persons in face-to-face contact. The systems of deviant sorting, spacing, and distancing restrict the range of association between different types and classes of deviants and also decrease the anonymity of like persons. These processes help develop a bond of trust between people with common interests.

The socio-operational entity for accomplishing these goals is the single-sex peer group comprised of female prostitutes. Street prostitutes work near each other for territorial defense and also for protection from the threat of outsiders (for example, dangerous johns and hangers-on) and the police. The single-sex peer group polices itself and serves as a force to control uncooperative or unruly peers. The group enforces street rules; for example, once a prostitute engages a potential john, other prostitutes are not permitted to interfere. A prostitute working alone at a location finds herself with little protection and hope for assistance, but groups of prostitutes can provide the social organization necessary to accomplish these objectives. This is one important reason why prostitutes gather and work near one another in small territorial enclaves. Of course pimps and men contribute to the overall security system, but front-line defense for most prostitutes is primarily their own responsibility.

Although the study was not specifically designed to test whether the area determines the behavior of prostitutes or whether prostitutes determine neighborhood characteristics, it may be inferred from the data that the area's patterns are dominant. The specific location attracts prostitutes who rapidly assume the characteristics and patterns of the process of prostitution at that particular location. The style, ethos, and subcultural values associated with a particular location seem to determine a prostitute's behavior. These include the fee, mode of operation, form of police regulation, and style of deviant management. Likewise for patrons. For example, johns in upper socioeconomic areas usually utilize hotels, whereas in lower socioeconomic areas they rely mainly on automobiles.

Notes

1. Dean Savage provided many excellent ideas and suggestions for this section.

2. See Clifford Robe Shaw and Henry D. McKay, *Juvenile Delinquency and Urban Areas* (Chicago: University of Chicago Press, 1942).

3. The theory of cultural transmission raises an issue not fully explored in the present research. Which comes first, the conditions associated with a delinquent area or the criminals and crime. It is my impression from the fieldwork that neither necessarily precedes the other, but rather these elements develop gradually and simultaneously in an interactive process. Criminals or prostitutes discover an area conducive for crime or deviance and then proceed to violate norms. Concurrently the area undergoes deterioration.

4. See Thomas Scheff, *Being Mentally Ill: A Sociological Theory* (Chicago: Aldine Publishing, 1966), pp. 31-101. The rationale behind Scheff's argument is that there is no single status of mental illness that can be castigated and condemned. Therefore he utilizes the term "residual deviance," which points to a variety of harmful acts by different types of actors.

5. Cloward and Ohlin's argument that certain types of illegitimate opportunity structures tend to surface only in certain neighborhoods deals with crime and neighborhood structure and not with relationships between different forms of crime as does the progression-regression hypothesis. See Richard A. Cloward and Lloyd E. Ohlin, *Delinquency and Opportunity: A Theory of Delinquent Gangs* (Glencoe, Ill.: The Free Press, 1960), pp. 156-158.

6. See Albert K. Cohen, *Delinquent Boys: The Culture of The Gang*, New York: The Free Press of Glencoe, 1955. Cohen argues that delinquent gangs are characterized by nonutilitarianism, a value not shared by most prostitutes.

11 Recommendations

Several recommendations emerged dealing with the management of deviant street locations. There is no reason to believe that these recommendations based on New York City could not be applied in principle to problems of street deviance in other large cities.

Discriminatory practices were uncovered in enforcement of laws prohibiting prostitution. Black and Hispanic prostitutes were more likely to be arrested than their white counterparts probably because of ethnicity. Current police tactics of harassment did not appear to accomplish its objective. Instead of controlling and containing street prostitution, it spread or at best displaced it to other neighborhoods. The sledgehammer approach utilized by police to disperse prostitutes sent them scurrying in all directions, extending this deviance to other neighborhoods.

Perhaps the greatest irony is that an arrest may bring the prostitute to court where she confronts a "revolving-door" policy. The prostitute often pays a fine, is released, and returns to the street sometimes even that same day. Now the prostitute must work harder, remain in the street longer, solicit more aggressively, and even be forced to commit violent crimes to pay the fines.

In addition, street prostitution evokes a myriad of other well-known, negative consequences including police malfeasance, pimping, venereal disease, a drain on limited police resources, disrespect for the criminal-justice system, community deterioration, and undesirable neighborhood role models for children.

One sensible solution is either to decriminalize street prostitution (that is, repeal all laws without imposing government regulation) or to legalize it (that is, repeal criminal sanctions but impose government regulations including periodic medical examinations, tax registry numbers, and so forth) and then introduce safeguards to assure the community that it will benefit by this legislation. Similar strategies have been tried in certain European cities, including Frankfurt and Amsterdam, and also in the United States in certain counties of Nevada. Other so-called victimless crimes have been decriminalized or legalized including gambling, marijuana abuse, abortion, and of course alcoholism, activities perhaps potentially more dangerous and injurious to individuals and society than prostitution. In fact, one of the most injurious aspects of prostitution is its present visible form scattered over city streets. The key is to identify a location or two where prostitution could be centralized, contained, and monitored. Each city burdened with street prostitution would have to determine the most suitable area for this purpose. The number of prostitutes could be controlled by licensing or other measures.

Until decriminalization or legalization is realized, an interim solution is to informally relax enforcement of laws prohibiting prostitution during time periods that do not interfere with residents or other neighborhood users. These hours are between midnight and 6:00 a.m. for most large cities. Total enforcement and stiff penalties would be imposed on prostitutes and johns at other times of day and night. This would at least obviate several severe by-products of prostitution, namely, unwanted neighborhood role models for children, harassment of businesses, shoppers, and residents, and unnecessary draining of police resources.

Another interim alternative to ease the transition away from criminalization is to strictly enforce laws prohibiting overt prostitution in the street but to lessen them for prostitutes working indoors. Prostitutes would be allowed to advertise their services in magazines and newspapers as in England so long as they remain in private quarters.

The police should review its policies of routine, spontaneous, and uncoordinated harassment, dispersal, and "street-sweep" tactics by sector cars, roving police vans and unmarked vehicles because these discretionary practices are ineffective and at times counterproductive. Instead of alleviating deviant street conditions these tactics appear to increase them. The police should follow a policy of nonintervention unless a deviant street location expands beyond the limits of community tolerance. Only then ought the police take meaningful action including arrest and prosecution.

A simple plan should be developed for police officers to conduct a crude survey of deviant street locations at set intervals (for example, monthly, quarterly) to estimate the approximate number of street prostitutes. The conduct of each survey should take no longer than a few minutes. The results would inform the police on seasonal variations in street deviance and whether deviant conditions are increasing, decreasing, or remaining at the same level. Appropriate steps could be taken to assure the community that a deviant street location does not expand and increase beyond its current level.

The police should undergo special training in vice control concentrating on how to enforce laws prohibiting prostitution in a fair and even-handed manner. Simply increasing the awareness of individual officers about discriminatory practices based on race would be a giant step forward. These actions would benefit not only prostitutes and patrons but also the police and the public in the long run.

Police officers should be trained to distinguish street prostitutes from other women utilizing the approach developed by this research. This strategy relies on several indicators for identification of prostitutes including location, time, gesture, walk, clothing, and reaction to police. This multiple indicator technique would reduce the chance of error whereby police officers arrest ordinary women mistaken for prostitutes.

==Police enforcement should concentrate on teenage prostitutes and prostitutes who engage in violence or theft.== Criminally prone prostitutes ought to be arrested but teenagers should be sent to a special agency established to counsel and assist them. Agency personnel should include carefully screened former prostitutes, trained in counseling and guidance.

The police should develop innovative investigation and arrest procedures for pimps who benefit from the proceeds earned by members of their stable. Improved arrest strategies might prove effective because there are fewer pimps than prostitutes in spite of greater difficulty in gathering evidence against procurers.

Police officers assigned to radio cars should be urged to provide more balanced patrol coverage to their assigned sector. The field observations disclosed that police officers in patrol cars tended to concentrate on those streets where prostitutes plied their trade, leaving much of the remaining parts of the assigned sector unprotected. Police supervisors in the field could assure even coverage by monitoring more closely patrol activities.

More female police officers should be assigned to sectors containing deviant street locations because the majority of arrests for prostitution involve women.

Vice officers should be trained in *network policing* and not be restricted to precinct or division boundaries that do not necessarily coincide with locations of street prostitution. Vice officers should be informed of the deviant street network concept and trained to cover entire networks or sets of networks. This could result in improved law enforcement and control over street prostitutes. Similarly, uniformed beat and motor patrol officers should be encouraged to cross precinct boundaries in order to pursue and arrest miscreant prostitutes who attempt to avoid them by simply crossing a street into an adjacent precinct.

The most propitious time for the police and the community to eliminate a deviant street condition is in its emergent phase when the condition is most vulnerable to outside forces. During this period the deviance has not yet had a chance to root itself in the community. The deviant condition should be suppressed by the police and the community before and not after subsequent phases of development, including expansion and equilibrium.

Prostitutes or johns who have been robbed or assaulted as a result of deviant street encounters should be encouraged to report these incidents to the police. Immunity from arrest under these circumstances for possible participation in acts of prostitution would go a long way in dispelling fear to report these crimes. Knowledge that partners to an illegal sexual contact may be subject to arrest for reporting related crimes tends to encourage victimization. Immunity from arrest for revealing criminal acts related to prostitution would make the streets and places for the sexual encounter safer for all parties including prostitutes, johns, and passersby.

A special organization should be formed with a twenty-four-hour-hotline-crisis-intervention center to assist street prostitutes who seek help. This organization should provide advice on medical, legal, and educational matters, alternatives to deviant management, and other problems or emergencies encountered by street prostitutes. The organization's program should be structured to provide job training referrals and individual group counseling. Similar organizations currently exist in the nation's largest cities but most are designed for all women in the "life," including call girls and bar prostitutes. The proposed organization would develop a program specifically suitable for street prostitutes and it would include on its staff carefully selected former prostitutes trained in social services.

More research should be undertaken on different forms of visible street deviance including drug abuse, gambling, male homosexual prostitution, transvestite prostitution, and alcoholism utilizing techniques of ethnometrics, selective participant observation, and mobile ethnography. Also, researchers ought to examine fully deviant spacing, sorting, and distancing because these processes probably occur in all social behavior including every form of crime and deviance.

Appendix A:
Prostitution: A Complex Phenomenon

Prostitution is a complex phenomenon that assumes a variety of forms based on the roles of prostitutes and relationships they have with their customers.[1] "It . . . may be performed by either males or females, for either males or females, . . . although in most cases, . . . acts of prostitution are commonly performed by females for males, or by males for males."[2] Although opinion varies, one recent estimate places the number of full-time prostitutes in the United States at about 250,000.[3]

H. Benjamin and R. Masters describe over eighteen types of prostitutes. They are categorized according to age, which ranges from the child prostitute to the elderly or "grandmother prostitute," the fees they charge, varying from a dollar or two to $100 for an evening (certain prostitutes today charge well over $100); and sexual specialization, which may be fricatrice (specializing in masturbating customers), fellatrice (oral sex), or sadomasochistic prostitutes.[4] Miller points out that although these eighteen types are instructive, they are not mutually exclusive, meaning for example, that the streetwalker, as well as call girl may deal with sadomasochistic clients.[5]

Miller believes that the organization of prostitution changes from society to society. He uses a classification system based on the variables of exclusivity and organizational affiliation.[6] *Exclusivity* refers to the extent to which a prostitute can reject clients who she feels are undesirable. *Organizational affiliation* refers to the prostitutes ties with larger systems of prostitution, such as massage parlors and escort services. Both variables can be rated along a scale ranging from low to high. According to this system, the prostitute who solicits customers by walking the streets is rated low in customer exclusivity because she accepts almost everyone. Male homosexual prostitutes who solicit on the streets are classified the same way. In Miller's system, organizational affiliation ranges between solo entrepreneurs and prostitutes who work in houses and brothels. Thus the prostitute who has a pimp is rated as an intermediate type. Prostitutes who work on the streets have the lowest status within the world of prostitution because they are quite explicit about what they are selling. In the present study only broad estimates could be obtained of the proportionate distribution of managed prostitutes and independents.

This literature review is based on a background paper prepared by Ronnie Shulman and used with permission.

The female heterosexual prostitute and in particular the streetwalker contacts her customers by walking the streets, and lingering around hotels, bars, and fast-food restaurants. Streetwalkers accept large numbers of clients and provide fast service in an impersonal setting.[7] These prostitutes are closest to the stereotyped "hooker" and are usually regarded as being at the bottom of the prostitution hierarchy. The fees commanded by the streetwalker tend to be lower than those received by most other types of prostitutes, and generally they are less attractive. Often the streetwalker is from a lower socioeconomic group. Because of her high visibility, she is more subject to arrest and harassment by the police.

Streetwalkers are quite visible to potential johns, as well as to police. They can be recognized just because they are on the street late at night and are obviously paying attention to male passersby.[8] Jennifer James points out that "Men may walk the streets freely wherever and whenever they wish; a woman downtown late at night, without a male escort is suspect."[9] However, it is no longer enough to identify a prostitute by her clothing, makeup, and manner alone because many streetwalkers today choose to look and behave subtly in order to avoid unwanted attention from the police.[10] In the reserach for this book prostitutes were identified by six indicators: location, time, gesture, walk, clothing, and reaction to police.

Winick and Kinsie note that in large cities, prostitutes try to work where there are the greatest number of potential male customers.[11] In New York City, they say, streetwalkers are concentrated on the blocks from 42nd to 57th Street between Lexington and Eighth Avenue. Winick and Kinsie explain that streetwalkers are concentrated in the entertainment district because white customers are afraid to go into ghetto areas to seek prostitutes. In this book a wider geographical distribution of prostitutes was found, however. Nearly two-thirds of the prostitutes were concentrated in locations outside the entertainment district but in mixed ethnic neighborhoods.

The elite female heterosexual prostitute is the call girl. These women may only deal with a small number of upper-class patrons. They are paid much more highly for their services, and the payment is not always transacted in cash as it is for the streetwalker. Payment may take the form of gifts such as coats, jewels, clothing, expensive nights on the town, or a month's rent.[12] The fleabag works in the most run down parts of a city. Her customers are often derelicts and she seems to feel quite comfortable with them. Generally, she is old, alcoholic, and unattractive.[13] The fees she receives are based on whatever she can get and the prostitute seldom receives more than two dollars from a customer. Usually, Benjamin and Masters note, she must settle for much less, such as fifty cents, and this is often after much bargaining. In addition, the customer sometimes supplies a bottle of cheap wine to enhance the party.[14]

Appendix A

According to Winick and Kinsie, prices charged for acts of prostitution vary from city to city but are usually more or less the same within one neighborhood.[15] Prices in larger cities tend to be higher than those asked in smaller ones, and white prostitutes sometimes charge more than nonwhites. Winick and Kinsie note that a short date (10 to 15 minutes) typically costs less than a long date (one hour or more). Bargaining often occurs even though prostitutes usually have a base price beneath which they will not go.[16] On the streetwalker level, business is almost always conducted with the customer paying cash in advance (up-front). This is to underscore the idea that this is a business transaction and also for the purpose of preventing the customer from leaving before he pays.[17] Prostitutes must first find out what the customer desires because the fee she asks is mainly determined by the type of sex act. Straight sex, is the least expensive, while every variation raises the cost.[18] The more unusual the act, the higher the fee.

Male counterparts to female streetwalkers are male homosexual prostitutes. They contact perspective clients mainly by walking the streets, or hanging out in gay bars. Generally, they accept all or most paying customers,[19] although they may charge higher fees with clients who are older or physically unattractive.[20] Those who solicit only on the streets or in parks and public bathrooms, sometimes discover that the *score* is a member of the police department.[21] Although this also happens in gay bars, Benjamin and Masters note that the risk is much greater on the outside. The majority of male homosexual prostitutes are in their late teens or early twenties. Some hustlers are clearly homosexuals "who dress and behave as effeminately as the police will allow."[22] Other hustlers, whether they are homosexual or not, try to exude a super masculine image by their style of dress, which is most typically leather jackets and tightly fitting jeans.[23] The area hustlers work, in major cities, is confined to particular streets, known as *meat blocks*. They were concentrated on certain blocks on 42nd Street, in Greenwich Village, and in the East 50s for the area covered by the present research. Occasionally, the police crack down on these locations and the hustlers are forced to work other areas. However, as soon as the police depart, they often return to the old favorite locations.[24] According to Benjamin and Masters, police in most cities concentrate more on apprehending female (heterosexual) than male (homosexual) hustlers.[25]

Another type of male homosexual prostitute is the adolescent boy (or *chicken*) who often is only twelve to fourteen years of age. Although not easily distinguished from regular boys in the Times Square area, chickens, according to Lloyd, outnumber female prostitutes five to one.[26] The boy prostitute does not usually contact his customers (or *chickenhawks*) in bars or hotels; rather he hangs out in places such as pinball arcades, where he waits for men to come in so that he can strike up a conversation, which often leads to the two going to a cheap hotel.[27]

Female homosexual prostitution by young girls and older women exists but is a comparatively rare phenomenon. Benjamin and Masters indicate that in many cases the lesbian patronizes a female prostitute who usually services men but is not unwilling to accept female customers as well.[28] Male heterosexual prostitutes, known as *gigolos*, are patronized by wealthy and older women.[29] Chesser points out that they must be "potent enough" to give women "the satisfaction they require," and if they can provide this service, then they are paid quite well.[30]

Transvestite Prostitutes

Transvestite prostitutes are predominently men who dress in women's clothing, and they may wear wigs, high-heeled shoes, earrings, and heavy makeup. Usually they solicit customers on the street, in bars, and in clubs. Miller notes that they are included in the male homosexual category but are different from other male homosexual prostitutes in several ways.[31] Although they partake in homosexual acts with their customers, the customers are not always aware of it during the encounter. In this way, the transvestite prostitute may fool the customer who is looking for a female prostitute. This is particularly the case for transvestite prostitutes who work near street locations of female heterosexual prostitutes and depend on them to attract johns. This was the main reason transvestite prostitutes worked adjacent to territory occupied by female prostitutes. According to Benjamin and Masters, transvestite prostitutes are common in Japan.[32] Some are known by their customers to be male, but others masquerade as women and try to deceive them as to their sex.[33] Transvestite prostitutes are not as common in American cities.

Feinbloom distinguishes between the homosexual and heterosexual transvestite.[34] The homosexual transvestite (or *drag queen*) cross-dresses for reasons of self-glorification and to sexually attract other men. These transvestites enjoy acting in very effeminate ways. Some have had hormonal treatments so that they have breasts and softer, curvier bodies. The heterosexual transvestite is different because he is attracted to women and attempts to make it absolutely clear that he is not homosexual.[35] Some heterosexual transvestites find they must "dress" in order to attain an orgasm. Others do not dress completely but have devotions to particular items of clothing such as a pair of panties or a pair of stockings. The one factor that both types of transvestites have in common is that they both perceive themselves as male.[36]

The transvestite, says Feinbloom, is deviant because of what he does, as well as how he looks. The deviance, she believes, is not only in wearing the clothing of the opposite sex, "but in keeping it on—in impersonating a woman, (femme personator), in enjoying it."[37]

Appendix A

Transvestites are often labeled prostitutes by police for merely walking in the street. Brierly notes, "the pointless behavior of transvestites who go out at night, often away from the main streets, with nowhere in particular to go, very often looks like the behavior of a prostitute to the distant observing policeman."[38] He adds that in most instances the policeman detecting a transvestite will not bother him, unless he feels that a disturbance is likely to occur. If he does confront the transvestite, he will probably tell him to go home and to keep off the streets. "If there is some disturbance, or if the transvestite is outrageously dressed, he might decide to take some action"[39] in the form of asking the transvestite to come with him to the station house. The transvestite is usually fearful and upset and usually goes along with the request, which often is issued like an order.[40]

Three Stages in Prostitution

According to Nannette Davis, who conducted research on young female streetwalkers, movement into prostitution is a process of an increasing number of sexual contacts, as well as the acceptance and identification with the prostitution work role.[41] Davis identified three stages in the career pattern of the street walker: "(1) Stage I—the process of drift from casual sex to first act of prostitution; (2) Stage II—transitional deviance and; (3) Stage III—professionalism."[42]

Stage I begins usually with the girl in her teens, and lasts until her first act of prostitution. During this stage, she has her first sexual experiences, which are often viewed by others to be promiscuous. As a result, she is negatively labeled a "bad girl" or "troublemaker" by her parents, teachers, and neighbors.[43] Because she is rejected by her community, she turns to others who have been similarly labeled and do not make her feel like an outcast. This new group not only supports her promiscuous way of life but may also encourage her to engage in her first act of prostitution. According to Davis, the dominant motives during this first stage are curiosity, the desire for new experience, an orientation toward living for the present, and an appreciation for the ethics and life style of the hustler.

Stage II in the career of the prostitute is characterized by ambivalence and vacillation.[44] In this phase, prostitutes show a zigzag pattern of deviance that alternates between occasional hustling and a return to conventional life. Many girls in this phase speak of going back to school or getting a legitimate job. During this time the person still feels that she has control over the situation and thus puts off defining herself as deviant. She may also learn some of the skills and values that go with the trade, including the ability to satisfy a broad range of client requests, overcoming fear of bizarre clients (such as sadomasochists); learning to deal with the police, avoidance of dangerous clients, and development of business ethics that replaces earlier excitement concerns.[45] Finally she may enter the final stage of a professional prostitute. Then she identifies totally with the role and views herself as a prostitute who works for a living.[46]

Some women, according to Miller, become full-time prostitutes for a short while but never reach Davis' third stage of professionalism where they fully identify with the career role of the prostitute. These women enter prostitution because they find the idea of sex as work exciting or because they believe they can make a lot of money in a short time.[47] Miller notes that although these women have also tended to be promiscuous just before becoming prostitutes, they differ from Davis' streetwalkers because they are often older and better educated (many have gone to college).[48] The reason, according to Miller, they never develop a deviant identity is that they are only in the occupation for a short time. Some leave when they become bored or disillusioned, and others leave when they have saved up enough money to buy what they would have otherwise not been able to afford. Because the occupation is only a temporary phase in their lives, they never internalize the concepts and values of prostitution to the extent that others do.[49]

Heyl notes that "arrest and public labeling of a novice prostitute may accelerate her estrangement from the conventional attitude toward prostitution and thus accelerate her identification with her new occupation."[50] She associates with others in the prostitution world, mainly other prostitutes and pimps. In this relevant group she is looked upon and accepted as a professional in the "game."[51]

Relationships between prostitutes range from very close—where prostitutes help each other—to competitive and hostile—where the girls fight and talk behind each other's backs.[52] Miller notes, "In some ways, prostitutes are encouraged to develop close ties and to cooperate with each other, but in other ways their work hinders such relationships."[53] One factor that encourages closeness and friendliness is that girls work in groups of two or three. Miller adds that several prostitutes who work in the same setting such as a party or convention develop a feeling of camaraderie. On the other hand, notes Miller, there are also factors, that lead to conflict and mistrust. Streetwalkers must compete for a limited number of customers and often "the gains of one prostitute are likely to be the losses of another."[54] In addition, pimps create situations which lead to jealousy and antagonism by forcing two or more women in their stable to compete for their attention. In sum then, according to Miller, prostitutes tend to develop the best relationships with women who are part of their group and who have occasion to work together on the street. For good relationships it seems essential that these other prostitutes "do not compete with her in too many ways."[55]

One of the best-known studies on prostitution was done by Kingsley Davis.[56] He claimed that prostitution is related to the organization of the family and especially to the ways in which sex is restricted and regimented in our society. According to Davis, "every society attempts to control, and for its own survival must control, the sexual impulse in the interest of social order, procreation, and socialization."[57] Furthermore he adds not everyone is born beautiful or handsome. There is a natural scale that ranges from extremely attractive to extremely ugly, with a majority being old and ugly. There is a small percentage of women who are young and attractive, and these women are sought after by the entire male population.[58] Davis claims that persons at the wrong end of the scale must and do use outside means to obtain sexual fulfillment. Davis argues that the institution of the family and prostitution go hand in hand because when the family system is strong, prostitution flourishes. However, when family controls are weak, it becomes easier to find sexual partners. He explains that women not under tight family supervision are more free to seek gratification. The more there are of these women, the easier it is for men to fulfill their own needs, whereas before they had to seek out prostitutes. In this way, Davis argues a decline of prostitution and a decline of the family are both linked with a rise of sexual freedom.[59]

The free indulgence of sex for the fun of it, for both sexes, threatens both the family and prostitution. Davis believes that prostitution will always persist despite efforts to suppress it for four main reasons: (1) There will always be kinds of reproductive institutions (that is, marriage) that place restraints on sexual freedom; (2) there will always be a supply-and-demand economy, which provides a motive for selling sex, and a scale of attractiveness, which creates a desire for buying this service; (3) prostitution is economical in that it allows a small percentage of women to service a large percentage of men; and (4) it is a necessary outlet for the physically undesirable. In sum, Davis says, prostitution "performs a function apparently which no other institution fully performs."[60]

James argues that the imbalance of customers from higher socioeconomic classes compared to prostitutes has led to "creation of a subclass of women who are simultaneously rewarded with money for participating in normal (for males) sex and punished as deviants for the same activity."[61] She points out, as does Kingsley Davis, that prostitution exists because there is a demand for it.

Winick and Kinsie found that mobility in prostitution tends to be downward.[62] Sometimes massage-parlor prostitutes resort to working in bars and on the streets when their places of business close. According to Winick and Kinsie, streetwalkers are typically unattractive and some even have fairly obvious flaws. They reported that the prostitutes arrested by the police over the last thirty years were often overweight and short. They frequently had poor teeth, blemishes, unkempt hair, and were otherwise slovenly about their personal appearance.[63] They often showed indifference about what would happen to them. These women may feel less capable of competing in more traditional jobs, and therefore, settle for a vocation where they sell something that is not really valuable to them.[64]

Winick and Kinsie also report that streetwalkers in large cities have always tended to be better dressed and more attractive than those who worked in less populated areas.[65] It would seem that customers in large cities, where there is more competition among streetwalkers, demand better grades of appearance. When a prostitute is forced to leave a big city because of public action or other reasons, she usually goes to work in another big city.[66] Little mobility was found among New York City's street prostitutes, and they tended to be attractive and most concerned about their day-to-day fate.

The prostitute's argot is often obscure such as: "How about a date?"[67] or "Going out?" The idea of "turning a trick" may have developed to infer that "the prostitute regards sexual intercourse with a customer as a kind of hoax."[68] Jargon is sufficiently important in the prostitution work role that one of the first things a prostitute learns is to speak openly and explicitly about sexual acts and preferences "and then to tie the new talk to the pricing of the specific activity that is requested."[69]

Gagnon and Simon note that once this style of speaking is learned, it becomes quite routine and second nature to the prostitute.[70] Prostitutes often refer to their clients as "suckers," which seems to imply that anyone who buys what she sells is a fool.[71]

Some prostitutes say that they would continue to be prostitutes even if they could make the same money in a conventional way "because anyone who works legitimately is a sucker."[72]

The age of working prostitutes varies from the middle teens into the sixties,[73] although the age of entry into prostitution is generally between seventeen and twenty-one.[74] Most prostitutes are single, although many are divorced or separated.[75]

Pimps

According to Jennifer James, "a prostitute needs a man for basic protection from harassment from other men in 'the life.'"[76] She further explains that a prostitute without a man is regarded as "up for grabs," by other pimps who will try to persuade her to join their stable. James notes, "Her pimp's name is significant as a 'keep away' sign in the same way that a 'straight' woman's wedding ring traditionally has been."[77] If he dresses well, drives a fancy automobile, is good looking, and handles himself well, she will be respected by others in the life; however, if he is not stylish and is unprofessional in playing his role, she will suffer accordingly.[78] Ideally the pimp is in charge of all business details; he decides how money is spent, pays the rent, and gives the woman an allowance.[79] He is expected to pay her bail if she is arrested and to provide support and encouragement if she has to serve time in jail. The prostitute turns to the pimp for affection. Prostitutes say that everyone needs someone to come home to, and for her, it must be someone in the life, who understands her work.[80] While the pimp does provide the prostitute with varying degrees of affection, it is often used as a weapon to control her.[81] James points out that "whatever their relationship, the woman is usually there by choice, not because of force."[82] For the most part, prostitutes are controlled by their pimps, and yet there are some ways that the pimp's influence is limited. The *bottom woman*, or pimp's favorite, has some part in influencing her pimp's actions and decisions. Miller writes, "Prostitutes can indirectly influence their pimp's behavior by giving or denying him status in the world of prostitution."[83] He further explains that a woman who creates a scene in public by being uncooperative or argumentative directly reflects on the status of her pimp. A prostitute can also control her pimp by walking out on him if he treats her unfairly or is unreasonably tough. In this case, Miller points out, the pimp ends up without any status or income, so he must not be so hard on his women that they leave him.

Benjamin and Masters cite sociologist Sara Harris, who estimates that 90 percent of all pimps in the United States are black.[84] Benjamin and Masters do not believe the percentage is quite that high but do agree that pimps are predominantly black. In the present study on New York City, about 72 percent of the deviant managers were black and 21 percent were Hispanic. Only 7 percent of the deviant managers were white. Benjamin and Masters argue that it is typically a less drastic step for a black man to turn to pimping than for a white man because it has been traditionally acceptable among blacks in this country for the wife to work and support the husband, who was either not working at the time or who worked only off and on. Thus the black man "has come to accept the idea of being supported by the earnings of a woman."[85] Also blacks seem to be less restrained by laws and social taboos (that is, blacks have a much higher illegitimacy rate than whites, black females begin having sex at an earlier age than do white females, and premarital virginity is not viewed as being as important by black families).[86] These are highly controversial viewpoints because blocked employment opportunities may be the most significant determinant for this pattern.

The role of the pimp, Miller explains, varies according to his personality and with each woman in his stable.[87] Teaching a woman to be a prostitute (or *turning her out*), "involves a variety of subtle techniques of social control and persuasion on the part of the pimp."[88] Initially the pimp uses his sexuality and money to attract the woman and later works on changing her previously held attitudes toward the profession. Once she is willing to work for him he tries to teach her the "proper" relationship between men and women; why men are dominant and how women cater to them.[89]

The successful pimp must be a clever and charming conversationalist as well as a "psychologist." If he is trying to *cop* (secure) a woman, he must be able to "tune into her," and size up her strengths and weaknesses.[90] Heyl notes that whatever their motivation, pimps must succeed in making potential prostitutes believe "that prostitutes earn large sums of money, that the occupation is not as dismal and degrading as she may have thought, and that the work provides opportunities for excitement, status, friendship, and perhaps love."[91]

A pimp will often tell his woman that her career as a prostitute will only be for a year or two, and then he will take her away from the life. An example of this is described in *Gentlemen of Leisure* where Silky, the pimp, says: "Because of my program, I have to sacrifice the girls for a certain length of time. Then I retire them and give them a business. . . . But I have plans for Linda to retire . . . She can have her own boutique."[92]

Officials charge pimps with turning prostitutes into drug addicts so that these women will be forced to work for them, but this is hardly the truth.[93] Pimps are aware that a drug addict is not a good prostitute because it is hard to motivate her to work unless she needs a fix. James writes, "A professional pimp will not let a heroin addict into his stable because the drug is in essence her pimp: It is what the woman is working for."[94] Many prostitutes, however, do take amphetamines, given to them by their pimps, in order to increase their self-confidence as well as their capacity to work long hours.[95]

The public is often told terrible stories that center around the idea that a prostitute cannot leave her pimp. In reality, however, James notes prostitutes often leave their pimps "and such situations are not very different from a divorce or the breakup of a love affair."[96] Benjamin and Masters also agree that most prostitutes, if they want to, are free to leave their pimps whenever they like.[97] When prostitutes walk out on pimps several things can happen. According to James, if both parties respect each other, their breakup is accepted, and the woman finds another pimp.[98] If the breakup leaves both parties bitter or angry, there may be fights, threats, and sometimes violence. "Infrequently a pimp will beat or kill a prostitute . . ." but James reminds us, "that even in socially accepted relationships husbands will infrequently beat or kill their wives."[99] James believes that prostitutes today are demanding better treatment or are opting to work alone, and pimps have learned that it is more effective to control a woman using psychology than physical violence. Women will work harder if they are striving to keep up a positive relationship with their pimp.[100] Dandy, a pimp is quoted as saying: "You could force a woman through dope—through injections in her arm. But there's very few kept that way and they've usually been junkies before. If a woman wants to be with you, she's going to be with you. If she ain't, she ain't.[101]

Appendix A

One prostitute who is not happy with the pimps she has known said: "... pimps make and spend a lot of money. ... I mean to spend $1,000, $2,000 a day is nothing for a pimp. They party. A pimp's whole life is a party. They do most of their partying with other pimps. The 'real' people, not the broads who make the money, mere employees ... "[102]

Fancy clothes, cars, and expensive jewelry are the trademarks of pimps. One pimp, Silky, remarked: "My tools are also very expensive. I'm continually sharpening my cars, my jewelry, and my clothes. ... If I didn't have the jewelry and the cars, I couldn't get the girls I get."[103] Silky also describes his car: "I have a Rolls-Royce grill, alligator-skin roof dyed gold, and the orange bubble."[104]

According to Winick and Kinsie, pimps are around to protect the prostitute when there is trouble. A customer who is drunk or is somehow creating a disturbance may have to deal with the prostitute's pimp, who can summon other pimps to help beat up the customer.[105] However, other evidence, including the findings from the research for this book, indicate that pimps are usually far away from the work scene and are typically not around if the girls have to deal with a difficult customer. Milner and Milner note, for example, that while their women are walking the streets, or hanging around hotel lobbies, the pimp is usually out "on the set" moving through the "scene" of the city's night life.[106] The reasons for this are: the client is not supposed to have any idea that the prostitute has a pimp; if the prostitute and the pimp both get arrested, there may not be anyone to post bail; pimps are more concerned about arrest than prostitutes because soliciting is a misdemeanor while pimping is a felony; and the professional pimp feels that he has more important things to do than to get involved with the trivialities of a prostitute's life style.[107]

Many prostitutes are dominated by pimps who tell them when to work and how much money they must earn. However, in the long run, according to James, more prostitutes than pimps are able to leave the profession without getting destroyed by it.[108] Prostitutes, once they leave, take low-status jobs, go on welfare, or get married. Pimps, on the other hand, tend to end up in jail, overdose on drugs, or get hurt on the street. James notes perhaps figuratively that unless pimps have another career, "they will rarely survive past the age of forty."[109]

Although it is comparatively rare, some prostitutes today work for female rather than male pimps. These female pimps are mainly black and of the *butch* (masculine) variety of lesbian. Moreover they are usually former prostitutes.[110] These relationships, according to Benjamin and Masters, often start when both girls become friends in jail. Then one continues working and supporting the other after both are released. In these cases it is unusual for the female pimp to have more than one girl.[111]

In sum then, the pimp-prostitute relationship may be diversified, and as time goes by, "it is likely to change in a number of directions."[112] Miller reports that while some pimps and prostitutes became very close and affectionate, others have relationships that remain cold and impersonal and function only for business reasons.[113] Because these relationships are vulnerable to outside forces, many are unstable and shortlived. According to Miller many prostitutes spend most of their time trying out different pimps and looking for the best financial and emotional arrangements. The literature does not distinguish between different types of deviant managers like a pimp and a man.

Johns

Gagnon and Simon believe that customers of different classes patronize prostitutes for different reasons.[114] For lower-class men, they point out, the reasons are mainly sexual relief, or the chance to try out a new female or a tabooed technique such as mouth-genital contact. For the middle-class customer who uses a prostitute, the reasons may be more complex. They may visit a prostitute because they desire sexual expression without any future commitments to the women. Some customers go to prostitutes because they have unusual desires (such as sadomasochism) that conventional women will not satisfy. Gagnon and Simon also point to the large number of men who only use prostitutes when they are away from the home, such as at conventions, to suggest that perhaps for these men, social controls must be eased before these contacts can occur.[115]

Benjamin and Masters have discovered an interesting situation in New York City.[116] It seems that there are a group of Puerto Rican prostitutes who only accept Latin and black customers. One streetwalker explained that too often clients have turned out to be police officers. All eleven Puerto Rican streetwalkers interviewed by Benjamin and Masters seemed to have unusually positive attitudes about their work. These women (aged eighteen to thirty-two) were engaging in prostitution, they said, as the single way available to them of making enough money to support their children.[117] They felt that prostitution was a legitimate way of earning a living. They enjoyed having sex with some of their clients, and they tried to choose men to whom they were attracted. Further they claimed that they would not partake in the more bizarre practices of the customers. No one said that she used drugs or alcohol to help cope with the profession. Overall, "they gave the impression of being 'level-headed' and emotionally stable."[118] Most had been working as prostitutes for less than one and one-half years.

Much research on prostitution indicates that patrons are usually "white, middle-aged, middle-class, and married."[119] Although they work

Appendix A

on all levels, a majority are white-collar workers.[120] The present New York City study found that age and background of customers depended on the particular neighborhood of a deviant street location. Younger and higher status johns seemed to patronize street prostitutes in higher socioeconomic areas. Winick and Kinsie note that there is a difference in age between the customer today and one of thirty years ago.[121] They write, "Today more customers are married men in their thirties, forties, and fifties, and the number of younger clients appears to have declined which is perhaps explained by the loosening of sexual mores."[122]

Jennifer James tells us, statistics confirm that prostitutes and johns come from different social classes; the streetwalker usually comes from a lower socioeconomic group, and the john is often from the middle-class and is most often white.[123] James suggests that we look at prostitution then, as not only a sex issue but also as a class issue. According to James the many books and articles written about the prostitute, as compared with the little material written about the customer, indicates that society views prostitution in terms of the perceived deviance of the prostitute, as opposed to the perceived normality of the client.[124] She points out that men break few societal rules when they visit a prostitute, while females break many. James argues that prostitutes are promiscuous and they engage in deviant sex acts for profit and not for love, acts that ordinary women are not expected to perform.[125]

Frequency of visits with a prostitute varies among different types of customers.[126] Some men will only see a prostitute during the course of a business trip. An occupation that requires a man to travel frequently, such as sales work, may permit him to be exposed to prostitutes more often. For some patrons, according to Winick and Kinsie, visiting a prostitute may be a regular and planned part of their lives. This type of customer is usually easy to satisfy because the customer allots a certain amount of time for the visit and sex is performed in a routine way. Winick and Kinsie also note that reactions of clients after seeing a prostitute may vary with the customer.[127] Some may resent the short time limit to fulfill their desires. Others do not mind having such a short time or that the place for the encounter may be dingy. Some men might even prefer to have sex in a seedy hotel than in surroundings that are more pleasant. Finally, some men have such a good time they hardly notice their surroundings.

The way a customer undresses, according to Winick and Kinsie, varies with the prostitute.[128] For prostitutes who are in great demand and do not have a lot of time to spend, the customer may only remove a minimum of clothing. Where some men like to undress down to their undershirt, others never even take off their shirt and tie. Benjamin and Masters make the distinction between "voluntary" and "compulsive" customers. *Voluntary customers* are those that go to prostitutes for practical, selective reasons, while *compulsive customers* go to prostitutes because of an emotional or psychological problem, as well as any other type of disability.[129] Men who are physically unattractive because of age, ugliness, or deformity may have to pay extra for sexual contacts.

One continuous problem the prostitute must deal with is control over the customer. The encounter with the customer is always a potentially dangerous situation because the prostitute is physically vulnerable to attack, as well as robbery.[130] Winick and Kinsie report that some prostitutes tell their pimps or their girl friends where they are going and for how long they plan to be gone.[131] They may leave word about what to do if they do not return at a certain time. Many carry tear gas pistols, knives, and other weapons.[132]

Winick and Kinsie also note that female heterosexual prostitutes often work in groups of two or three.[133] There are several reasons for this. The obvious reason is for protection. Another reason is that one girl in the trio or pair may be able to spot a vice-squad officer who the others do not know. The third reason is that the girls feel a certain legitimacy walking with other prostitutes, as opposed to being out alone. Some prostitutes, notes Miller, travel with customers only in public transportation such as cabs and buses because the john's car is partly shielded from public view.[134] In one sense then street deviance depends partly on its visibility; its public character prevents it from becoming overly deviant and subsequently suppressed.

Another way in which control over the customer is gained is by keeping the time spent with the customer at a minimum. Miller writes "thus many prostitutes consciously stimulate the customer while checking him for venereal disease or while putting on the condom, in order to speed his achievement of orgasm."[135] The prostitute learns to control the meeting by taking the lead and not allowing the customer to slow down the pace of the encounter.[136]

The Police

Winick and Kinsie report that legislation concerning prostitution has become much tougher over the last twenty years.[137] Its enforcement, however, varies depending on the degree of community tolerance as well as changes in the policies of different administrations. Kate Millet writes that prostitution arrests vary a great deal from day to day; during "clean-up" campaigns, entire groups are sometimes brought in.[138] She says that it is as if "somebody called up and said, 'West Forty-fourth Street' is bothering me, would you go over and clean it up."[139]

During times when laws concerning prostitution are strictly enforced, it becomes difficult for prostitutes and clients to fulfill each others needs.

Appendix A

Winick and Kinsie report that some clients travel a substantial distance in order to find a prostitute.[140] When law enforcement became tougher in New York City, they report, many customers drove to Scranton, Bethelehem, and Easton in Pennsylvania, and to Hudson in New York.[141]

Streetwalkers are subject to most arrests by the police.[142] One of the first-learned skills of new prostitutes who work the streets is to learn to detect and avoid the police. To make it harder for prostitutes to utilize this expertise, police use disguises to conceal their identity. Winick and Kinsie note that since most police do not wear glasses, vice-squad agents may wear them.[143] "They may limp, slump in order to look shorter, or exhibit other characteristics that a policeman is unlikely to have."[144]

In addition to being able to recognize vice-squad members on sight, prostitutes have also tried to develop other methods of identifying them.[145] For example, "In some cities police are not allowed to strip or kiss a prostitute before making an arrest";[146] prostitutes in these places will try to detect a decoy by kissing him on the lips. When a prostitute is arrested for the first time, she is likely to be worried and embarassed, but after subsequent arrests she comes to accept it as a regular feature of her work. Her later "reaction is often that of a Los Angeles prostitute who shrugged, 'Damn, what lousy luck,'"[147] or a New York prostitute who remarked, "What can you do; that's life."

Atkinson and Boles detail some strategies used by both vice officers and prostitutes, so that each group can do their job while only minimally interfering with each other.[148] In this "ecological balance," vice officers are able to meet goals such as making arrests, filling quotas, minimizing civilian complaints, and avoiding personal danger. At the same time prostitutes can achieve their objectives, including making money and avoiding hassles, arrests, and personal injury.[149] Each party cooperates with the other so that both can play the game. The vice officer, like the prostitute, is engaged in a sophisticated confidence game where he must convince his superiors and the general public that he is doing his job.[150] Here, the prostitute can either help him, or discredit his performance. She has two ways of dealing with vice officers. One is keeping away from them. However, it is more rewarding for her to be their friend. Atkinson and Boles state, "The prostitute must structure her game so as to convince the vice officers that she can provide services that in turn help them satisfy their superiors."[151] Prostitutes can provide information concerning the drug scene and gambling operations. Frequently police officers will request their hooker friends to talk to troublesome prostitutes who are acting up, for example, soliciting too aggressively, being offensively drunk, or otherwise creating a disturbance. Atkinson and Boles note that prostitutes will not try to cover up for those who jeopardize their own unstable positions. One streetwalker said, "some girls deserve to be arrested every night."[152] The "good" prostitutes look down upon those who steal from johns, fight with other girls, or are too conspicuous in the way they dress and behave. Some prostitutes provide sexual favors for police officers, and some of the more attractive girls are selected by vice officers to service judges and politicians. One hooker said, "I didn't charge for the [having sex with a state legislator]; that was public relations."[153] In New York City similar practices were at a minimum.

Vice officers also help prostitutes by dropping or reducing charges in exchange for information, helping prostitute's friends in court, providing inside accounts of the nature of charges, and helping prostitutes resolve personal problems.[154] At times this system does not work; "unsocialized prostitutes come into town, raids are called for by the police administrators for their own purposes, a murder occurs which draws the public's attention to prostitution, a crusading reporter does a story on prostitution."[155] However, the ecological balance again takes over, and conditions return to normal.

Marilyn Haft believes the prostitutes should not be arrested in the first place because the staggering outlay of time and money by police, courts, and corrections agencies has not resulted in a significant reduction in prostitution.[156] One major factor in the community's position toward prostitution is the widespread absence of public complaint. Haft believes that as with all victimless crimes, enforcement of the laws prohibiting prostitution only serves to increase the work for the police and the entire legal system. Jennifer James writes, "The customer who actively seeks a service is not a victim. . . ." and that ". . . persons who refer to the prostitute as a victim, do so in a non-legal sense."[157] The prostitute is termed a victim because of her way of life and her immorality but not as the victim of a crime. James believes that it is unreasonable that the person regarded as the victim in prostitution is arrested and sent to jail. The person "who files a complaint in prostitution is the police officer, who, after masquerading as a customer, is solicited by a prostitute."[158]

Certain cities even pay "civilian agents" to have sex with prostitutes over a period of several weeks and then to testify against these prostitutes in court. Jennifer James also points out that "since most civilian agents are married, they break adultery, fornication, and sodomy laws in many states in order to facilitate a prostitution arrest."[159] James also believes that the police have strong interests in keeping prostitution an illegal activity for the following reasons: prostitution arrests and convictions boost the total clearance rate;[160] a high conviction rate often masks the fact that the clearance rate for more serious crimes is considerably low; some policemen would rather chase prostitutes than go after criminals who commit more dangerous and violent crimes; arresting prostitutes involves little risk, and some police may find the sexual element stimulating; and prostitutes can be coerced into being a lucrative source of payoffs. James also mentions that many officers believe the myth that by arresting prostitutes, other street crimes, such as larceny, assault, drug abuse, and robbery will be reduced. This research found that street prostitution tends to suppress rather than increase serious crime.

According to Winick and Kinsie, prostitutes are often more concerned about the possible sentence they will receive than the arrest itself.[161] They point out that if a fine is severe and recurs, the woman often leaves the territory. However, if it is very low, she may almost feel that it is a license to continue. In the courts, judges may radically differ in their attitudes toward prostitution and this is reflected in the way they dole out penalties.[162] Judges, whose goals are structured more toward rehabilitation than punishment, may dismiss many cases because they feel that these women are better off on the outside than in jail where they would come into contact with more experienced prostitutes. Some judges send prostitutes to prison to get them off the streets and out of the vocation if only for a while.[163] Still other judges may sentence a prostitute to prison to get her away from a pimp who is harassing her.

Laws against soliciting tend to discriminate against poor prostitutes and those belonging to minority groups. Haft says, "racism is as prevalent in the business of prostitution as everywhere else in our society."[164] She believes that because many bar owners, hotel workers, and landlords do not permit black prostitutes to conduct business on their premises, these women are forced to work the streets, where the frequency of arrest is greatest.[165] It is more likely nationally that prostitution arrests will involve black women (53 percent of total) than all other races together.[166] In New York City for the area studied, approximately 69 percent of the arrests for prostitution involved members of minority groups although they comprised only about 50 percent of all street prostitutes. Winick and Kinsie agree that nonwhites are more often apprehended in prostitution arrests.[167] They cite Los Angeles, where about 33 percent of arrested prostitutes were black, although they made up only 9 percent of the population. Winick and Kinsie also point out that the rate of arrest for prostitution among blacks corresponds with their rate of arrest for other crimes, which may indicate that similar factors are at work in other law-enforcement areas.[168]

Winick and Kinsie argue that the media, such as the press, and the arts, reflect our country's changing attitudes toward prostitution.[169] However, since the media emphasize unusual occurrences, the public has distorted perceptions on prostitution. It is a world from which most are shielded. Kate Millet's perceptions on this subject are most appropriate: ". . . what is it like to stand on Broadway tonight . . .? Perhaps the rest of us are merely deceiving ourselves—it is ultimately an experience we all share. But diluted. I think many of us, maybe all of us, are really selling and not knowing we're doing it. The question lies then in who among us *could* stand, or will *have* to stand on Broadway tonight."[170]

Notes

1. Gale Miller, *Odd Jobs: The World of Deviant Work* (Englewood Cliffs, N.J.: Prentice-Hall, Inc., 1978), p. 123.
2. John H. Gagnon and William Simon, *Sexual Conduct* (Chicago: Aldine Publishing Company, 1973), p. 217.
3. Gail Sheehy, "The Economics of Prostitution: Who Profits? Who Pays?," (Adapted from *Hustling*, by Gail Sheehy, New York: Delacorte Press, 1973), in *Sexual Deviance and Sexual Deviants*, eds. Erich Goode and Richard Troiden (New York: William Morrow & Company, 1975), pp. 110-123.
4. Harry Benjamin and R.E.L. Masters, *Prostitution and Morality* (New York: Julian Press, 1964), Ch. 5.
5. Miller, *Odd Jobs*, p. 126.
6. Ibid., p. 127.
7. Ibid., pp. 127-131.
8. Jennifer James, "Prostitutes and Prostitution," in *Deviants: Voluntary Actors in a Hostile World*, eds. Edward Sagarin and Fred Montanino (N.J.: Silver Burdett Co., 1977), p. 384.
9. Ibid., p. 410.
10. Ibid., p. 384.
11. Charles Winick and Paul M. Kinsie, *The Lively Commerce: Prostitution in the United States* (Chicago: Quadrangle Books, 1971), pp. 166-167.
12. Miller, *Odd Jobs*, p. 130.
13. Benjamin and Masters, *Prostitution and Morality*, p. 138.
14. Ibid.
15. Winick and Kinsie, *Lively Commerce*, pp. 150-151.
16. Maxine Atkinson and Jacqueline Boles, "Prostitution as an Ecology of Confidence Games: The Scripted Behavior of Prostitutes and Vice Officers," in *Sexual Deviancy in Social Context*, ed. Clifton D. Bryant (New York: Harper and Row, 1977), p. 225.
17. Winick and Kinsie, *Lively Commerce*, p. 151.
18. Atkinson and Boles, *Sexual Deviancy in Social Context*, p. 225.
19. Miller, *Odd Jobs*, p. 128.
20. Benjamin and Masters, *Prostitution and Morality*, p. 293.
21. Ibid., p. 293.
22. Ibid., p. 291.
23. Ibid., p. 292.
24. Ibid.
25. Ibid., p. 293.
26. Robin Lloyd, *For Money or Love* (New York: Ballantine Books, 1976), p. 11.

Appendix A

27. Ibid., p. 12.
28. Benjamin and Masters, *Prostitution and Morality*, p. 290.
29. Eustace Chesser, *Strange Loves: The Human Aspects of Sexual Deviation* (New York: William Morrow and Co., 1971), p. 194.
30. Ibid.
31. Miller, *Odd Jobs*, p. 129.
32. Benjamin and Masters, *Prostitution and Morality*, p. 298.
33. Ibid.
34. Deborah Heller Feinbloom, *Transvestites & Transsexuals: Mixed Views* (New York: Delacorte Press, 1976), p. 16.
35. Ibid., p. 20.
36. Ibid., p. 18.
37. Ibid., p. 91.
38. Harry Brierley, *Transvestism* (New York: Pergamon Press, 1979), pp. 151-152.
39. Ibid., p. 153.
40. Ibid.
41. Nanette J. Davis, *"Prostitution: Identity, Career, and Legal-Economic Enterprise,"* in *Studies in the Sociology of Sex*, eds. James M. Henslin and Edward Sagarin (New York: Shocken Books: 1978), pp. 195-222. Also cited in Miller, *Odd Jobs*, pp. 133-136.
42. Ibid., p. 197.
43. Miller, *Odd Jobs*, p. 134.
44. Ibid.
45. Ibid.
46. Ibid.
47. Ibid., p. 135.
48. Ibid.
49. Ibid., p. 136.
50. Barbara Sherman Heyl, *The Madam as Entrepreneur* (N.J.: Transaction Books, 1979), p. 226.
51. Ibid.
52. Miller, *Odd Jobs*, p. 147.
53. Ibid.
54. Ibid.
55. Ibid., p. 148.
56. Kingsley Davis, "The Sociology of Prostitution," *American Sociological Review* 2 (October 1937):744-755.
57. Ibid., p. 754.
58. Ibid.
59. Ibid., p. 755.
60. Ibid.
61. James, *Deviants*, p. 412.
62. Winick and Kinsie, *Lively Commerce*, pp. 29-30.

63. Ibid., p. 30.
64. Ibid.
65. Ibid.
66. Ibid.
67. Ibid., p. 41.
68. Ibid., p. 40.
69. Gagnon and Simon, *Sexual Conduct*, p. 228.
70. Ibid.
71. Winick and Kinsie, *Lively Commerce*, p. 42.
72. Ibid.
73. Ibid., p. 31.
74. Bernard J. Oliver, Jr., *Sexual Deviation in American Society: A Social Psychological Study of Sexual Non-Conformity* (New Haven, Conn.: New Haven College and University Press, 1967), p. 157.
75. Ibid.
76. Jennifer James, "Answers to the 20 Questions Most Frequently Asked about Prostitution," in *The Politics of Prostitution*, Jennifer James, Jean Withers, Marilyn Haft, Sara Theiss, and Mary Own, (Washington: University of Washington, 1975), p. 57.
77. Ibid.
78. Ibid.
79. Ibid.
80. Ibid.
81. Ibid., p. 58.
82. Ibid.
83. Miller, *Odd Jobs*, p. 145. His discussion of a pimp's influence relies heavily on Christina Milner and Richard Milner, *Black Players* (Boston: Little, Brown and Co., 1972).
84. Benjamin and Masters, *Prostitution and Morality*, pp. 227-228.
85. Ibid., p. 228.
86. Ibid.
87. Miller, *Odd Jobs*, p. 141.
88. Ibid., p. 142.
89. Ibid.
90. Christina Milner and Richard Milner, "Black Players," in Goode and Troiden, *Sexual Deviance and Sexual Deviants*, p. 129.
91. Heyl, *Madam as Entrepreneur*, p. 213.
92. Susan Hall and Bob Adelman, *Gentleman of Leisure* (New York: The New American Library, 1972), p. 108.
93. James, *Deviants*, p. 419.
94. Ibid., pp. 419-420.
95. Ibid., p. 420.
96. Ibid.

Appendix A

97. Benjamin and Masters, *Prostitution and Morality*, p. 238.
98. James, *Deviants*, p. 420.
99. Ibid.
100. Ibid.
101. Hall and Adelman, *Gentleman of Leisure*, p. 43.
102. Kate Millett, *The Prostitution Papers* (New York: Ballantine Books, 1976, p. 126.
103. Hall and Adelman, *Gentleman of Leisure*, p. 15.
104. Ibid.
105. Winick and Kinsie, *Lively Commerce*, p. 109.
106. Milner and Milner, *Black Players*, p. 126.
107. Ibid., p. 127.
108. James, *Deviants*, p. 419.
109. Ibid.
110. Benjamin and Masters, *Prostitution and Morality*, p. 229.
111. Ibid., p. 230.
112. Miller, *Odd Jobs*, p. 144.
113. Ibid.
114. Gagnon and Simon, *Sexual Conduct*, p. 230.
115. Ibid., p. 231.
116. Benjamin and Masters, *Prostitution and Morality*, p. 137.
117. Ibid., footnote 10.
118. Ibid.
119. James, *Politics of Prostitution*, p. 49.
120. Ibid.
121. Winick and Kinsie, *Lively Commerce*, p. 186.
122. Ibid.
123. James, *Deviants*, p. 410.
124. Ibid., p. 401.
125. Ibid., pp. 409-410.
126. Winick and Kinsie, *Lively Commerce*, p. 186.
127. Ibid., p. 187.
128. Ibid., p. 188.
129. Benjamin and Masters, *Prostitution and Morality*, p. 129.
130. Miller, *Odd Jobs*, pp. 140-141.
131. Winick and Kinsie, *Lively Commerce*, pp. 69-71.
132. Ibid., p. 69.
133. Ibid., p. 166.
134. Miller, *Odd Jobs*, p. 140.
135. Ibid., p. 141.
136. Ibid.
137. Winick and Kinsie, *Lively Commerce*, p. 212.
138. Millet, *Prostitution Papers*, p. 145.

139. Ibid., p. 146.
140. Winick and Kinsie, *Lively Commerce*, p. 186.
141. Ibid.
142. Ibid., pp. 212-213.
143. Ibid., p. 214.
144. Ibid.
145. Miller, *Odd Jobs*, p. 149.
146. Ibid., p. 150.
147. Winick and Kinsie, *Lively Commerce*, p. 218.
148. Atkinson and Boles, *Sexual Deviance and Sexual Deviants*, pp. 219-231.
149. Ibid., p. 222.
150. Ibid., p. 221.
151. Ibid., p. 226.
152. Ibid.
153. Ibid., p. 227.
154. Ibid., p. 228.
155. Ibid., p. 229.
156. Marilyn G. Haft, "Legal Arguments: Prostitution Laws and the Constitution," in James, *Politics of Prostitution*, p. 23.
157. James, *Politics of Prostitution*, p. 39.
158. Ibid.
159. Ibid., pp. 50-51.
160. Ibid., pp. 54-55.
161. Winick and Kinsie, *Lively Commerce*, p. 218.
162. Ibid., pp. 218-219.
163. Ibid., p. 219.
164. Haft, ("Legal Arguments"), p. 21.
165. Ibid.
166. *Crime in the United States, 1977 Uniform Crime Reports* (Washington, D.C.: U.S. Government Printing Office, 1978), p. 198.
167. Winick and Kinsie, *Lively Commerce*, pp. 216-217.
168. Ibid., p. 217.
169. Ibid., p. 21.
170. Millet, *Prostitution Papers*, pp. 89-90.

Appendix B:
Letter of Identification

QUEENS COLLEGE
of THE CITY UNIVERSITY OF NEW YORK

FLUSHING · NEW YORK 11367

DEPARTMENT OF SOCIOLOGY

TELEPHONE: 212-520-7088
212-520-7089

May 23, 1978

To Whom It May Concern:

The bearer of this letter, Dr. Bernard Cohen of Queens College, City University of New York, is conducting a study of criminal street conditions in New York City. This study requires that he conduct field observations of criminal street conditions in the area encompassing 59th Street to the lower tip of Manhattan. Please extend your cooperation to him in order that Dr. Cohen may successfully complete this study which expires on August 31, 1979.

Sincerely,

Chairman, Sociology Department

Appendix 3.
Notes of Identification

Bibliography

Atkinson, Maxine and Jacqueline Boles. "Prostitution as an Ecology of Confidence Games: The Scripted Behavior of Prostitutes and Vice Officers." In *Sexual Deviancy in Social Context*, edited by Clifton D. Bryant. New York: New Viewpoints, 1977, pp. 219-231.

Bartell, Ann, P. "Women and Crime: An Economic Analysis." *Economic Inquiry* 17, no. 1 (January 1979):29-51.

Benjamin, Harry and R.E.L. Masters. *Prostitution and Morality*. New York: Julian Press, 1964.

Berger, Alan, S. *The City*. Iowa: C. Brown, 1978.

Brierly, Harry. *Transvestism: A Handbook with Case Studies for Psychologists, Psychiatrists and Counsellors*. New York: Pergamon Press, 1979.

Bryan, James, H. "Apprenticeships in Prostitution." In *Sexual Deviance*, edited by John H. Gagnon and William Simon. New York: Harper & Row, 1967. pp 146-159.

Buder, Stanley. Forty-Second Street at the Crossroads: A History of Broadway to Eighth Avenue. In *West 42nd Street: The Bright Light Zone*, edited by William Kornblum, et al. New York: Graduate School and University Center, City University of New York, 1978. Unpublished monograph.

Carter, Ronald, L. and Kim Q. Hill. "The Criminals Image of The City and Urban Crime Patterns," *Social Science Quarterly* 57, no. 3 (December 1957):597-607.

Census Tracts New York, N.Y. Standard Metropolitan Statistical Area 1970, Census Population and Housing, Parts I, II, III.Washington, D.C.: United States Department of Commerce, Bureau of the Census, 1970. pp. 99-117, 603, 698-717, 801, 835-843.

Chaiken, Jan and Bernard Cohen. *Police Civil Service Selection Procedures in New York City: An Ethnic Comparison*. Santa Monica, Calif.: The Rand Corporation, 1973.

Chesser, Eustace, M.D. *Strange Loves: The Human Aspects of Sexual Deviation*. New York: William Morrow and Co., 1971

Cohen, Albert, K. *Delinquent Boys: The Culture of the Gang*. Glencoe, N.Y.: The Free Press, 1955.

Cohen, Bernard and Stephen Leinen. *Research on Criminal Justice Organizations: The Sentencing Process*. Santa Monica, Calif.: The Rand Corporation, R-2018DOJ, 1976, pp. 8-10.

Cressey, Paul, G. *The Taxi-Dance Hall*. Chicago: University of Chicago Press, 1932.

Crime in the United States, Uniform Crime Reports, 1977. United States Department of Justice, Washington, D.C.: U.S. Government Printing Office, 1978.

Crime in the United States, Uniform Crime Reports, 1978. United States Department of Justice, Washington, D.C.: U.S. Government Printing Office, 1979.

Dahl, Robert, *Modern Political Analysis.* Englewood Cliffs, N.J.: Prentice-Hall, 1963.

Davis, Kingsley. "The Sociology of Prostitution." *American Sociological Review* 43, no. 2 (October 1937):746-755.

Davis, Nannette, J. "Prostitution: Identity, Career, and Legal-Economic Enterprise." In *Studies in the Sociology of Sex,* edited by James M. Hanslin and Edward Sagarin. New York: Shocken Books, 1978, pp. 195-222.

Erickson, Kai, T. "A Comment on Disguised Observation in Sociology." In *Qualitative Methodology,* edited by William J. Filstead. Chicago: Markham Publishing Co., 1970.

Feinbloom, Deborah, Heller. *Transvestites & Transsexuals: Mixed Views.* New York: Delacorte Press, 1976.

Filstead, William, J., ed. *Qualitative Methodology.* Chicago: Markham Publishing Co., 1970.

Gagnon, John, H. and William Simon. *Sexual Conduct.* Chicago: Aldine Publishing Co., 1973.

Goffman, Erving. *Relations in Public.* New York: Basic Books, 1971.

———. *Behavior in Public Places,* New York; The Free Press, 1963.

Gold, Raymond, L. "Sex Roles in Sociological Field Observations." *Social Forces* 36, no. 220 (March 1958):217-223

———. "Roles in Sociological Field Observations." In *Issues in participant Observation,* edited by George J. McCall and J.L. Simmons. Reading, Mass.: Addison-Wesley Publishing Co., 1967, pp. 30-38.

Hall, Susan and Bob Adelman. *Gentlemen of Leisure.* New York: New American Library, 1972.

Heyl, Barbara, Sherman. *The Madam as Entrepreneur.* New Jersey: Transaction Books, 1979.

Humphrey, Robert, E. *Children of Fantasy.* New York: John Wiley and sons, 1978.

Ianni, Francis, A.J. *Black Mafia.* New York: Simon and Schuster, 1974.

Jacobs, Jerry. *Deviance: Field Studies and Self-Disclosures.* California: National Press Books, 1974.

Jacobs, June. *The Death and Life of Great American Cities.* New York: Vintage Books, 1961.

James, Jennifer, Jean Withers, Marilyn Haft, Sara Theiss, and Mary Owen. *The Politics of Prostitution.* Washington: University of Washington, 1975.

Bibliography

———. "Prostitutes and Prostitution." In *Deviants: Voluntary Actors in a Hostile World*, edited by Edward Sagarin and Fred Montanino. New York: Silver Burdett Company, 1977, pp. 368-428.

Jeffery, C., Ray. *Crime Prevention Through Environmental Design*. Beverly Hills, California: Sage Publications, 1971.

Kapsis, Robert, E. "Black Street Corner Districts." *Social Forces* 57, no. 4 (June 1979):1212-1228.

Karmmen, Michael. *Colonial New York*. New York: Charles Scribner & Sons, 1975.

Kornblum, William, et al. *West 42nd Street: The Bright Light Zone*. New York: Graduate School and University Center, City University of New York, 1978. Unpublished monograph.

Kreiner, Alcira. "Environmental Preferences: A Critical Analysis of Some Research Methodologies." *Journal of Leisure Research* 9, no. 2 (1977):88-97.

Liebow, Elliot. *Tally's Corner: A Study of Negro Street-Corner Men*. Boston: Little, Brown and Co., 1967.

Light, Ivan and Charles Choy Wong. "Protest or Work: Dilemmas of the Tourist Industry in American Chinatowns." *American Journal of Sociology*. 80, no. 6 (May 1975):1342-1368.

Lloyd, Robin. *For Money or Love*. New York: Ballantine Books, 1976.

Marcuse, Maxwell, F. *This Was New York*. New York: Carlton Press, 1965.

McCall, George, J. and J.L. Simmons, eds. *Issues in Participant Observation*. Reading, Mass.: Addison-Wesley Publishing Co., 1969.

McDarrah, Fred, W. *Greenwich Village*. New York: Cornith Books, 1973.

Mech, David, L. "Wolf-Pack Buffer Zones As Prey Reservoirs." *Science* 198, no. 21 (October 1977):320-321.

Melbin, Murray. "Night As Frontier." *American Sociological Review* 43, no. 1 (February 1978):3-22.

Miller, Gale. *Odd Jobs: The World of Deviant Work*. Englewood Cliffs, N.J.: Prentice-Hall, 1978.

Millet, Kate. *The Prostitution Papers*. New York: Ballantine Books, 1973.

Milner, Christina and Richard Milner, "Black Players." In *Sexual Deviance and Sexual Deviants*, edited by Erich Goode and Richard R. Troiden. New York: William Morrow and Co., 1975, pp. 124-134.

Newman, Oscar. *Defensible Space*. New York: Macmillian Publishing Co., 1972.

New York City Planning Commission, Plan for New York City. Vol. 4. Manhattan, 1969.

O'Connor, Richard. *Hell's Kitchen*. Philadelphia: J. B. Lippincott Co., 1958.

Oliver, Bernard, J. *Sexual Deviation in American Society*. New Haven, Conn.: Connecticut, College University Press, 1967.

Park, Robert E., Ernest W. Burgess, and Roderick D. McKenzie. *The City*. Chicago: University of Chicago Press, 1925.

Ponte, Meredith, R. "Life in a Parking Lot: An Ethnography of a Homosexual Drive-In." In *Deviance: Field Studies and Self- Disclosures*, edited by Jerry Jacobs. Palo Alto, Calif.: National Press Books, 1974, pp. 7-29.

Reppetto, Thomas, A. "Crime Prevention through Environmental Policy." *American Behaviorial Scientist* 20 (November/December 1976):275-288.

Roth, Julius, A. "Comments on Secret Observation." In *Qualitative Methodology*, edited by William J. Filstead. Chicago: Markham Publishing Company, 1970.

Rubinstein, Jonathan. *City Police*. New York: Ballantine Books, 1973.

Scheff, Thomas. *Being Mentally Ill: A Sociological Theory*. Chicago: Aldine Publishing Co., 1966.

Schur, Edwin, M. *Interpreting Deviance*. New York: Harper & Row, 1979.

Shaw, Clifford, R. and Henry D. McKay. *Juvenile Delinquency and Urban Areas*. Chicago: University of Chicago Press, 1967.

Sheehy, Gail. "The Economics of Prostitution: Who Profits? Who Pays?" In *Sexual Deviance and Sexual Deviants*, edited by Erich Goode and Richard R. Troiden. New York: William Morrow and Co. 1975, pp. 110-123.

Skolnick, Jerome. *Justice Without Trial: Law Enforcement in Democratic Society*. New York: John Wiley and Sons, 1966.

Suttles, Gerald, D. *The Social Construction of Communities*. Chicago: University of Chicago Press, 1972.

_____. *The Social Order of the Slum*. Chicago: University of Chicago Press, 1968.

Task Force Report: Crime and Its Impact-An Assessment. The President's Commission on Law Enforcement and Administration of Justice. Washington, D.C.: U.S. Government Printing Office, 1967.

Tauber, Gilbert and Samuel Kaplan. *New York City Handbook*. New York: Doubleday and Co. 1968.

The Knapp Commission Report on Police Corruption. New York: George Braziller, 1973.

The *New York Times*, 3 August 1980, Section 4, p. 6E.

_____. 19 April 1980, p. 27.

_____. 10 November 1979, p. 27.

_____. 4 August 1978, p. 24.

_____. 5 February 1978, p. 6.

_____. 16 October 1976, p. 27.

_____. 16 April 1976, p. 27.

_____. 10 March 1976, p. 23.

Thrasher, Frederic, M. *The Gang*. Chicago: University of Chicago Press, 1927.

Wax, Rosalie, H. *Doing Fieldwork*. Chicago: University of Chicago Press, 1971.

Weber, Max. *The Theory of Social and Economic Organization*, edited by Talcott Parsons. Glencoe, Ill.: The Free Press, 1947.

Weppner, Robert, S., ed. *Street Ethnography*. Beverly Hills, Calif.: Sage Publications, 1977.

Whyte, William, F. *Street Corner Society*. Chicago: University of Chicago Press, 1943.

Wilson, James, Q. *Varieties of Police Behavior*. Cambridge, Mass.: Harvard University Press, 1968.

Winick, Charles and Paul M. Kinsie. *The Lively Commerce*. Chicago: Quadrangle Books, 1971.

Wirth, Louis, H. "Urbanism as a Way of Life," *American Journal of Sociology* 44, no. 1 (July 1938):1-24.

Index

Abortions, 155
Academicians, role of, 3
Addicts and addictions: drug, 9, 18, 85-90, 106, 148, 151, 168; heroin, 168
Adult art movie theaters, 32, 128
Adultery, factor of, 145
Advertisements, prostitution services, 156
Age: approximation of, 18, 51-52; of customer patrons, 61, 171; entry into prostitution, 166; factor of, 87, 99, 115-116, 159, 172; of managers, 59-60; of prostitutes, 60, 95-96, 166; of prostitutes by race, 51-52; of transvestite prostitutes, 53-55
Agencies: city, 132, 136; corrections, 174; criminal justice, 82; official data of, 3; public, 137; social control, 2-3; special, 157
Aggressiveness, levels of, 64
Aid, mutual among prostitutes, 89
Alcohol, alcoholics, and alcoholism, 1, 4, 11, 14, 85-86, 146-148, 155, 158, 170
Allen Street, 123
Alleys and alleyways, 6, 19, 65, 108, 121, 126-127
Amphetamines, use of, 168
Amsterdam, legalized prostitution in, 155
Anal sex, 96
Anonymity, factor of, 111, 117, 134, 152
Antagonism, factor of, 164
Apathy, public attitude of, 141
Appearance and attractiveness, scale of, 99, 107-108, 165-166
Arrest(s), 1, 106, 125, 132, 156, 160; avoidance of, 4-5; data on, 18, 80; fear of, 20-21; immunity from, 157-158; for loitering, 89; of pimps, 157; for prostitution, 71-73, 76-77, 80, 82, 155, 157, 164-165, 174-175; by race, 76-82; risk of, 48, 140; threats of, 65
Assault and battery, 9, 24, 56, 125, 146-147, 175; aggravated, 2, 85; risk of, 135; sadistic, 142
Atkinson, Maxine, 173
Attitudes: changing, 175; community neighborhoods, 2, 136, 141-142; police, 134
Automobiles: theft of, 1, 85; use of, 17, 55, 63, 152. *See also* Cars
Auxiliary Police Force, activities of, 71

Bank Street, 16
Bargaining, acts of, 97, 160-161
Barnes, J.A., 10
Bars: cheap, 30, 132-134; gay, 161; prostitute hangout areas, 4, 6, 9, 21, 31, 34, 56, 113, 118-119, 124, 128, 147, 158, 160, 162
Behavior: law-violating, 1, 3, 10; in public places, 3; social, 158
Benjamin, Harry, 159-162, 167-171
Bethlehem, Pennsylvania, 173
Black Mafia (Ianni), 10
Blacks, 11, 30-31; age of prostitutes, 51; arrest of, 80, 82, 155; derelicts, 92; disadvantaged, 46; discrimination against, 81; hangers-on, 66, 68, 103; males, 34; managers, 57; pimps, 167; prostitutes, 14, 39-40, 42, 44, 46, 50, 76, 79, 175; transvestite prostitutes, 53
Blouse and open-halter dress attire, 21
Bodily harm, threats of, 20, 140. *See also* Violence
Boles, Jacqueline, 173
Bookstores, Pornographic, 31
Boots, wearing of, 21
Bottom Woman, 167

Bowery Street area, 10-11, 20, 25, 30, 39, 44, 50, 57, 63, 65, 77, 83-86, 96-97, 101, 103, 106-107, 113-114, 119-125, 135, 137, 142-143
Breasts, exposure of, 53
Bribery, accusations of, 142, 174
Brierly, Harry, 163
Broadway and surrounding area, 11, 35
Bronx, Borough of the, 29, 40
Brooklyn, Borough of, 29, 40
Broome Street, 85-86
Brothels, legal and illegal, 80-81, 159
Budgeting of time, 148
Buildings: abandoned, 6, 30, 114, 117; deteriorated and use of, 90, 98, 133, 136
Bums, activities of, 85-86, 103
Burgess, Ernest W., 3, 87, 111
Burglars and burglaries, 1, 85
Bus depots and shelters, 114, 132. *See also* Port Authority Bus Terminal
Business transactions, 6, 99-100, 105, 135, 164
Bystanders, factor of, 89, 150

Call girls, 4, 158-160
Career roles, 144, 164
Cars: johns' use of, 149; oral sex in, 97, 100; parked, 112, 121; police, 71-72, 74, 78; radio-motor-patrol (RMPs), 71-74, 157; and research tactics, 25-26
Census-tract data, 116-117
Central Park area, 9, 29
Chatham Square area, 136
Checks and balances, system of, 72
Chelsea district, 29, 136
Chesser, Eustace, 162
Chicago, Illinois, 83; gangs in, 18
Chicago Urban School, 3, 87, 111
Chicken and *chickenhawks*, (adolescent boys), 161
Child molestation and children, 2, 6, 142

Chinatown, area of, 136-137
Chinese ethnic group, 30, 42, 118, 136-137
Christie Street, 121, 134
Churches, factor of, 127-128
Circuits, street, 10-14
Citizens, 2; complaints of, 73, 148
City agencies, 132, 136
Civil rights, individual, 71, 91
Class issues and stratification, 139, 148-151, 171
Clinton mid-fifties area, 33
Clothing and dress attire, 20-21, 96, 102-103, 157, 160
Clubs, 162; after-hours, 9; private, 32
Clusters, street, 83
Coffee shops as hang-outs, 6, 21, 24, 31-32, 48, 56, 85, 105, 113, 118, 121, 123, 125-127, 147
Community: acceptance, 111; action, 5, 108; attitude, 2, 136, 142; controls, 5; deterioration, 155; expectations, 87, 90; opposition, 6, 135; residential, 127-128; resistance, 141-143; sense of, 128, 134, 136-137; tolerance, 117-121, 139, 172
Community Planning Districts (CPD), 115
Competition, 111, 166; business, 135; economic, 87-89, 148; intense, 100, 140; pressures, 73, 135; among prostitutes, 56, 103, 148
Complaints: citizen, 73, 148; public, 173-174
Contacts per prostitute, 99-100
Control(s): community, 5; customer, 171-172; family, 165; mechanism, 149, 151; prostitute, 97; social, 1-3, 151, 167, 170; traffic, 80; vice, 156
Conversations, negotiating, 108
Conviction rates, 174
Cooper Square area, 30-31
Core location positions, 105-108, 112-113, 119, 125, 135, 143
Corner groups, 2, 20
Corrections officers and agencies, 3, 174

Index

Cost prices for sexual services, 96-98, 106-161
Counseling guidance facilities, 157-158
Court system, 3, 72, 174-175; revolving door policy, 155
"Coyote" (Call Off Your Old Tired Ethics), National Organization of Prostitutes, 91
Crackdowns, police, 125, 131
Crime(s): direct observation of, 3; entrenchment of, 143; incidence of, 71, 75, 144-145; major against males, 2; marginal, 1; moderate, 120; organized, 3, 102; predatory, 1-2; statistics on, 1-2; street, 1-2, 85, 147-148; victim-less, 1-3, 56, 155-156, 174; violent, 174
Criminal: interests, 134; justice system, 3, 82, 155
Crises, man-made, 42
Cruising johns, 14, 63, 102; routes of, 124
Crusading reporters, 174
Cultural factors and values, 87, 103, 128, 143-144
Customers and clients: age of, 61, 171; compulsive, 172; control over, 171-172; dangerous, 164; fidelity of, 140; requests by, 163; solicitation of, 132, 159, 162; sporadic, 141; time spent with, 172; voluntary, 171

Danger: from clients, 164; personal, 151-152, 173
Data: arrest, 18, 80; census-tract, 116-117; official agency, 3
Davis, Kingsley, 164-165
Davis, Nannette, 163-164
Dead Rabbit gang, 33
Decriminalization of prostitution, 155-156
Delancey Street, 10-11, 20, 25, 30, 39, 44, 50, 57, 63, 65, 77, 83, 85-86, 96-97, 101, 106-107, 113-114, 116-125, 135, 137, 142-143
Delinquency and delinquents; areas of, 9, 83; gang, 3, 6, 120, 147-148

Demography, factor of, 4, 111, 124
Dependency on johns, 86
Depressed and deteriorated areas, 117, 155
Derelicts: accosted by, 2, 9, 88; black, 92; problem of, 6, 73, 85-86, 89-91, 103, 124, 148, 151, 160
Desirability, rating of, 96
Detention records, 5
Disadvantaged personnel, 46
Discretion: police, 2; of prostitutes, 2, 4
Discrimination, patterns and practice of, 81-82, 155-156
Disorderly conduct, charges of, 1-2
Dissolution of location, 136-138
Distancing, deviant, 108-109, 151, 158
Distribution, spatial of street deviance, 83-85, 111
Domestic disputes, problems of, 3
Doorways, deserted, 20, 108, 121
Drag queens and heshes, 52, 162
Drug: abuse, 1-6, 11, 147, 151, 158, 175; addiction, 9, 18, 85-90, 106, 148, 151, 168; amphetamine use, 168; habits, 56, 137; and heroin use, 168; industry, 98, 119, 170, 173; pushers, 2, 9; sales, 9, 120, 146
Drunkenness, problem of, 1-2, 83. See also Alcohol, alcoholics, and alcoholism
Durkheim, Emil, 87, 111

Earnings of prostitutes, 92, 99-100, 132
East Side, area of, 11, 14, 19, 29, 39-42, 95, 113, 117. See also Lower East Side
Easton, Pennsylvania, 173
Ecology: balance of, 173-174; characteristics, 19; elements of, 3-5; factors of, 111-114, 117
Economy, the: advantages, 149; base, 111, 115, 117, 120; competition in, 87-89, 148; covert, 147-148; hierarchy in, 91-92; legitimate, 147; requirements, 135; social models,

139-143; supply-and-demand theory in, 165
Eight Avenue, 10-11, 14, 22, 25,33-35, 39-42, 46-51, 57, 65, 74, 77, 85, 90, 95-104, 112, 114, 116, 118, 128, 131-132, 136, 138, 140, 160
Eldridge Street, 118-119, 137
Eleventh Street, 98
Emergence of deviant street locations, 131-133
Emergency Service Division, police, 71
Employment opportunities, blocked, 167
Empty lots, use of, 6
Enforcement: campaigns, 136; law, 2, 5, 71, 155-157, 173-175; patterns of, 4, 156; police, 65, 76, 132-133, 137, 157
England, prostitution in, 156
Entertainment district, 34, 160
Entry age for prostitutes, 166
Environment, ecological and social, 3
Equilibrium of location, 135-136
Erikson, Kai T., 24
Escape routes and means, 19, 113, 121, 126-127
Escort services, 159
Ethics and ethical issues, 23-25, 164
Ethnic areas and ethnicity, 77, 79, 155; characteristics, 11, 87, 103; of johns, 61; neighborhoods, 160; of police, 81; of prostitutes, 51; racial, 11, 87
Ethnography, mobile, 4, 17, 158
Ethnometrics, techniques of, 18, 158
Ethnostatistics, 74, 77, 96, 116
Examinations, medical, 155
Exclusivity, territorial, 139, 146-148, 159
Expansion, location renewal, 133-135
Expectation, community, 87-90
Eye movements, attraction method, 108

Factories, 85
Family: controls, 165; exodus from cities, 2; status, 2, 6, 87, 164-165

Fast-food-take-out stores, 118, 128, 134, 147, 160
Favors, sexual, 74
Fear of arrest, 20-21
Fees: hotel, 97, 112; sexual services, 97, 101, 106, 113, 149, 152, 159-160; transvestite, 55
Feinbloom, Deborah, 162
Fellatio and fellatrice, *See* Oral sex
Felony, crimes of, 169
Female(s): heterosexual, 2-4, 11, 172; homosexual, 162; impersonators, 52-54, 86; pimps, 169; street prostitution, 5, 14, 95-100; unattractiveness, 6, 105-106, 162
Fidelity of customer patrons, 140
Field observations, 5, 16-18, 37, 74, 92, 111, 116, 157
Fifth Avenue, 10-11, 14, 21, 25, 31-32, 39, 42, 46-53, 57, 61, 63, 65, 73-75, 89-90, 95-103, 113-117, 120, 125-127, 137, 140, 149
Fiftieth Street, 11, 32, 34, 39, 42, 63, 128, 140, 161; East, 10
Fifty-ninth Street, 9-10, 14, 22, 76, 83, 128; East, 39; North, 29; South, 29; West, 39
Fifty-seventh Street, 160
Fifty-third Street, 83, 86, 95; East, 11
First sexual experience, 163
Floaters, problems of, 150
Flophouses, existence of, 30
Foot patrols, police, 72-77, 119
Foreign diplomats, 102
Forsythe Street, 11, 30, 44, 63, 77, 97
Forty-eight Street, 131, 133
Forty-fifth Street, 33, 53, 55, 61, 100-101, 119
Forty-first Street, 53, 86, 100
Forty-fourth Street, 11, 23, 32, 39, 42, 44, 63, 96, 98, 140; West, 172
Forty-ninth Street, 11, 25, 34, 39, 41, 50, 57, 63, 75, 77, 104, 116, 118, 128, 140; West, 10
Forty-second Street, 2, 11, 14, 33-34,

Index

Forty-second Street: (*cont.*) 39, 41-44, 50, 55, 57, 63, 75, 77, 86, 90, 104, 113-116, 136, 140, 160-161; West, 2, 10
Forty-seventh Street, 85
Forty-sixth Street, 33, 44, 50, 55, 77, 83, 103, 119, 133, 137-138; West, 10
Fourteenth Street, 11, 30-31, 39, 44, 57, 63, 75, 77, 86, 97, 103, 116-117, 123-126
Fourth Street, 29, 53, 85, 101, 124
Frankfurt, Germany, 155
Freedom, sexual, 165
Full-time prostitutes, 40-41, 134, 159, 164

Gagnon, John, 166, 170
Gamblers, street, 18, 85-90, 145
Gambling operations, 1-2, 11, 147, 155, 158, 173
Gangs: in Chicago, 18; delinquency of, 3, 6, 120, 147-148; roving, 9; youth members of, 146-147
Gay liberation movement, 91, 161
Gemeinschaft, 111
Gentlemen of Leisure (Hall/Adelman), 168
Geography, factor of, 83
Germany and the Germans, 29, 33
Gesellschaft, 111
Gestures, verbal and body, 20, 55, 64-65, 108, 157, 160
Ghetto areas, 19, 160
Gifts, payments for sexual favors, 160
Gigolos, role of, 162
Goffman, Erving, 18
Gold, Raymond L., 24
Goods and services, illegal, 1
Gopher street gang, 33
Grand Street, 30, 116, 118
Greece and the Greeks, 11, 33
Greenwich Village area, 16, 29, 55, 86, 90, 161

Haft, Marilyn, 174-175
Hair styles and wigs, 21
Hand and head signals, overt, 20

Hangers-on: black, 66, 68, 103; Hispanic, 66, 103; problem of, 89, 102, 107, 126, 146, 150, 152; by race, 67-68; white, 66, 68, 103
Hanging out, factor of, 17-18, 25
Harassment, 5, 132, 160; by johns, 20; by police, 68, 81, 90, 135, 140, 150; of prostitutes, 81, 90; risk of, 106
Harlem, area of, 29
Harris, Sara, 167
"Hell's Kitchen" district, 32-34
Heroin, use of, 168
Heterogeneity, 111, 117
Heterosexual: females, 3-4, 11, 172; males, 162; transvestites, 162
Heyl, Barbara, 164, 168
Hierarchy: economic, 91-92; in prostitution, 105, 107, 148, 160
High socioeconomic factors: areas of, 46, 51, 73, 80, 91, 97-98, 100, 103, 165, 171; of johns, 102; of pimps, 56-57; status network, 56-57, 61, 65, 95-96, 104
Hispanic ethnic group, 11, 30-31, 46; age factor in, 51; arrest record, 155; community of, 118-119; hangers-on, 66, 103; males involved, 34, 101; managers, 57-60; prostitutes, 39-42, 44, 51-52, 60, 63, 76, 79, 81; transvestites, 53
Homicides, problem of, 1-3, 6, 9, 147, 151
Homosexuality and homosexuals, acts of, 4, 9, 11, 88-91, 146, 148, 158-162
"Hookers," 160, 173. *See also* Prostitutes
Hormone treatments, transvestites, 162
Hotel(s): closing of, 137-138; pros, 65, 112, 132; rates and fees, 97, 112; surrogate, 102; unseemly, 6, 30, 34, 90, 118, 131-132, 142, 171; use of, 21, 104-107, 112, 121, 123, 125, 147, 152; walk-up, 124; welfare, 31, 127-128
Hotline crisis-intervention center, 158
Hot pants, wearing apparel, 21, 52

Hourly basis and rates, 37-38, 40, 46-49, 75
Household composition, factor of, 115-117
Housing and Port Authority police, 71
Houston Street, 86, 117, 123-124, 173
Hustlers, life styles of, 161, 163

Ianni, Frank, 10
Illegal goods and services, 1
Illegitimacy, rate of, 167
Illnesses and injuries, likelihood of, 23-24, 146
Immigrant groups and immigration, 103
Immunity, 157-158
Impersonators, female, 52-54, 86, 162
Income, factor of, 87, 132, 148
Independent prostitutes, 101, 107-108, 133, 159
Indian prostitutes, 42, 61
Indicators of prostitution, 19-22
Integrity and fidelity, traits of, 64, 140
Interactions, patterns of, 83, 111
Intercourse, sexual, 53, 55, 65, 96, 98, 125
International Ladies Garment Workers Union, 136
Interpersonal affiliations, extent of, 108
Interracial conflicts, 59, 61
Interviews, unstructured, 3, 17-18
Intimacy, levels of, 108
Intraracial activities, 59
Irish ethnic group, 11, 29, 33
Italian ethnic group, 29, 31, 33; neighborhoods, 118-119, 123

James, Jennifer, 160, 165-169, 171, 174
Japan, prostitution in, 162
Jealousy, factor of, 164
Jewish ethnic group, 29-31
Job training referrals, 158

John Hour program, 64
Johns: chronic, 144; cruising, 14, 63, 102, 124, 149; dangerous, 81, 151-152, 164; dependence on, 86; ethnic composition of, 61; harassment by, 20; pool of, 11, 56; and prostitutes, 60-65, 140-141; and robbery, 157; role of, 102-103, 170-172; sidewalk, 65; socioeconomic status, 102, 106; and solicitation, 48; steady, 144
Judges, decisions of, 175
Juvenile delinquency, 120

Kapsis, Robert, 3
Kinsie, Paul M., 160-161, 165-166, 169, 171-173, 175
Kissing, acts of, 96
Koch, Edward, 64

Language problem, handicap of, 57, 101
Larceny, crime of, 1, 146, 175
Laws: enforcement of, 2, 5, 71, 155-157, 173-175; violation of, 1, 3, 10, 146, 175
Lesbianism and lesbians, 162, 169
Lexington Avenue, 10-11, 21, 23, 32, 39, 42, 44, 48, 53, 57, 61, 63, 83, 96, 98, 104, 120, 140, 149, 160
Licensing procedures, 156
Liebow, Elliot, 18, 23, 68
Life styles, variant, 111
Lincoln Tunnel, area of, 33, 55, 114
Live sex shows, 35
Lloyd, Robin, 161
Location(s): area covered, 105; core positions, 105-108, 112-113, 119, 125, 135, 143; dissolution of, 136-138; emergence of, 131-133; equilibrium of, 135-136; expansion of, 133-135; order within, 105-107; precinct boundaries of, 72; satellite, 125; stability of, 14, 16; status of, 65; and time factor, 48-51
Loitering and loiterers, 2, 66, 89
Loners as prostitutes, 133, 135

Index

Lookouts, need for, 56
Los Angeles, California, 173, 175
Lower East Side, 10-11, 14, 29-31, 39, 42, 46, 48-53, 56-57, 61, 63, 65, 68, 74-75, 80, 95-103, 114, 117-118, 124, 134, 142, 149
Lower Socioeconomic areas and status, 44, 53, 56, 61, 80, 83, 90, 96-101, 104, 149-152, 160, 171

Mace, use of, 25
Madison Avenue, 20, 126, 137
Madison Square Garden district, 31-34, 136
Makeup, excessive use of, 21
Male(s): black, 34; crimes against, 2; heterosexual prostitutes, 6, 14, 83-90, 162; hispanic, 34, 101; homosexual prostitutes, 4, 11, 88, 91, 146, 148, 158-162; transvestites, 4, 100-101, 124
Management: of prostitutes, 59, 101-108, 125, 133, 158-159; self, 40, 101
Managers and managerial functions, 55-60. *See also* Pimps
Manhattan, 29; southern tip of, 9-10, 14, 19, 83
Manhattan Plaza district, 34, 136
Marijuana, abuse of, 155
Marketplace for sex, 139, 141-142
Massage parlors, 35, 81, 112, 118, 128, 134, 136, 142, 159, 165
Mass media, influence of, 1, 175
Masters, R. E. L., 159-162, 167-171
Masturbation, acts of, 159
McKay, Henry D., 3, 83
Meat blocks, term of, 161
Medical examinations, periodic, 155
Men, line supervisors of prostitutes, 56, 59, 65, 101, 106, 133, 135, 152
Metropolitan Life Insurance Company, 32
Midtown Tunnel area, 114, 126
Miller, Gale, 159, 162, 164, 170, 172
Millet, Kate, 172, 175
Milner, Christina and Richard, 169
Mini-skirts dress attire, 21

Minnesota Strip, 34, 140
Minority: group members, 53, 76, 81-82, 175; neighborhoods, 120
Mobile ethnography, 4, 17, 158
Mobility among prostitutes, 148-150, 165-166
Moral standards, 116
Mores, changing, 72, 117, 171
Morningside Heights district, 29
Motorized police patrols, 71-74, 78, 119
Mouth-genital contact. *See* Oral sex
Movie houses and theaters, 32-35, 118, 128
Muggings, possibilities of, 6, 9, 120, 146, 148
Murder, crime of, 85, 135, 137, 142, 174
Murray Hill Section, 31
Mutual: integrity, 64, 140; protection, 87-89, 103

Narcotics, use of, 2
National Organization of Women, 91
Neighborhood(s): cohesion, 134; ethnic, 160; Italian, 118-119, 123; minority, 120; parks, 121; residents, 142; typing of, 133-134
Nevada, legalized prostitution in, 155
New York Coliseum cultural center, 128
New York Life Insurance Company, 32
Nightclubs, factor of, 32, 34
Ninth Avenue, 10-11, 14, 32-34, 39, 42, 44, 46-48, 51-57, 65, 74-77, 83, 95-101, 103, 114, 116-120, 131, 133, 136-137, 140
Ninth Street, 31, 86, 124
Noncommercial homosexual encounters, 4
Normative Succession, theory of, 139, 143-146
Norms, social, 143-146
Novice prostitutes, 164

Obesity, typical prostitute, 106
Observations: direct of crime, 3; field research, 5, 16-18, 37, 74, 92, 111, 116, 157
Obtrusiveness and offensive types, 2, 22-23, 71
One-sex peer group, 151
One-timers prostitutes, 141
Opportunity, 5; employment, 167; short-run, 87
Opposition to deviant behavior, 6, 135
Oral sex (fellatio), 53, 55, 65, 96, 106, 125, 159, 170; in cars, 97, 100; price for, 97
Order: maintenance of, 71, 73; stratified street location, 90, 105-107
Organization affiliations, 159
Organized crime, 3, 102
Oriental ethnic groups, 61. *See also* Chinese ethnic group

Pandering techniques, 55, 92
Pantyhose, seductive wearing of, 21
Parisitic structures, 86, 92, 147
Park Avenue, 3, 10-11, 14, 25, 31-32, 39, 42, 44, 46, 48-53, 57, 61, 63, 65, 73-75, 83, 87, 90, 95-104, 111, 114, 117, 120, 125-127, 135, 149
Parked cars for deviant behavior, 112, 121
Parking lots, use of, 31, 108, 112, 124, 126, 133-134, 147
Parks, deviant use of, 6, 19, 111, 113, 121, 161. *See also specific parks by name*
Part-time prostitutes, 40-41, 134, 151
Passersby, 2, 5, 16, 50; accosting of, 9
Patrons, role of, 4, 16, 18, 60-66, 102, 126, 147, 160. *See also* Customers and clients
Pawn shops, 31
Payoffs, sources of, 142, 174
Peep shows, 35, 128
Peer groups, 150-151
Penalties, assessment of, 156

Pennsylvania, 173
Perseverance, trait of, 107-108
Personal: appearance, 107-108, 165-166; danger, 173; safety, 120; social-psychological interaction, 2-3
Physical: power, 91; segregation, 108; violence, 168
Pimps and pimping: arrest procedures for, 157; black, 167; a felony, 164, 169; female, 169; influence of, 167; management by, 56, 101-103, 105, 107; mobility of 56; professionalism, 55-56; recruitment, 140; role of, 11, 16, 18, 40, 44, 91, 96, 125-126, 133, 137, 144, 147, 152, 155, 166; socioeconomic status of, 56-57; trademarks of, 168-170
Pinball arcade hangout areas, 161
Pioneer prostitutes in location, 132-133
Pizza parlors, 147
Police: attitudes, 134; auxiliary, 71; bribery charges, 142, 174; crackdowns, 125, 131; departments, 24; discretion; 2; enforcement policies, 65, 76, 132-133, 137, 157; escape from, 113, 121; ethnic composition, 81; harassment by, 68, 81, 90, 135, 140, 150; malfeasance of, 155; motorized, 71-74, 78, 119; network, 71-76, 157; plainclothes, 73; pressures, 73, 133; reaction to, 20, 135, 157; role of, 18, 79, 172-175; and sexual favors, 74; sightings and sweeps, 71, 74, 77
Polish ethnic group, 11, 30-31
Politics and political imperatives, 91, 140, 145
Population density, factor of, 71, 75, 87, 111, 117
Pornography and pornographic shops, 31, 35, 128, 134, 142, 145
Port Authority Bus Terminal, 33-34, 86, 114; police force of, 71
Posturing, seductive, 21
Poverty, effects of, 143
Power, 6, 91; balance of, 97

Index

Predatory street crimes, 1-2
President's Commission on Law Enforcement and Administration of Justice, 1
Press. *See* Crusading reporters; Mass media
Pressure: competitive, 73, 135; police, 73, 133
Private: clubs, 32; rented rooms, 97-98
Professionalism, deviant, 55-56, 163-164
Progression-regression hypothesis, 147
Promiscuity, acts of, 163-164, 171
Property losses and proprietary rights, 1, 147-150
Prosecutorial system, 3, 155-156
Pros hotel, 65, 112, 132
Prostitutes and prostitution, 1-2, 18, 37-42; age, 47, 51-52, 55, 59-60, 95-96, 166; arrest record, 71-73, 76-77, 80, 82, 155, 157, 164-165, 174-175; average working life, 150; black, 14, 39-40, 42, 44, 46, 50-53, 76, 79-82, 155, 175; career, 144; competition, 56, 103, 148; contacts, 99-100; control, 97; core, 106-107; decriminalization, 155-156; earnings, 99-100; entry into, 166; ethnic composition, 51; female, 5, 14, 95-100; full time, 40-41, 134, 159, 164; harassment, 81, 90; hierarchial order, 105, 107, 148, 160; Hispanic, 39-40, 42, 44, 51-52, 60, 63, 76, 79, 81; hourly factor, 46-47; independent loners, 101, 133, 135, 159; indicators, 19-22; and johns, 60-65, 140-141; male homosexual, 4, 6, 11, 14, 83-91, 100-101, 124, 146, 148, 158-162; managers and management, 59-60, 101-103, 105-108, 125, 158-159; miscreant, 150-151, 155-156; novice, 164; one-timers, 141; part time, 40-41, 134, 151; pioneer, 132-133; protection, 169; Puerto Rican, 170; by race, 43, 45, 47, 51-54, 60, 62; regular single, 9, 141; soliciting, 2, 9; status and supply of, 140, 145; teenage, 157; transvestites, 4, 11, 14, 37-55, 86, 88, 90, 92, 100-101, 106-107, 124, 146-148, 158, 162-163; white, 39-40, 42, 44, 50, 53, 76, 79, 81
Prostitutes of New York (PONY), 91
Protection, provisions for, 56, 103, 108, 169, 172
Pseudonyms, street, 144
Psychology, factor of, 168, 172
Public: agencies, 137; complaints, 173-174; places, 3; transportation, 140-141, 172
Puerto Rican ethnic group, 30, 33, 170
Pushers, drug, 2, 9
"Pussy Posse," 72

Queens, Borough of, 29, 40, 126
Questionnaires, use of, 3

Racial and ethnic characteristics, 11, 87, 96, 116; arrests by, 76-82; hangers-on by, 67-68; managers by, 58-60; prostitutes by, 42-48, 51-54, 60, 62
Racism, prevalence of, 175
Radio-motor-patrol cars (RMPs), 71-74, 157
Rape and rapists, 1-3, 9, 85, 148
Reaction to police activity, 20, 157
Recruitment in deviant behavior, 140
Redevelopment areas, 136
Red light zones, 11
Refuge, places of, 126, 132, 141
Regression hypothesis, 147
Regulations: deviance, 71; governmental, 155-156
Rehabilitation, attempts at, 175
Repression models, 5-6, 143
Reputation. *See* Status
Requests, clients' range of, 163
Research techniques, 16-26
Residential areas and neighborhoods, 5, 9, 29, 65, 83-85, 127-128, 142
Resistence, community, 141-143

Restaurants, hangouts in, 127, 142, 147
Richmond, Borough of, 29, 40
Risk: of arrest, 48, 140; of assault, 135; of harassment, 106
Robbery, possibilities of, 1-2, 9, 24, 56, 64, 85, 140, 145, 147, 151, 157, 172, 175
Rooming houses, use of, 6
Roosevelt Park, 30, 121-122, 134, 137
Roth, Julius, 24
Runaway females, 140
Rural areas, 111

Sadomasochism and sadomasochists, 142, 163, 170
Safety: measures of, 25-26, 64; personal, 120
St. Clement's Church, 119
St. Mark's Place, 31, 86, 125
Sales and selling of drugs, 2, 9, 120, 146
Satellite street locations, 125
Scapegoats, need for, 91
Scores and scoring, 161
Scranton, Pennsylvania, 173
Screening process, need for, 64
Second Avenue, 124
Security: measures for, 25-26, 65, 97-98, 149, 152; mutual, 87-89; sense of, 148; threats to, 73
Segregation: deviance, 85-86, physical, 108; territorial, 86, 88, 104
Self-confidence and glorification, 162, 168
Self-management, prostitute, 40, 101
Seniors and seniority, factor of, 107-108, 133
Sense of community and safety, 128, 134-137, 148
Sensory stimulation, use of, 111
Seventeenth Street, 29
Seventh Avenue, 14, 35, 90
Seventh Street, 53, 55, 100-101, 124
Sex and sexual activities, 92, 115; as favors, 74; freedom, 165; mores, 171; posturing, 21; services, 53, 55, 65, 92, 96-98, 106, 115-116, 125, 161; shows, 32, 35, 128; specializations, 159; unnatural, 148. *See also* Prostitutes and prostitution
Shaw, Clifford, 3, 83
Shoppers, annoyance to, 5-6
Shulman, Ronnie, 159
Sidewalk johns, 65
Sightings, police, 74, 77
Signals, subtle and discreet, 2, 4, Simmel, 111
Simon, William, 166, 170
Site selections, 131-132
Sixteenth Street, 131-132
Sixth Street, 11, 14, 30-31, 39, 41, 44, 53, 63, 75, 97, 101, 124-125, 140; East, 10, 137
Slum areas, 1, 18-19, 33, 117, 120-121
Social: characteristics, 3, 124, 128, 158; classes, 9, 102, 171; control, 1-3, 151, 167, 170; determinants, 4, 111; interaction, 2-3, 103; models, 139-143; norms, 143-146; order, 90-91, 165; organization, 152; relations, 87; services, 158; status, 92, 148; taboos, 167
Society, 90-91, 144-146
Sociodemographic characteristics, 5, 10, 18, 87, 115-117, 120, 124, 128
Socioeconomic areas: high upper, 44, 56-57, 61, 65, 80, 83, 95-96, 104, 117, 152; low, 55, 53, 56, 61, 80, 90, 96-101, 104, 149-152, 160, 171; neighborhood status, 4-6, 11, 14, 65, 82, 90, 95, 104, 115, 117
Sociology, 141-142
Solicitation, street, 2, 9, 48, 105, 132, 145, 148, 155, 159-162, 169, 175
Sorting process, deviant, 87-90, 108-109, 151, 158
Space and spacing, 103-109, 151, 158
Spanish Harlem area, 90
Spatial: distribution, 83-86; 111; signals, 108
Special: agencies, 157; task forces, 71
Specializations, sexual, 86-87, 159

Index

Spillovers and spinoffs, 125, 133-134
Stability: of locations, 14, 16; market, 141
Standards and standardization, 74, 116
Stanton Street, 134
Statistics, crime, 1-2
Status and reputation: area and personal, 4-6, 11, 14, 20, 65, 82, 90, 92, 95, 102, 104, 115, 145
Stigma, element of, 135, 142, 144
Stimulation, overt, 111
Stratification: deviance, 139, 148-151, 171; street location order, 90-92, 105-107
Streetwalkers, 4, 81, 159-166, 170-173
Suburban areas, 2, 111
Supply-and-demand hypothesis, 139-140, 165
Suppression, political, 140
Surrogate hotels, 102
Surveys: street, 10; urban, 2
Suttles, Gerald, 3, 18
Sweep tactics, street, 71, 156

Taboo subjects, 167, 170
Tally's corner (Liebow), 68
Tape recorders, use of, 16
Task-force vehicles, police, 71
Tax-registry numbers, 155
Teenagers, problem of, 140, 157
Tenth Avenue, 10-11, 16, 31-34, 44, 53, 75, 86, 113, 131, 133
Tenth Street, 11, 31, 39, 44, 55, 57, 63, 77, 97, 101, 103, 116, 123-126, 136; East, 10
Territorial: affiliations, 149-150; exclusivity, 139, 146-148, 159; segregation, 86, 88, 104; stake-outs, 88, 106
Testing, phases of, 131-134, 138
Theater district, 11, 34-35, 57, 136. *See also* Movie houses and theaters
Theft and thieves, problem of, 1, 85, 147, 157
Third Avenue, 10-11, 30-31, 39, 41, 53, 55, 57, 77, 83, 86, 89-90, 98, 101, 108, 124-125, 131-132, 137, 140

Thirteenth Street, 31, 124, 137
Thirtieth Street, 136
Thirty-eighth Street, 11, 34, 44, 50, 63, 104, 114, 116, 118, 128; West, 10
Thirty-fifth Street, 127-128
Thirty-first Street, 136
Thirty-fourth Street, 32, 114, 131-132; West, 39
Thirty-ninth Street, West, 33, 42
Thirty-second Street, 11, 20-21, 32, 39, 42, 44, 50, 53, 57, 61, 63, 89, 96, 103, 113, 116, 120, 125-128, 137, 140, 143; East, 10
Thirty-seventh Street, 14, 131, 133
Thirty-third Street, 127-128, 136
Thrasher, Frederic, 18
Time factor, element of, 49-51, 77, 79, 157, 160; budgeting of, 148; police, 9; traveling to location, 112; work contact, 46-48, 100, 105-107, 113, 172
Times Square area, 11, 34, 85, 161
Tolerance: community, 117-121, 139, 172; of deviant behavior, 143-145
Tonnies, 111
Tourists as clients, 102
Trademarks of pimps, 168-170
Traffic layout patterns, 71, 80, 141
Transitional deviance, 163-164
Transit strikes, effects of, 141
Transportation networks, 114, 120, 140-141, 172
Transvestites, 9, 83, 145; age of, 53-55; black, 53; earning power of, 55, 92; heterosexual, 162; Hispanic, 53; homosexual, 162; hormonal treatments for, 162; as prostitutes, 4, 11, 14, 37-55, 86, 88, 90, 92, 100-101, 106-107, 124, 146-148, 158, 162-163, by race, 54; white, 53
Truck drivers, out-of-town, 55
Trust, bond of, 141, 152
Twelfth Street, 31, 86, 89, 108, 124-125, 137
Twenty-fifth Street, 11, 21, 32, 44, 53, 57, 63, 83, 96, 104, 120, 149; East, 10

Twenty-ninth Street, 136
Twenty-sixth Street, 11, 32, 44, 50, 53, 57, 63, 83, 96, 104, 120, 135-136; East, 10
Twenty-third Street, 32, 95, 136; East, 11

Unattractive older women, 6, 105-106, 162
Unnatural sexual acts, 148
Upper middle class residential areas, 83, 160
Urban community studies, 1-2

Venereal disease, contracting of, 140, 155, 172
Vice-squad agents, 157, 172-173
Victimless crimes, 1-3, 56, 155-156, 174
Violations: norms, 145-146; weapons, 1
Violence, real or potential, 1, 146-147, 157, 168, 174
Voluntary customers, 171

Walk and voice come-ons, 20, 55, 108, 157, 160

Walk-up hotels, use of, 124
Washington Heights area, 29
Wealth, factor of, 6
Weapons, 1, 172
Weather, effects of, 21, 41
Weber, Max, 111
Welfare: hotels, 31, 127-128; recipients, 136
West Side circuit, 14, 19, 29, 42
West Side Highway area, 16
West Street, 16
White(s): arrest record, 80; hangers-on, 66, 68, 103; johns, 61; managers, 57; prostitutes, 39-40, 42, 44, 50-51, 53, 76, 79, 81; transvestites, 53
Whyte, William, 18
Williamsburg Bridge area, 114, 119, 121, 123-124
Winick, Charles, 160-161, 165-166, 169, 171-173, 175
Wirth, Louis, 3, 87, 111
Working-class members, 5, 171

X-rated movie films, 35, 118, 128

Youth-gang members, 146-147
Yugoslavian ethic group, 33

About the Author

Bernard Cohen is a professor of sociology and criminology at Queens College, City University of New York. He received the A.M. and Ph.D. degrees in sociology from the University of Pennsylvania and the master's degree in Hebrew literature from Yeshiva University. Dr. Cohen was a visiting professor in the Faculty of Law at the Hebrew University of Jerusalem in 1974-1975.

Dr. Cohen served for many years as the director of the Police Personnel Program at the Rand Corporation, where he completed numerous research projects on the selection, assignment, and promotion of police officers. The findings and recommendations of these studies have been implemented by the New York City Police Department. He was a staff member for the National Advisory Committee on Criminal Justice Standards and Goals, U.S. Department of Justice, and he wrote part of its task-force report, *Research on Criminal Justice Organizations: The Sentencing Process*.

Dr. Cohen has coauthored two books, *Crime and Race* and *Police Background Characteristics and Performance*, and he has written extensively on the police, crime, and juvenile delinquency. His most recent publications include an article on police commanders in *Journal of Police Science and Administration* and a chapter in *Perspectives on Criminal Justice*.

DATE DUE